MW01000191

MALOUF

NEW MIDDLE EASTERN FOOD

MALOUF

GREG & LUCY MALOUF

hardie grant books

TO CHALICE, BRONTE AND TARKYN
AND TO GEORGE

This edition published in 2013 by Hardie Grant Books
First published in 2011

Hardie Grant Books (Australia)
Ground Floor, Building 1
658 Church Street
Richmond, Victoria 3121
www.hardiegrant.com.au

Hardie Grant Books (UK)
Second Floor, North Suite
Dudley House
Southampton Street
London WC2E 7HF
www.hardiegrant.co.uk

publisher paul mcnally
project editor gordana trifunovic
designer sarah odgers
editor janine flew
photographer mark roper
stylist leesa o'reilly

A Cataloguing-in-Publication entry is available from the catalogue of the
National Library of Australia at www.nla.gov.au
Malouf: new Middle Eastern food
ISBN 978 1 74270 145 5

Printed and bound in China by 1010 Printing International Limited.
Colour Reproduction by Splitting Image Colour Studio

CONTENTS

It's now more than twenty years since I grabbed the reins of my very own restaurant kitchen, full of youthful determination to forge a new kind of Middle Eastern cooking. I had a dream to take it out of the ubiquitous falafel shop, to break away from the limitations of traditional Lebanese restaurants, and to set it free in the contemporary dining room — and it's a dream that has come true in more vivid and exciting ways than I could ever have imagined.

INTRODUCTION

MY FAMILY IS LEBANESE-AUSTRALIAN, and I grew up eating food cooked by my mum, my two grandmothers and by a bevy of aunts, cousins and other female members of my extended family, so I knew just how exciting the flavours and dishes of my own heritage could be.

While still an apprentice, I read and was inspired by Claudia Roden's seminal *Book of Middle Eastern Food*, and learnt that there was a whole world of culinary discoveries to make in these ancient and enticing lands. I could hardly wait to get there and explore it all for myself.

My training took me around Europe and South-East Asia, where I was lucky enough to hone my skills and extend my culinary repertoire, but I found that I was gradually being drawn back to the food of my childhood. By the time I took on my first head chef position, I was convinced that if more people were able to taste these dishes — and to understand that the Middle East has so much more to offer than tabbouleh and kebabs — they would love them as much as I do.

With all the arrogance of youth, I wanted to do things my own way. My food would not be about reinventing classics — and nor, really, would it be about tradition. Instead, I was bursting with ideas for a new kind of Middle Eastern food: subjective and personal interpretations, yes, but dishes that would absolutely capture the essence of the Middle East, but express it in a fresher, more inventive — and even, perhaps, a more Western — manner.

And I have certainly not been the only one wanting to open up this particular world of flavour, aroma and colour. Over the last ten years or so, the dishes and ingredients of the Middle East, North Africa and Eastern Mediterranean have come out of the shadows and into the limelight, thanks not just to Claudia Roden's body of work, but also to a growing brigade of restaurateurs, cookbook authors and food writers, all keen to share their own discoveries and enthusiasm for these rich and complex culinary traditions.

As a result, more and more people are familiar with filo pastry and flower waters, with couscous, pomegranate molasses, saffron, sumac and harissa. And reflecting this growing popularity, formerly 'exotic' ingredients are far more widely available. Even suburban supermarkets now stock a reasonably broad range of Middle Eastern staples, spices and aromatics.

Since those giddy early days of my career, I've been fortunate to have cooked my own style of modern Middle Eastern food all around the world. I've also co-authored five food and travel books with my former wife, Lucy. And the journeying we've undertaken to research our books — around North Africa, Moorish Spain, Turkey, Iran, Lebanon, Syria and Jordan — has not only provided a rich seam of inspiration for my restaurant menus and our books, but has underscored my deep love and respect for the food cultures of this extraordinary and exciting part of the world.

Over the years I've been thrilled to see so many of the young chefs who have worked with me embrace these ingredients and ideas and take them out into their very own restaurant kitchens. But I think my greatest joy comes when diners at the restaurant express their surprise and delight at the dishes and ingredients they have tried, or when I receive letters and emails from people telling me that they've enjoyed cooking recipes from my books, and how pleased they've been to try 'something new'.

This book, then, is an attempt to bring together a comprehensive collection of my and Lucy's best and favourite dishes from all five of our earlier books. Many of the recipes have been slightly refined or updated (after all, *Arabesque*, our first book, was published twelve years ago and my own cooking style has evolved and matured since then), and there are also new ones added, for good measure.

The recipes in this book are exactly the kind of 'new' Middle Eastern food that I started dreaming about all those years ago. They reflect my own culinary journey, which I have loved, and I hope that you will enjoy sharing it too.

GREG MALOUF
November 2011

The recipes that follow have been inspired, in one way or another, by the countries that make up — loosely — the Middle East. These influences begin in Moorish Spain and North Africa and reach eastwards to Turkey, the countries of the Levant, the Arabian Peninsula and Persia. While each cuisine stands alone — and several are as refined and complex as any in the world — there are common threads that weave through and bind them. For us, the strongest and most significant of these threads is the spirit of generosity and sharing that underpins mealtimes, especially if guests are present. As such, food is always abundant, and dishes are nearly always shared, rather than served in individual portions, as we do in the West.

THE NEW MIDDLE EASTERN WAY OF EATING

WE HAVE STRUCTURED THE BOOK TO reflect this philosophy of abundance, and to approximate, roughly, the Middle Eastern approach to eating. But we also want to avoid being overly prescriptive. These recipes are absolutely not about full-on immersion into culinary traditions that are, after all, quite different from our own. Instead, they are about ways of using Middle Eastern flavours and ideas to transform a meal from the mundane to the exotic, often with the simplest addition or replacement. And while we're not expecting you to whip up an elaborate mezze banquet for every meal, we do hope that you will see the appeal of a looser, less structured way of eating, where dishes are served from the centre of the table and everyone helps themselves to a few spoonfuls of whatever they like.

With this in mind, we've divided the recipes into seven sections — soups, small dishes, large dishes, side dishes, bakery, sweet and larder — and we encourage you to mix and match them in any way you wish. The recipes are mostly designed for sharing — especially within the small, large and side dish sections — but most could also be served as individual portions, if you prefer.

For a larger meal, or when you're entertaining, we recommend you select a few dishes from each of these three sections, ensuring you include a vegetable or salad, and perhaps a rice or grain dish as well. Most of the savoury pastries also make delicious starters, as do some of the lighter soups. So be as generous or restrained as you like!

For light meals, too, it's lovely to put together a selection of one or two dishes — even if it's just a simple basket of herbs, fresh cheese and bread, followed by a hearty soup, an omelette or a risotto. Many of the breads, pide, pizzas and savoury pastries also make terrific snacks or light lunches.

Vegetarians are well served, as in many Middle Eastern countries salads, vegetables, pulses and grains comprise the bulk of a meal, with meat, poultry and seafood served as a more occasional treat, or in much smaller quantities than we consume in the West. So you'll find a large number of vegetarian dishes among the small dishes and in the bakery sections, while many of the side dishes would do excellent double-duty as a meat-free main course.

Although most Middle Easterners have a very sweet tooth, most ordinary mealtimes finish with fruit, and desserts are rarely eaten in the way that we do in the West; they are usually reserved for special occasions and celebrations. This, then, is the section in which we take the biggest liberties with tradition! There are a number of our favourite sorbet and ice creams, as well as a selection of fruit-based desserts, dairy desserts and heartier puddings. We also include some delectable goodies, many of which make excellent gift ideas or which you could serve with tea or coffee.

The larder plays an important role in every Middle Eastern household, where, even in these modern times, many families preserve homegrown summer fruits and vegetables to last through the leaner winter months. This is the section where you'll find frequently used spice blends and pastes, popular dressings and sauces and pickled vegetables, relishes and preserved fruits. Finally, there are recipes for cordials, and even some of our favourite cocktails.

ABOUT INGREDIENTS

In general, the range and quality of fresh produce available in Middle Eastern countries is extraordinary. The cooking there is still largely seasonal; people understand that food follows the natural rhythm of the seasons and the expectation is that produce will have been grown or reared within a few kilometres of their own kitchen. Middle Easterners tend to shop in small amounts daily and they demand the best, freshest and most intensely flavoured ingredients. For us, too, freshness and quality are everything and these are two of the key elements of any of our recipes. Luckily, this approach is gaining in popularity in many Western countries as well, and so we encourage you to choose your ingredients carefully.

Although some of the spices and ingredients in these recipes might be new to you, most of them are readily available these days — even many larger supermarkets stock a good range of Middle Eastern ingredients. There are some more unusual items that you might have to track down in Middle Eastern or specialist food stores, but it will always be worth the effort to help you achieve an authentic result. There is a glossary (page 408) to help you with some of these ingredients.

SOUPS

A good stock is the key to making a good soup (and also many braised dishes and savoury sauces) as it provides a richness and depth of flavour that just won't be there otherwise. And although some butchers' shops and delicatessens sell good 'homemade' stocks, neither these, nor the supermarket variety, will give as much flavour as a stock you make yourself.

Stocks are not technically hard to make — you just put everything in a pot and simmer away until all flavour and body are extracted from the bones and vegetables. However, you can't just rustle one up when you fancy making a soup, so you need to be organised enough to have stock on hand in the fridge or freezer.

There are a few key things to remember when making a stock to achieve a clear, richly flavoured result. First, don't allow the stock to boil or it will turn cloudy. As it simmers, skim away any impurities that rise to the surface, and finally, when it's ready, ladle the liquid out so as not to disturb the solids.

CHICKEN STOCK

3 kg chicken carcasses | 1 onion, cut into quarters | 2 sticks celery, roughly chopped
1 leek, white part only, roughly chopped | 2 cloves garlic, halved
1/2 teaspoon black peppercorns | 1 bay leaf | 3 sprigs thyme

RINSE THE CHICKEN CARCASSES and then put them in a 5 litre stockpot. Pour on enough water to cover the bones generously, then add the remaining ingredients. Bring to the boil, skimming away any fat and impurities that rise to the surface, then lower the heat immediately. Cover the pot and simmer very gently for 2 hours, skimming from time to time.

Carefully ladle the stock into a container, discarding the solids. (Don't be tempted to tip it all into a sieve: the less you disturb the solids at this stage, the clearer the final stock will be. I find the best method is to use a sieve to keep the solids submerged while you ladle out the liquid.)

Refrigerate for up to 3 days or freeze for later use.

MAKES **2.5 litres**

Many seafood dishes are immeasurably improved by using a good seafood stock. We tend not to use fish stocks, as they can be rather overpowering. Instead, we use crabs as the base, which have a sweeter, almost nutty flavour.

CRAB STOCK

2 kg crabs | 150 ml olive oil | 4 sticks celery, roughly chopped | 2 onions, roughly chopped | 4 cloves garlic, roughly chopped | 1/2 teaspoon fennel seeds, roughly crushed | 400 g can diced tomatoes | 125 ml dry sherry | long piece of zest from 1 orange | 20 saffron threads, roasted and crushed | 2 bay leaves | 12 sprigs thyme | 4 litres water

REMOVE THE UNDERBODY FROM THE crabs and pull away the spongy gills ('dead man's fingers'). Cut each body in half and bash the shells and claws into large pieces.

Heat the oil in a large, heavy-based saucepan to smoking point. Sauté the crab pieces briefly over a high heat, then add the celery, onion, garlic and fennel seeds and sauté for 2 minutes. Stir in the tomatoes, sherry, zest, saffron, bay leaves and thyme, then add the water. Bring to the boil, skimming away any fat and impurities that rise to the surface, then lower the heat immediately. Simmer, uncovered, for 1 hour, skimming from time to time.

Carefully ladle the stock into a container, discarding the solids. (Don't be tempted to tip it all into a sieve: the less you disturb the solids at this stage, the clearer the final stock will be. I find the best method is to use a sieve to keep the solids submerged while you ladle out the liquid.) Refrigerate for up to 3 days or freeze for later use.

MAKES 2.5 litres

GOLDEN MUSSEL CHOWDER

1 kg black mussels | 1 onion, sliced | 2 sticks celery, sliced
2 cloves garlic, chopped | 1 teaspoon Golden Spice Mix (page 378)
30 ml olive oil | 200 ml white wine | 2 medium potatoes, peeled and diced
2 small leeks | 200 ml cream (35% fat)
1 preserved lemon (page 394), rind only, washed and diced finely
10 saffron threads, roasted and crushed | 1 tablespoon thyme leaves
2 medium tomatoes, seeded and diced small
freshly ground black pepper | 4 small bacon rashers | soft brown sugar
thin rounds of small leek, crisply fried, to garnish

SCRUB THE MUSSELS CLEAN AND pull off the beards. Discard any mussels that refuse to close after a sharp tap.

In a heavy-based saucepan, sauté the onion, celery, garlic and golden spice mix in the oil for about a minute, then add the wine and the mussels. Cover, turn the heat up high and steam for 3 minutes. Turn the mussels well, replace the lid and steam for a further 2 minutes, or until the mussels have opened.

Remove the pan from the heat and allow to steam for a further minute before taking off the lid and straining the liquor through a fine sieve to catch any dirt. Reserve the liquor. Throw any unopened mussels back into the pot and steam for another minute or two. Discard any that stubbornly refuse to open. Allow the mussels to cool and then remove them from their shells and cut in half.

Steam the potatoes and whole leeks for 10–15 minutes, or until tender. Remove from the heat and allow to cool a few minutes. Split the leeks in half lengthwise then cut them into 1 cm slices.

Return the mussel liquor to the pot, add the cream and bring to the boil. Add the potatoes, leeks and preserved lemon, then the saffron and thyme. Heat thoroughly. Add the diced tomatoes and mussels and warm through briefly. Season with pepper.

Sprinkle the bacon rashers liberally with soft brown sugar and grill until golden brown. Shred and sprinkle on the soup. Garnish with crisp fried leeks.

SERVES 4–6

SHELLFISH SOUP WITH FENNEL AND SAFFRON

SPICE MIX 1 teaspoon ground turmeric | 1 teaspoon chilli powder
1 teaspoon ground coriander | 1 teaspoon ground cumin | 1/2 teaspoon ground ginger
1/2 teaspoon saffron threads

1 kg black mussels | 60 ml olive oil | 1 onion, finely chopped
1 leek, white part only, finely chopped | 1 clove garlic, finely chopped
2 small fennel bulbs, cut lengthwise into wedges
15 king prawn tails, split in half | 4 blue swimmer crabs, head and gills removed, cut in half
100 ml white wine | 1.5 litres good-quality chicken stock
2 ripe tomatoes, seeded and diced | 1/3 cup roughly chopped flat-leaf parsley leaves
1 tablespoon roughly chopped celery leaves | few sprigs thyme
100 ml cream (35% fat) | juice of 1-2 lemons
sea salt and freshly ground black pepper | extra-virgin olive oil to serve

MIX ALL THE SPICES TOGETHER.

Scrub the mussels clean and pull off the beards. Discard any mussels that refuse to close after a sharp tap.

Heat the oil in a large, heavy-based saucepan and add the onion, leek, garlic, fennel and the spice mix. Stir over a medium heat for a few minutes, then tip in the mussels, prawns and crabs, shaking the pan to move them around over the heat. Pour in the wine, cover the pan and turn up the heat. Steam for 3–4 minutes, shaking the pan vigorously from time to time.

Remove the lid and stir around well. Pick out and discard any mussels that have not opened, then put the lid back on and steam for a further 2 minutes. Take the pan off the heat and remove the mussels, prawns and crabs. Pick the meat from the body and claws of the crabs and discard the shells. Remove the mussel meat from the shells.

Add the chicken stock, tomatoes, parsley, celery leaves and thyme to the pan and put it back on the heat. Bring to the boil and simmer for 10 minutes. Pour in the cream and lemon juice and lightly season with salt and pepper. Return the prawns, mussels and crab meat to the soup. Serve sprinkled with fruity extra-virgin olive oil.

SERVES 4–6

Egg and lemon sauces and soups are a distinctive feature of both Turkish and Greek cookery. Using eggs to add richness was a common feature of medieval cooking, and the egg-lemon combination is believed to have been a Byzantine idea, taken up by the sophisticated kitchens of the Ottoman sultans.

The appeal of avgolemono (as they are known in Greek) or terbiye (Turkish) sauces and soups is that they are rich and velvety smooth, with a refreshing lemony flavour.

GOLDEN AVGOLEMONO WITH PRAWNS, CHICORY AND RICE

1.2 litres Crab Stock (page 13) | 150 g short-grain rice
1/2 teaspoon freshly ground black pepper | 4 free-range egg yolks | juice of 2 small lemons
1 cup shredded chicory leaves | 1 tablespoon finely chopped dill | 1 teaspoon dried mint
240 g raw prawn meat | 40 g unsalted butter | good pinch of sweet paprika

HEAT THE STOCK IN A LARGE, heavy-based saucepan, then add the rice and pepper and bring to the boil. Lower the heat and simmer, uncovered, for 20 minutes.

In a small mixing bowl, whisk the egg yolks with the lemon juice. Ladle a spoonful of the hot stock into the egg mixture and whisk gently. Pour this back into the barely simmering soup, whisking continuously. Cook at a bare simmer, whisking gently, until the soup starts to thicken. Be sure not to let the soup boil or the mixture will curdle. Add the chicory, dill, dried mint and prawn meat to the pan and simmer gently for 3 minutes, or until the prawns are barely cooked.

Meanwhile, quickly heat the butter in a small frying pan until it foams, then add the paprika. When ready to serve, ladle the soup into warmed serving bowls and swirl on the sizzling butter.

SERVES 8

We spent a fascinating afternoon in Istanbul with Turkish food journalist Engin Akin, who showed us how to make manti, a sort of Turkish ravioli. Although most Turkish women make the silky, soft dough themselves and deftly roll it by hand into paper-thin fineness, for the novice, it's probably easier to use a pasta machine. Just work the dough through each setting until you reach the finest one. If you don't feel brave enough to make your own dough, then gyoza dumpling wrappers make a good substitute and are readily available from Asian grocers; you'll need about 24 for this recipe.

When made correctly, manti dumplings are about the size of a grape, and it takes great patience and dexterity to shape and seal them into the traditional four-cornered star-like shape — but it's worth having a go!

TURKISH RAVIOLI IN A CRAB AND SAFFRON BROTH

MANTI DOUGH 2–3 large free-range eggs | 250 g baker's flour | 1 teaspoon sea salt

SEAFOOD STUFFING 300 g raw prawn meat, finely chopped
100 g raw crab meat, finely chopped | 1 tablespoon chopped mint leaves
2 tablespoons chopped dill | 1/2 teaspoon dried mint
1 long green chilli, seeded and finely chopped | finely grated zest of 1 lime
2 hard-boiled free-range eggs, roughly chopped | 1 tablespoon extra-virgin olive oil
drizzle of honey | sea salt and freshly ground black pepper

800 ml Crab Stock (page 13) | sea salt | 2 tablespoons extra-virgin olive oil
1/4 teaspoon sweet paprika | pinch of hot paprika
chervil sprigs to garnish | 1 purple carrot, sliced into wafers, to garnish (optional)

TO MAKE THE MANTI DOUGH, lightly beat two of the eggs, then put these into the bowl of an electric mixer with the flour and salt. Use the dough hook to work it to a stiff dough — if the dough is too stiff, add the remaining egg, lightly beaten. Knead for about 5 minutes, then tip the dough onto a lightly floured work surface and knead by hand for a further 5 minutes or so until smooth and elastic. Place the dough in a lightly oiled bowl, then cover with plastic wrap and leave to rest for about 1 hour.

Divide the dough into pieces the size of a golf ball. Working with one piece at a time, roll the dough on a lightly floured work surface to form a large, paper-thin rectangle. Cut into strips about 4 cm wide. Repeat with the remaining dough. Stack the strips on top of each other and cut into 4 cm squares. (If you have a pasta machine, roll the dough through the settings, then trim the sheets to end up with 4 cm squares.)

To make the stuffing, combine all the ingredients in a large bowl. Refrigerate for 30 minutes to chill thoroughly.

To make the mantı, put a teaspoon of filling into the centre of each dough square or gyoza wrapper.

We've gone with a simple ravioli shape, but if you're brave enough to attempt the traditional shape, bring two opposite corners together over the filling and press to join at the top. Repeat with the other two corners, carefully moistening the side 'seams' with a little water as you go and pinching them together to seal them. You should aim to end up with a four-cornered star-like shape. For an easier option, simply moisten the edges with a little water and fold the pastry over the filling to create little triangles, then squeeze to seal. Whichever shape you decide to make, ensure that the edges are sealed well so the filling doesn't come out as the mantı cook. Place the mantı on a lightly floured tray as you complete them and repeat until all the dough and filling are used up.

Bring the stock to a simmer in a large, heavy-based saucepan. Taste and adjust the seasoning by adding salt, if required. Reduce the heat to a very gentle simmer. Bring another large saucepan of salted water to the boil. Add the mantı to the water and poach for 4–5 minutes, or until they are cooked and rise to the surface. Use a large slotted spoon to lift them out and transfer to a colander to drain.

Meanwhile, gently heat the oil and two paprikas to blood temperature in a small saucepan. Tip the bright-red oil into a small tea strainer lined with paper towel over a small bowl.

To serve, ladle the stock into four warmed bowls. Divide the mantı among the bowls and drizzle with a little of the paprika oil. Garnish with chervil and wafers of purple carrot, if using, and serve straight away.

SERVES **4**

OPPOSITE TURKISH RAVIOLI IN A CRAB AND SAFFRON BROTH (PAGE 18)

Versions of creamy hot yoghurt soup can be found across the Middle East. At their simplest, they may be flavoured with dried mint and thickened with rice, chickpeas, burgul or barley, while other more complex versions include stuffed dumplings (see page 30). We add sweet corn kernels and threads of chicken to this recipe to make it more substantial.

HOT YOGHURT SOUP WITH CHICKEN THREADS AND CORN

1 large chicken breast on the bone | 1 small onion, cut into quarters
1 stick celery | 1/2 lemon | 1 sprig thyme | 2 bay leaves | 1 small cinnamon stick
1/2 teaspoon white peppercorns | 1.5 litres good-quality chicken stock
100 g short-grain rice | 1/2 cup sweet corn kernels | 500 g thick natural yoghurt
2 teaspoons cornflour | 60 ml water | 1 free-range egg, lightly beaten
sea salt and freshly ground black pepper | 40 g unsalted butter | 1 tablespoon dried mint
dried red pepper flakes to serve (optional)

PUT THE CHICKEN, VEGETABLES, lemon, herbs, cinnamon, peppercorns and stock into a large, heavy-based saucepan. Bring to the boil, skimming away any fat and impurities that rise to the surface, then lower the heat immediately. Simmer very gently, covered, for 5 minutes. Turn off the heat and leave the chicken in the stock for 20 minutes.

Pull the chicken meat off the bone and shred it as finely as you can. Set aside for later. Strain the stock into a large, heavy-based saucepan, then add the rice and slowly bring to the boil. Simmer gently, covered, for 30 minutes, or until the rice has broken down and begun to thicken the soup. Add the corn kernels.

To stabilise the yoghurt, beat it in a large bowl until smooth. Mix the cornflour with the water, then stir it thoroughly into the yoghurt with the egg. Gently stir a spoonful of the hot soup into the yoghurt mixture, then pour this back into the barely simmering soup. Cook at a bare simmer for about 10 minutes, stirring in one direction only. Be sure not to let the soup boil or the mixture will curdle.

When ready to serve, add the shredded chicken to the soup and season with salt and pepper, then ladle the soup into warmed serving bowls. Quickly sizzle the butter in a small frying pan, then add the mint and heat until foaming. Swirl the sizzling butter into each bowl of soup, sprinkle with red pepper flakes, if using, and serve.

SERVES **6–8**

Similar to a traditional Moroccan harira, this soup is chock-full of nutty chickpeas and lamb, and thick with couscous. Throw in some fresh mint and parsley and serve it with warm Arabic flatbread and a big dollop of creamy yoghurt for a filling winter lunch.

NORTH AFRICAN COUSCOUS SOUP

60 ml olive oil | 250 g lamb leg steak, cut into small chunks
1 medium onion, finely chopped | 2 cloves garlic, crushed with 1 teaspoon sea salt
1 tablespoon coriander seeds, roasted and ground
1 tablespoon cumin seeds, roasted and ground | 1 teaspoon ground allspice
1 teaspoon chilli powder | 1 teaspoon sweet paprika | 400 g can crushed tomatoes
1 green chilli, seeded, scraped and finely shredded | 1 teaspoon honey
100 g chickpeas, soaked overnight and drained | 800 ml good-quality chicken stock
500 ml water | sea salt and freshly ground black pepper | 50 g couscous
1 tablespoon finely chopped flat-leaf parsley leaves
1 tablespoon finely chopped fresh mint | juice of 1 lemon

HEAT THE OLIVE OIL AND SAUTÉ THE lamb pieces. Remove them with a slotted spoon and drain on paper towel. Add the onion and cook over a gentle heat until soft. Then add the garlic, coriander, cumin, allspice, chilli powder and paprika, and mix well with the onion. Cook for a further 2 minutes and then return the lamb to the pan. Add the tomatoes, chilli and honey.

Stir well before adding the chickpeas, stock and water. Cover and simmer on a low heat for 45–60 minutes, or until the chickpeas are tender. When you are ready to serve, taste and adjust the seasonings. Add the couscous to the pot, cover and allow it to sit for 5 minutes. Serve garnished with parsley and mint and sprinkled with lemon juice.

SERVES **6**

Let's be honest, there's nothing remotely Middle Eastern about Scotland's favourite soup! Although he turned his nose up at the idea of the prunes, which feature in the original, Greg did like the idea of popping dried fruit into a savoury soup — it's a theme that is popular all around the Middle East and in North Africa. After a few days mulling it over, he came up with the following wonderfully fragrant soup, which uses fresh dates to add little nuggets of toffee sweetness.

The fried cheese sandwiches are also delicious. If you have a sandwich maker, then the accompanying croques monsieurs are simple to make. Otherwise you can fry them for a lovely rich toasty crust.

COCK-A-LEEKIE WITH DATES AND CROQUES MONSIEURS

SOUP **50 ml olive oil | 4 leeks, white part only, shredded | 100 ml dry sherry | 1/2 teaspoon ground allspice | 1/2 teaspoon grated nutmeg | 1/2 teaspoon ground ginger | sea salt | 1/4 teaspoon ground white pepper | 6 fresh dates, pitted and diced | 1.5 litres good-quality chicken stock | 1 tablespoon finely chopped flat-leaf parsley leaves | edible pansies (optional) and thin rounds of small leek, crisply fried, to garnish**

CROQUES MONSIEURS **softened butter | 12 slices white bread, crusts removed | Dijon mustard | 6 slices good-quality leg ham | 250 g grated gruyère cheese | 50 g unsalted butter | 50 ml olive oil**

TO MAKE THE SOUP, HEAT THE OIL in a large saucepan and lightly sauté the leeks for a few minutes until they soften. Increase the heat and add the sherry, then let it all bubble away for a minute or two. Stir in the spices, salt and pepper and the dates. Add the chicken stock and bring to the boil. Lower the heat and simmer very gently for 10–15 minutes, or until the leeks are nice and tender and the dates and spices have infused their sweetness to the soup.

Towards the end of the cooking time, make the croques monsieurs. Butter the bread and spread with mustard. Lay on the ham and plenty of cheese and press the top slice of bread on firmly. Melt the butter and oil together in a frying pan and fry the sandwiches on both sides until they are golden brown.

When ready to serve, taste the soup and adjust the seasoning as necessary. Ladle into serving bowls and sprinkle with parsley, edible pansies, if using, and crisp fried leeks. Serve with the croques monsieurs.

SERVES **6**

This hearty soup, known as beyran, comes from Gaziantep in the south-east of Turkey, where it's eaten as a warming breakfast dish, especially during the long, cold winters. Beyran is served in soup restaurants known as metanet lokantasi, a phrase that translates as building strength of body as well as spirit.

It requires a fair amount of strength and spirit to eat a traditionally made beyran, as it includes sheep's cheek and the solid tail fat from the fat-tailed sheep found all around the Middle East. This solid white fat is the cooking medium of choice in the eastern and southern parts of the country, but it is rather terrifying to Western palates. An authentic beyran is also full of garlic, and you'll probably be offered a couple of sweet and spicy cloves to munch on as a breath freshener as you head off to join the world again. This tamed-down version uses lamb shanks, which provide a similarly melting texture without the fat. For a truer Gaziantep experience, add the extra garlic clove at the last minute.

SLOW-COOKED LAMB SOUP WITH GARLIC AND GREEN CHILLIES

3 lamb shanks | 1 whole head garlic, cut crosswise | 1 onion, cut into quarters
1 carrot, cut into quarters | 2 bay leaves | 2 litres water | 150 g short-grain rice
1 1/2 teaspoons extra-virgin olive oil | additional 1 clove garlic, roughly smashed (optional)
chilli flakes, lemon wedges, long green chillies and Turkish bread to serve

PUT THE LAMB SHANKS, GARLIC, onion, carrot, bay leaves and water in a large, heavy-based saucepan. Slowly bring to the boil, skimming away any fat and impurities that rise to the surface, then immediately lower the heat. Simmer very gently, covered, for 1$1/2$ hours, skimming from time to time. Check after an hour and top up with more water if necessary.

Remove the pan from the heat, then carefully ladle the stock into a container, discarding the solids but reserving the lamb shanks. (Don't be tempted to tip everything into a sieve; the less you disturb the solids at this stage, the clearer the final soup will be. I find the best method is to use a sieve to keep the solids submerged while you ladle out the liquid.)

Rinse the rice thoroughly under cold running water. Bring to the boil with 300 ml reserved lamb stock in a small saucepan, then lower the heat and drizzle in $1/2$ teaspoon of the extra-virgin olive oil. Simmer gently, covered, for 15 minutes or until the rice is tender.

While the rice is cooking, remove the meat from the lamb shanks and tear it into small shreds. Bring the remaining stock, the shredded lamb, smashed garlic clove, if using, and remaining extra-virgin olive oil to a gentle simmer.

When ready to serve, place a spoonful of rice in the centre of each warmed bowl and distribute the shredded lamb evenly among them. Pour on the hot stock, then sprinkle the soup with chilli flakes and serve with lemon wedges, long green chillies and plenty of soft Turkish bread alongside. Squeeze on the lemon, then crunch on the chillies and chew on the bread as you slurp up the soup.

SERVES **6–8**

This is a version of a Renaissance soup that I learnt in Mantova, Italy. The original uses cock's combs instead of sausage.

ARTICHOKE SOUP WITH SPANISH SAUSAGE AND ROASTED PISTACHIOS

6 large artichokes | juice of 4 lemons mixed with 1 litre water
2 medium onions | 2 cloves garlic | 2 medium leeks | 100 ml olive oil
2 litres good-quality chicken stock | sea salt and freshly ground black pepper
3 semi-dried chorizo sausages, grilled and sliced into 1 cm diagonal pieces
2 free-range egg yolks | 150 ml cream (35% fat) | juice of 2 lemons

GARNISH **100 g unsalted pistachio kernels, dry roasted and coarsely crushed**
1/2 teaspoon allspice (freshly ground, if possible) | 60 ml extra-virgin olive oil

TO PREPARE THE ARTICHOKES, remove the outer hard leaves as well as the choke and immediately place the heart into the lemon water.

Slice the onions, garlic and leeks finely. Heat the olive oil in a heavy-based pot.

Drain the artichokes and very quickly slice into thin (2 mm) slices. Sauté them in the hot oil with the onions, garlic and leeks, then cover and simmer for 5–8 minutes. Do not allow the artichokes to colour.

Add the chicken stock. Bring to the boil and gently simmer for 30 minutes. Taste and season with salt and pepper.

When ready to serve, bring the soup back to the boil and then add the grilled chorizo pieces. Mix the egg yolks with the cream and then add to the soup. Slowly return the soup to just below boiling, stirring constantly. Remove from the heat and adjust seasoning with salt, pepper and lemon juice.

As you serve, finish each bowl with a sprinkling of crushed pistachios and ground allspice, and a drizzle of extra-virgin olive oil.

SERVES **8**

This soup, known as dizi, became one of our favourite quick-and-easy lunch dishes on our travels around Iran, and we would actively seek out specialist restaurants. Dizi is a simple enough idea: small chunks of meat on the bone are simmered slowly over several hours with potato, tomatoes, beans and lamb tail fat, which releases an unctuous richness. To serve, the broth is poured into a bowl onto pieces of flatbread and slurped up with a squeeze of sour orange or lemon. The bone is then fished out and discarded, and the remaining meat, fat and vegetables are pounded to a coarse paste. This tasty mush (for want of a better word) is eaten with plenty more flatbread, pickles, onion, sour orange (or any citrus, really) and fresh herbs (try tarragon, mint and basil). It's far from refined, but unspeakably delicious.

This version omits the lamb tail fat to suit Western palates, and it is probably a tad more spiced than authentic dizi. The longer you can simmer the lamb, the better the result.

MORTAR AND PESTLE SOUP WITH CHICKPEAS, LAMB AND FLATBREAD

3 tablespoons olive oil | 3 lamb shanks | 1 teaspoon sea salt | 8 small shallots, peeled
6 cloves garlic, peeled | 1 1/2 teaspoons ground turmeric | 1 teaspoon ground cinnamon
1 teaspoon freshly ground black pepper | 1 tablespoon tomato paste
250 g dried chickpeas, soaked overnight and drained | 8 sprigs thyme
2 bay leaves | 2 litres water | 2 potatoes, peeled and cut into chunks
12 small tomatoes | flatbread, fresh herbs, onion wedges and citrus wedges to serve

PREHEAT THE OVEN TO 160°C (GAS 3).

Heat the oil in a large, heavy-based casserole dish over a high heat. Add the lamb shanks and season with salt, then brown all over and remove from the pan.

Add the shallots, garlic and spices to the pan and fry over a medium heat for a few minutes until the vegetables soften. Stir in the tomato paste and fry for a minute, then stir in the chickpeas. Return the lamb shanks to the pan with the thyme and bay leaves and pour in the water. Cover the pan and cook in the oven for 2–3 hours, or until the meat is falling away from the bones.

Tuck the potatoes and tomatoes in among the lamb shanks and return the pan to the oven for another 30 minutes, or until the potato is tender.

Lift the lamb shanks from the soup and remove the meat from the bones. Break the meat roughly into smallish chunks and return it to the pan.

Encourage everyone to eat the dizi the authentic Iranian way. After you've drunk the soup, you could use a mortar and pestle, or just mash the meat and vegetables in your bowl with a fork. Scoop it all up with flatbread, then add herbs and onion and a squeeze of citrus juice — delicious!

SERVES **6**

This ancient dish, chiche barak, has its roots in pre-Islamic Persia and is thought to have been introduced to Lebanon by the Ottomans. Traditionally, it is served with rice and makes a hearty meal. We find the dumplings quite filling, and prefer to serve them in a soup. They are partially baked in the oven, which gives a rustic, rather chewy result. If you prefer a smoother, more refined dumpling, poach them in water for 5 minutes before finishing the cooking in the soup.

LEBANESE-STYLE DUMPLINGS IN YOGHURT SOUP WITH SILVERBEET

LAMB DUMPLINGS **1 tablespoon olive oil | 1/2 onion, finely chopped**
1 small clove garlic, finely chopped | 200 g lean lamb, finely minced
1/2 teaspoon ground allspice | 1/2 teaspoon ground cinnamon
sea salt and freshly ground black pepper | 50 g pine nuts, lightly toasted
36 round white wonton wrappers

YOGHURT SOUP **2 tablespoons olive oil | 1 onion, finely chopped**
1 clove garlic, finely chopped | 1 bunch silverbeet (Swiss chard), leaves roughly chopped
1 red bullet chilli, seeded, scraped and finely chopped
1/2 teaspoon ground allspice | 250 ml good-quality chicken stock
juice of 1 lemon | 500 g natural yoghurt | 1/2 tablespoon cornflour
50 ml water | 1 free-range egg, lightly beaten

TO MAKE THE DUMPLING FILLING, heat the oil in a non-stick pan and sauté the onion and garlic until soft. Add the lamb and continue to sauté, stirring constantly to break up any lumps. Add the spices and season lightly with salt and pepper. When the juices have evaporated, remove the pan from the heat and stir in the toasted pine nuts. Set aside and leave to cool.

Preheat the oven to 180°C (Gas 4). Place a teaspoon of filling in the centre of each wonton wrapper. Moisten the edges and fold over into a crescent shape. Use your fingers to press the edges together and seal well. Arrange the dumplings on a lightly oiled baking tray and bake for 10–15 minutes until very lightly browned, but not cooked through.

To make the soup, heat the olive oil in a large pan and sauté the onion and garlic until they soften. Add the silverbeet, chilli, allspice, chicken stock and lemon juice and cook over a gentle heat for about 20 minutes, until the silverbeet is tender.

To stabilise the yoghurt, tip into a large bowl and stir briskly until smooth. Mix the cornflour with the water and add to the yoghurt with the egg. Stir well, then tip into the hot silverbeet mixture. Lower the heat and cook, stirring in one direction only, for about 10 minutes, or until the soup has thickened. Add the dumplings and simmer gently for a further 5 minutes, or until they are cooked through.

SERVES **8**

This spicy soup was created when the American band was touring Australia in 1992. Use between one and three chillies — or more, of course — depending on your stamina. Squat, thick-skinned capsicums are best for this soup, as they are easy to skin.

'RED HOT CHILI PEPPER' SOUP

3 large red capsicums (peppers) | 2 medium onions | 2 cloves garlic
1–3 bullet chillies | 60 ml olive oil | 4 whole tomatoes, skinned and diced | 40 ml dry sherry
600 ml vegetable or good-quality chicken stock | sea salt and freshly ground black pepper
6 sprigs thyme, tied with string | 2 whole bay leaves | 1 teaspoon honey
goat's cheese and extra-virgin olive oil to serve

ROAST THE WHOLE CAPSICUMS OVER a gas flame, or under the griller, turning constantly until they are blackened and blistered all over. This takes about 20 minutes. Put them into a bowl, cover with plastic wrap and allow them to steam and soften for another 10 minutes.

In the meantime, slice the onions finely and chop the garlic and chillies, seeds included. Sauté in the oil over a low–medium heat until they are soft and translucent. Then add the peeled, roughly diced tomatoes and sauté for a further 20 minutes. (To skin the tomatoes, pour boiling water over them, pierce the skin and peel it off.)

Once the capsicums are cooled, peel off the skins, making sure you remove any blackened bits that will make the soup bitter and unattractive. Remove the seeds too, then roughly chop the capsicums and add them to the tomato-onion mixture.

Add the sherry and stock and cook for a further 5 minutes. Season with salt and pepper. Add the bundle of thyme and the bay leaves. Simmer for 15 minutes. Remove from the heat and stir in the honey. Taste and adjust seasoning if necessary. Blitz the mixture in a blender or food processor until it is very smooth, which will take about 3 minutes on high speed.

If you are fussy about presentation, tip the soup through a fine sieve, which will also remove any chilli seeds. Thin the soup with a little extra stock or water if required.

Serve it with a blob of goat's cheese and a drizzle of extra-virgin olive oil.

SERVES **6**

There are many garlic soups to be had all around the Mediterranean. Some are simple bread soups. Other, more sophisticated versions use a flavourful stock, instead of water, and others still are enriched with egg yolks. Some soups are served hot, others warm or even chilled. One hot day in Seville we ate a delicious version thickened in true Moorish style with almond meal, sharpened with vinegar and served with a sprinkling of currants.

ANDALUSIAN WHITE SOUP

200 g day-old good-quality white bread, crusts removed | 150 ml milk
150 g blanched almonds | 3-4 cloves garlic, crushed with 1/2 teaspoon sea salt
120 ml olive oil | 500-750 ml iced water | 3 tablespoons sherry vinegar
sea salt and freshly ground black pepper | 12 small black grapes, frozen
2 teaspoons pistachio slivers | 2 tablespoons currants, soaked in 2 tablespoons dry sherry

SOAK THE BREAD IN THE MILK FOR a few minutes, then squeeze it dry. Place the almonds in a food processor and whiz to a coarse meal. Then add the bread and garlic paste and whiz to a smooth paste. With the motor running, slowly pour in the olive oil, drop by drop, as if making a mayonnaise. When all the oil has been incorporated, add the iced water until the soup is the consistency of pouring cream. Add the vinegar and season with salt and pepper if needed.

Keep the soup chilled until you are ready to serve. You can make it a day ahead if it suits. Vigorously whip it just before serving, and serve chilled on a hot summer's day, with frozen black grapes, pistachio slivers and sherry-plumped currants.

SERVES **4-6**

Wonderfully refreshing on a hot summer's day, ice-cold yoghurt and herb soups are popular all around the Middle East, with slight variations from country to country. Iranian versions such as this one often include chopped walnuts and raisins, which make the soup richer and more filling; a little goes a surprisingly long way. Serve with plenty of warm flatbread.

CHILLED YOGHURT SOUP WITH SUMMER HERBS

3 Lebanese cucumbers, peeled | 1 small clove garlic, crushed with 1 teaspoon sea salt
800 g thick natural yoghurt | 2 tablespoons chopped tarragon leaves
2 tablespoons finely snipped chives | 1 tablespoon chopped chervil | 1 teaspoon dried mint
sea salt | 1/4 teaspoon freshly ground white pepper | 40 g finely chopped walnuts
2 tablespoons currants | up to 300 ml ice-cold water | squeeze of lemon juice
slivered pistachios, fresh or dried rose petals or 1 small radish, thinly shaved, to garnish
warm flatbread to serve

SPLIT THE CUCUMBERS LENGTHWISE and scoop out and discard the seeds. Grate the cucumber coarsely into a colander set on a plate and refrigerate for 30 minutes.

Whisk the garlic paste into the yoghurt until evenly distributed, then whisk in the herbs. Squeeze the grated cucumber firmly to remove as much moisture as you can, then stir into the yoghurt. Season with salt and pepper and refrigerate for at least 1 hour to let the flavours develop.

Just before serving, stir the walnuts and currants into the yoghurt and whisk in enough of the ice-cold water to achieve a soupy consistency — you may not need it all. Add a big squeeze of lemon juice, then taste and adjust the seasonings to your liking once more.

Sprinkle with pistachios, rose petals or radish as you please, and serve straight away.

SERVES 6

This is our twist on a simple, rustic onion soup known as eshkeneh that we ate on a chilly spring evening at the Apadana Hotel at Persepolis. Eshkeneh is an ancient dish thought to date back several thousand years. Onions traditionally give courage and strength in battle and legend has it that eshkeneh was the daily diet of Persian soldiers under the Parthian King Arsaces back in the third century. It was bulked up with pieces of dry bread that would soften in the soup — similar to the way that croutons are used in French onion soup. In some eshkeneh recipes the eggs are whisked into the hot broth, where they create long eggy strands. Poaching them, as we've done here, makes this a more elegant dish, and we can't resist the way the creamy yolks ooze into the warming, golden broth.

Serve with a small jug of verjuice or mild vinegar, and perhaps a few tiny sour grapes as an extra tangy garnish.

PERSEPOLIS ONION SOUP WITH SOFT-POACHED EGGS

2 tablespoons olive oil | 20 g unsalted butter | 2 onions, finely sliced
2 cloves garlic, finely sliced | 1/2 teaspoon ground turmeric
1/2 teaspoon fenugreek seeds, lightly crushed | freshly ground black pepper
250 g kipfler or other waxy potatoes, peeled and cubed
1.25 litres good-quality chicken stock | few sprigs thyme | 1 bay leaf
1 long strip of zest from 1/2 orange, all pith removed | sea salt | 2 tablespoons verjuice
juice of 1/2 lemon | 6 small free-range eggs, at room temperature
flatbread, lemon wedges or additional verjuice and tiny sour grapes (optional) to serve

HEAT THE OIL AND BUTTER IN A large, heavy-based saucepan over a low heat. Add the onion and garlic and fry gently until soft and translucent. Stir in the spices and 1 teaspoon ground black pepper and cook for another couple of minutes. Add the potato and cook for a minute, stirring to coat well with the onion mixture. Add the stock, herbs and orange zest. Add salt to taste and simmer gently for 30 minutes.

Just as you are ready to serve, remove the bay leaf and orange zest, then stir in the verjuice and lemon juice. Crack the eggs, carefully slip them into the simmering soup and poach gently for 3–4 minutes or until the yolks are barely set — they will continue to cook in the broth after you remove the pan from the heat.

Ladle the soup straight from the pan at the table, ensuring everyone has an egg. Season with salt and pepper and serve with flatbread and lemon wedges or verjuice, and a few tiny sour grapes, if you like, to garnish.

SERVES 6

Who knew that the English word 'spinach' derives from the Farsi word 'esfenaj'? In this Iranian dish known as ash-e sak, though, it is called sak, an Indian word — suggesting that the dish might have come to Persia from India, a reversal of the seventh-century trend that saw Persian recipes taken with Zoroastrian exiles who became Parsis in their new homeland.

Tasty little meatballs are found all around the Middle East, where they are known, variously, as kifta, köfte or, as here, koofteh. They are very popular in Persian cooking, and the word itself derives from the Farsi verb 'to pound', which describes the desired paste-like consistency. The secret is to mince the meat twice; ask your butcher to do this for you, or do it yourself at home. The mince must then be energetically and thoroughly kneaded so that the fat is evenly distributed throughout the meat and it turns into a soft, sticky paste. You can do this quickly in a food processor if you like, but chill the bowl and blade in the fridge first.

SPINACH SOUP WITH LITTLE BEEF KOOFTEH

2 tablespoons olive oil | 1 small onion, finely diced | 1 clove garlic, finely chopped | 1/2 teaspoon ground turmeric | 1/2 teaspoon freshly ground black pepper | 1.5 litres good-quality chicken stock | sea salt | 250 g spinach leaves, finely shredded | 1/2 cup coriander leaves | 2 free-range eggs, lightly whisked | 3 tablespoons verjuice | generous squeeze of lime juice

BEEF KOOFTEH **300 g lean beef, minced twice | 1 small onion, grated | 1 clove garlic, grated | 1/2 teaspoon dried mint | 1/2 teaspoon freshly ground black pepper | 1/2 teaspoon ground turmeric | 1/2 teaspoon sea salt | splash of extra-virgin olive oil**

TO MAKE THE KOOFTEH, COMBINE all the ingredients in a large bowl and knead thoroughly for at least a minute (alternatively, pulse in a chilled food processor). When everything is well combined, cover and refrigerate for 30 minutes.

Heat the oil in a very large, heavy-based saucepan over a low heat. Add the onion and garlic and fry gently until soft and translucent. Stir in the turmeric and pepper and cook for another couple of minutes. Add the stock and salt to taste, then simmer gently for 10 minutes.

While the soup is simmering, use wet hands to roll the beef koofteh mixture into smooth, even dumplings, about the size of a small walnut. You should get 24 dumplings from the mixture.

Pop the dumplings into the soup and bring to the boil. Lower the heat and simmer gently for 12 minutes, skimming away any impurities that rise to the surface.

Add the spinach to the pan and increase the heat to a rolling boil. Cook for 2 minutes, then stir in the coriander and eggs. Stir gently to distribute the egg threads. Add the verjuice and lime juice and season to taste. Serve immediately, making sure that everyone gets four koofteh.

SERVES **6**

We love fennel for its sweetness and subtle aniseed flavour. Here, it is transformed into a delightful lemony soup with a comforting cinnamon fragrance. It is made a little richer by adding cream and egg yolks towards the end of the cooking.

FENNEL SOUP WITH LEMON AND CINNAMON

60 ml olive oil | 2 onions, sliced | 2 cloves garlic, roughly chopped
2 leeks, roughly chopped | 3 large bulbs fennel, sliced
2 potatoes, peeled and cut into chunks | 1.5 litres good-quality chicken stock
1 cinnamon stick | zest of 1/2 lemon | 1/2 teaspoon ground allspice | 2 bay leaves
sea salt and freshly ground black pepper | 2 free-range egg yolks
150 ml cream (35% fat) | juice of 2 lemons | extra-virgin olive oil
1 teaspoon ground cinnamon | 1 tablespoon roughly chopped flat-leaf parsley leaves

HEAT THE OIL IN A LARGE, HEAVY-based saucepan and sauté the onions, garlic, leeks and fennel for a few minutes until they soften. Add the potatoes and chicken stock, then the cinnamon stick, lemon zest, allspice and bay leaves. Bring to the boil, then lower the heat and simmer gently for 20 minutes. Remove and discard the cinnamon stick, lemon zest and bay leaves, and season to taste with salt and pepper.

In a separate bowl, mix the egg yolks with the cream, then ladle in a spoonful of the hot soup. Whisk together well, then tip the egg mixture into the soup. Slowly return the soup to just below boiling, stirring it all the time. Remove from the heat and adjust the seasoning with extra salt and pepper and the lemon juice.

As you serve, drizzle each bowl with extra-virgin olive oil and sprinkle with a little cinnamon and parsley.

SERVES **6**

Known as harira, this soup is a Moroccan favourite, particularly popular during Ramadan, when it is served after a day of fasting. Harira is traditionally eaten with dates and a wedge of lemon or lime. It is often made with lamb in a hearty meat stock. This is a lighter version, all lemony and peppery. Garnish, if you like, with grilled seafood — delicate fillets of red mullet or garlicky prawns work well.

MOROCCAN CHICKPEA SOUP

SOUP 60 ml olive oil | 1 medium brown onion, diced | 2 cloves garlic, crushed
100 g brown lentils | 100 g chickpeas, soaked overnight and drained
2.5 litres vegetable or good-quality chicken stock | 400 g can crushed tomatoes
1/4 teaspoon ground cinnamon | 1/4 teaspoon ground ginger
1 pinch ground saffron (about 10 threads), lightly roasted and crushed | sea salt
1/2 teaspoon freshly ground black pepper | 60 ml dry sherry | juice and zest of 1 lemon
1 tablespoon chopped flat-leaf parsley leaves | 1 tablespoon chopped coriander leaves
1 tablespoon chopped celery leaves

GARLIC PRAWNS 1/4 teaspoon chilli flakes | 2 cloves garlic, crushed with 1/2 teaspoon salt
12 king prawns, tails and heads removed | 40 ml olive oil

HEAT THE OLIVE OIL IN A LARGE saucepan and gently sweat the onion and garlic until they soften. Add the lentils, soaked chickpeas and 2 litres of the stock. Simmer for an hour, or until the lentils and chickpeas are soft and beginning to break down. Use a hand-held electric beater on low speed to crush the pulses, but make sure not to turn them into a smooth purée. Add the tomatoes, cinnamon, ginger and saffron. If need be, adjust the consistency with additional stock. Bring the liquid to the boil, season with salt and pepper and finish off with the sherry, lemon juice and zest, parsley leaves, coriander and celery leaves.

Mix the chilli and garlic to a paste and rub it into the prawns. Allow them to sit for half an hour before cooking.

Heat a grill, pan or wok, add the oil and, when it is smoking hot, add the prawns. Cook them on a high heat for 2 minutes. Serve on top of the soup.

SERVES 6

SMALL DISHES

Yoghurt is an essential part of the Middle Eastern diet and appears on the table in many guises — mixed with water as a refreshing drink, or served as a thin, runny sauce or a thick, creamy dip as part of a mezze selection. It is often flavoured with fresh herbs or vegetables. There are plenty of quality commercial brands around, but home-made yoghurt tastes sweeter and fresher. To make it, all you need is milk and good-quality, natural live yoghurt to start things off — not a flavoured, sweetened variety.

HOME-MADE YOGHURT

1 litre full-cream milk | 1 tablespoon natural live yoghurt

PUT THE MILK IN A LARGE SAUCEPAN and bring to the boil. When the froth rises, turn off the heat and leave to cool. As you are dealing with a living 'culture', the bacteria will only grow within a certain temperature range — between 32°C (90°F) and 49°C (120°F). If you don't have a thermometer, the traditional way of testing the temperature is to dip your finger into the milk. You should be able to leave it for a count of 15 seconds. When the milk has cooled sufficiently, remove any skin that has formed on the surface.

In a glass or earthenware mixing bowl, beat a few tablespoons of hot milk into the yoghurt, then pour in the rest of the milk and beat again.

Cover the bowl with a tea towel or plastic wrap and leave it in a warm place, undisturbed, for at least 8 hours — overnight is ideal. It should thicken to a custard-like consistency. Transfer to the fridge, where it will keep for up to a week. If you want to keep making your own yoghurt, reserve a little to make another batch within 4 days.

MAKES 1 kg

STRAINED YOGHURT

1 kg thick natural yoghurt | 1 teaspoon sea salt | extra-virgin olive oil to serve

STIR TOGETHER THE YOGHURT AND the salt, then put the yoghurt into a clean muslin or cheesecloth square or tea towel. Tie the four corners together and suspend the bundle from a wooden spoon over a deep bowl. Refrigerate overnight, or for about 8 hours, to drain. To serve, tip into a bowl and flatten the surface. Make a little well in the top and fill with extra-virgin olive oil.

MAKES about 350 g

HAYDARI

Tip 350 g Strained Yoghurt (opposite) into a large bowl. Beat in 1 clove garlic crushed with 1 teaspoon sea salt, 1/2 cup finely chopped dill and 1 seeded and shredded long green chilli. Taste and adjust seasoning if necessary. Chill, covered, until ready to eat. Transfer to a serving bowl or plate and garnish with a sprinkle of sweet paprika and a drizzle of extra-virgin olive oil. Serve on little toasts or toasted flatbread. It's also delicious with köfte and all sorts of grills — meats, seafood, poultry and kebabs.

SERVES **4-6 as part of a mezze selection**

TZATZIKI

In a large bowl, mix together 350 g Strained Yoghurt (opposite), 2 seeded and grated small Lebanese cucumbers (skin left on), 1 clove garlic crushed with 1 teaspoon sea salt, 1 teaspoon dried mint, 1/2 cup roughly chopped mint leaves and the juice of 1 lemon. Season with a little sea salt and freshly ground black pepper. Chill until required and serve as a dip or with grilled meats. You can vary the final result by using different herbs. Instead of using chopped mint and dry mint, try substituting 1/2 cup chopped basil leaves to make basil tzatziki or 1/2 cup chopped tarragon leaves with a splash of arak or Pernod to make tarragon tzatziki.

SERVES **4-6 as part of a mezze selection**

WHIPPED FETA DIP

Soak 220 g sheep's feta in cold water for about 10 minutes to remove excess salt, changing the water twice. Crumble the feta roughly into a food processor and purée for a minute, pushing the mixture down from the sides once or twice. Add 150 g Strained Yoghurt (opposite) and a generous teaspoon of Dijon mustard and purée again until very smooth and creamy. Chill, covered, until needed. This dip will keep for up to a week. Serve with raw vegetables or warm or toasted flatbread. You could even thin it down with olive oil and use it to dress a robust cos lettuce salad. If you want to add another dimension of flavour, add a teaspoon of mild honey while puréeing.

SERVES **4-6 as part of a mezze selection**

Labneh (yoghurt cheese), the simplest of cheeses, is made regularly around the Middle East. In Lebanon and Syria, for instance, people eat it daily and it is widely available in the souks, dairies and supermarkets. It's hard to find commercially made labneh in western countries, but it is easy to make at home. The result will vary depending on how long you leave it to strain, which may be between 24 and 72 hours (the longer the time, the firmer the result).

After 24 hours' straining it makes a delicious spread, drizzled with olive oil and served with crusty bread and olives. Or serve it as an accompaniment for spicy dishes such as tagines, Indian curries or most rice dishes.

At the end of 72 hours you will have a very firm lump of fresh cheese. When ready to serve, form it into smooth round balls or quenelle shapes using spoons. Make an indentation in the top and fill it with rosewater and a big drop of extra-virgin olive oil. Alternatively, roll the firm labneh into small balls with oiled hands. Place the balls in jars with olive oil and the herbs of your choice. They will keep for up to 2 weeks in the refrigerator.

Labneh is infinitely versatile and lends itself to both savoury and sweet flavourings. You could try adding a teaspoon of garlic purée, for instance, or swirl in a spoonful of harissa, a hint of saffron or fresh herb purées such as mint, basil, oregano or dill. Sweet versions can be made with a splash of rosewater, orange-flower water or a fragrant honey.

YOGHURT CHEESE

1 kg thick natural yoghurt | 1 teaspoon sea salt | 50 ml extra-virgin olive oil to serve

MIX THE YOGHURT WITH THE SALT. Spoon into a clean muslin or cheesecloth square or a tea towel. Tie the four corners together and suspend the bundle from a wooden spoon over a deep bowl. Put it in the refrigerator and allow it to drain for 24–72 hours. The longer the hanging time, the firmer the result.

To serve, tip into a bowl and flatten the surface. Make a little well and fill with extra-virgin olive oil.

SERVES **4 as part of a mezze selection**

MINT LABNEH

Put 200 g thick natural yoghurt into a blender and add 1/2 cup mint leaves and 1/2 cup flat-leaf parsley leaves. Blitz to make a nice, fine, pale green purée. Put 500 g yoghurt cheese that has been strained for 24 hours into a mixing bowl with 1 teaspoon dried mint and 1 teaspoon sea salt. Stir together well, then swirl in the green purée for a pretty marbled effect. Serve to accompany spicy soups and braises, grilled poultry and meats, and traditional Middle Eastern favourites such as stuffed vine leaves and cabbage rolls.

SERVES **4 as part of a mezze selection**

SAFFRON LABNEH

Spoon 1 kg thick natural yoghurt (use sheep's milk for a richer result) into a clean muslin or cheesecloth square or a tea towel. Mix in 1 clove garlic crushed with 1 teaspoon sea salt, then sprinkle 10 saffron threads, lightly roasted and crushed, over the top and swirl it in roughly. Strain the yoghurt for 24–48 hours, as described opposite. To serve, use a spoon to make a well in the surface of the yoghurt cheese. Fill with extra-virgin olive oil then add a splash of rosewater. Serve with Seven-Vegetable Tagine (page 250).

SERVES **4 as part of a mezze selection**

SWEET LABNEH

In a mixing bowl, beat 1 kg thick natural yoghurt with 2 tablespoons honey, a generous splash of orange-flower water and the lightly crushed seeds of 4 cardamom pods. Spoon into a clean muslin or cheesecloth square or a tea towel. Strain the yoghurt for 24–48 hours, as described opposite. Serve with fresh strawberries or as accompaniment to syrupy cakes or puddings instead of cream.

SERVES **4 as part of a mezze selection**

No Middle Eastern cookbook would be complete without a homemade hummus recipe. It's so simple, there really is no excuse for not making your own.

If you want a shortcut, use a 400 g can of chickpeas, but be sure to rinse them well to get rid of the 'tinny' flavour. This version uses a lot of bicarbonate of soda in the soaking process, which helps break the pulses down. They are then cooked to a mush and blitzed, skins and all. The result is a superlative, super-smooth dip.

HUMMUS WITH TAHINI

250 g dried chickpeas | 2 tablespoons bicarbonate of soda
juice of up to 2 lemons | 1 clove garlic crushed with 1 teaspoon sea salt
100 ml tahini paste, well stirred | freshly ground black pepper

SOAK THE CHICKPEAS OVERNIGHT in twice their volume of cold water and the bicarbonate of soda. The next day, rinse the chickpeas very thoroughly. Don't rush this step — you should take at least 2 or 3 minutes rinsing them under cold running water. You can rub them to help remove the bicarb.

Place the chickpeas in a large pan with plenty of fresh water and bring it to the boil. Then lower the heat and simmer for up to 2 hours, until they have disintegrated into a porridge-like mush. Keep an eye on them during the cooking process, and top them up with extra water every 20 minutes or so.

Tip the chickpeas into a food processor with the lemon juice, garlic paste and tahini and whiz until the mixture is very smooth. Taste and adjust the seasoning until you get the right balance of nuttiness, acid and pungent garlic. As it cools, the hummus will thicken, so thin it down with a little more lemon juice or water as needed.

SERVES **4 as part of a mezze selection**

HUMMUS WITH CRUSHED CHICKPEAS, PINE NUTS AND CUMIN

As described opposite, soak 250 g dried chickpeas overnight in water to which 2 tablespoons bicarbonate of soda has been added, then thoroughly rinse. Put the chickpeas in a large pan of fresh water and bring to the boil. Lower the heat and simmer for 1–2 hours, until the chickpeas are tender — the timing will depend on how old they are. Don't cook them to a mush, but you should be able to squish them easily between your fingers. When cool enough to handle, swish them around to loosen the skins and remove as many as you can. The more skins you can remove, the better. Drain the chickpeas and reserve 1/2 cup to garnish. Tip the rest into a food processor with 1 small clove garlic crushed with 1 teaspoon sea salt, 1/2 teaspoon ground cumin, the juice of 1 1/2 lemons and 50 ml olive oil. While still warm, blitz to a smooth purée.

To prepare the garnish, heat 50 ml olive oil in a small pan and fry 2 finely sliced garlic cloves and 50 g pine nuts until they start to colour. Remove from the heat and allow to cool slightly. Tip onto the hummus and squeeze on the juice of 1/2 lemon. Serve immediately with plenty of Arabic flatbread.

SERVES **6–8 as part of a mezze selection**

HUMMUS WITH SPICED MARINATED LAMB AND PINE NUTS

Heat a splash of extra-virgin olive oil in a hot frying pan and fry 1 quantity Minced Lamb Manoushi filling (page 281) for 5 minutes, stirring continuously, until well browned. Leave the meat to cool slightly while you toast 2 tablespoons pine nuts. To serve, put 500 g Hummus with Tahini (opposite) into a serving dish, make a well in the centre and mound in the spicy mince. Scatter on the pine nuts and drizzle generously with extra-virgin olive oil. Serve with Onion and Sumac Salad (page 161) and lots of warm Arabic flatbread.

SERVES **6 as part of a mezze selection**

Versions of this superb dip are found throughout the Middle East and Eastern Mediterranean, and local variations abound. The earthy tahini, sharp lemon or pungent garlic should not dominate, but all should meld into one rich, creamy, smoky whole, which is infinitely greater than the sum of its parts.

One thing which we are adamant about, though, is that the eggplants must be roasted over a direct flame. This direct heat chars and blackens the skin and results in that exciting, mysterious smokiness. If you have a gas stove, cook them directly on the top burners. A similar effect can be obtained on the coals of a barbecue or in the white-hot ashes of a bonfire. If you have an electric stove, you will have to roast them in the oven, but you won't get the same result.

BABA GHANOUSH

4 medium eggplants (aubergines), about 1 kg
1 large clove garlic crushed with 1/2 teaspoon salt | 200 g natural yoghurt
juice of 3 lemons | 3 tablespoons tahini | sea salt and freshly ground black pepper
extra-virgin olive oil and Arabic flatbread to serve

PRICK THE EGGPLANTS ALL OVER with a fork then sit them directly on the naked flame of your stove burners. Set the flame to low–medium heat and cook for at least 10 minutes, constantly turning until the whole eggplant is blackened and blistered and has collapsed in on itself. Remove from the flame and place on a small cake rack in a sealed container or plastic bag (so juices can drain off). Allow to cool for about 10 minutes. For a milder smoky flavour, you can char the eggplants on the flame for 5 minutes and then finish off the roasting in a preheated 180°C (Gas 4) oven for 10 minutes.

When the eggplants are cool, gently peel away the skin from the flesh with a small sharp knife. Allow the skin to come away naturally, and do not scrape the flesh directly off the skin, as it will have a burnt flavour. For this reason too, be careful not to allow any pieces of the skin itself into the mixture. Sit the pulp in a colander and allow to stand for 5–10 minutes to drain further.

When you are ready to assemble the dish, mix the garlic paste with the yoghurt then mix this into the eggplant pulp with the lemon juice and tahini.

Season with salt and pepper and mix to combine — the dip should be coarse, not smooth. Don't be afraid to taste and adjust seasonings, as it should taste sharp. Serve with a big splash of extra-virgin olive oil as a dip with plenty of Arabic flatbread, or as a deliciously different accompaniment to grilled or roast lamb.

As a nice variation, try making a Persian eggplant and walnut dip. Omit the tahini and garnish with 80 g roasted walnuts, roughly chopped, just before serving.

SERVES **4 as part of a mezze selection**

In its true form, taramasalata is a creamy smooth, pinky-golden purée, tangy with garlic and lemon juice, and bursting with flavours of the sea. And it couldn't be easier to make, requiring nothing more than a little blitzing in a food processor. When you've tasted the light, fluffy and far subtler homemade version, you may never buy a ready-made version again!

Tarama itself is the salted preserved roe of grey mullet (commercial versions are often made from less expensive cod's roe) and comes as a very firm, hot-pink paste. Avoid any that seems to have an orange tinge, as it is likely to be bitter. We used to rinse the tarama to remove some of the excess salt. But it is rather fragile, and we've come to the conclusion that rinsing is not really necessary.

TARAMASALATA

2 thick slices good-quality white bread | 100 g tarama
1 clove garlic, roughly chopped | juice of 1-1½ lemons | 250 ml olive oil
250 ml vegetable oil | about 100 ml water

REMOVE THE CRUSTS FROM THE bread and chop the bread roughly. Put it into a mixing bowl and pour on enough water to cover. Then fish out the bread and squeeze it tightly. Put the scrunched-up bread into a food processor with the tarama, garlic and the juice of 1 lemon and whiz everything to a paste.

Mix the two oils together and start to drizzle them into the processor. Begin with about 100 ml of oil, then loosen the mixture with about 2 tablespoons of water. Continue adding first the oil, then the water in similar quantities, and finish with the remaining lemon juice. The purée should be light and fluffy and the prettiest pale pink-gold colour.

Taste the taramasalata and adjust the balance if necessary. Tip it into a container, cover and refrigerate, where it will keep for 4–5 days.

SERVES **4 as part of a mezze selection**

This is a Persian borani — a kind of yoghurt 'salad' or side dish made with endless different vegetables and herbs. This is a particularly brilliant combination — serve it as an accompaniment to grilled or roast lamb, spread it onto little toasts or flatbread as a pre-dinner nibble or serve it as a dip with fresh vegetables.

SPINACH, TURMERIC AND GOLDEN-RAISIN DIP

2 scant tablespoons golden raisins, roughly chopped | 1 tablespoon olive oil
2 large shallots, finely chopped | 1/4 teaspoon ground turmeric | 250 g spinach leaves
200 g thick natural yoghurt | sea salt and freshly ground black pepper
squeeze of lemon juice

SOAK THE GOLDEN RAISINS IN A little warm water for 15 minutes, then drain.

Heat the oil in a heavy-based frying pan over medium heat. Fry the shallots until soft and translucent. Stir in the turmeric and golden raisins and fry for another 2–3 minutes. Remove from the heat and leave to cool.

Bring a large saucepan of salted water to a boil and blanch the spinach for 20 seconds. Refresh in cold water, then squeeze firmly to extract as much liquid as you can. Chop the spinach finely, then mix into the yogurt. Season with salt and pepper to taste and add lemon juice.

Mound the spinach and yoghurt into a small bowl and spoon the turmeric, shallot and golden raisin mixture over the top. Alternatively, mix it all together.

SERVES **6 as part of a mezze selection**

Preserved lemons add a wonderful tang to guacamole. Serve as part of a mezze selection, or as a more formal starter with strips of smoked eel and toasted baguette slices.

PRESERVED LEMON GUACAMOLE

GUACAMOLE 1 large ripe but firm avocado, cut into 5 mm dice
1 small tomato, skinned, seeded and cut into 5 mm dice | 1/3 cup coriander chopped leaves
1 long green chilli, seeded, scraped and finely chopped | juice of 1 lime
1 clove garlic crushed with 1/2 teaspoon sea salt
1/2 preserved lemon (page 394), skin only, finely chopped
1/2 medium purple onion, finely chopped
extra-virgin olive oil for drizzling | 1 teaspoon ground sumac (optional)
sea salt and freshly ground black pepper (optional)

GENTLY COMBINE THE AVOCADO, tomato, herbs, lime juice, garlic paste, preserved lemon and onion in a large mixing bowl. Drizzle a little extra-virgin olive oil around the plate and sprinkle with sumac and salt and pepper, if desired.

SERVES 4 as part of a mezze selection

ALMOND TARATOR

250 g blanched almonds | 3 cloves garlic crushed with 1 teapoon sea salt
juice of 1 lemon | 50 ml champagne vinegar | 1 tablespoon honey | 4 egg yolks
525 ml olive oil | 100-150 ml lukewarm water | freshly ground black pepper

BLITZ THE ALMONDS IN A FOOD processor until roughly crushed. Add the garlic paste, lemon juice, vinegar, honey and egg yolks and blitz until smooth and creamy. With the motor running, slowly drizzle in about half the oil, followed by half the water to loosen and stabilise the mixture. Slowly drizzle in the rest of the oil to form a thick, creamy mayonnaise — add a little more water if it is too thick. Season with pepper and check for salt — you may need to add a little more. To give the tarator a smoother, finer texture, you can process it in a blender on high for a few minutes.

Tarator is great served as a dip with raw vegetables or to accompany Kibbeh (page 116), seafood or lamb dishes.

SERVES 6 as part of a mezze selection

In the West we have an attitude towards fresh vegetables and herbs which is ambivalent, at best. In the Middle East they embrace them, and most meals will begin with a platter of crudités — fresh chunks of carrot, cucumber, pepper, radish and wedges of cos lettuce.

In Iran a basket of fresh, unadorned herbs — sabzi khordan — are the first thing to appear on the table. Eaten with tangy, feta-like white cheese and flaps of soft flatbread, it's a totally addictive way of starting a meal. As the fresh, vital flavours sharpen the appetite, you can't help but feel somewhat virtuous, munching on all that greenery.

Obviously, this approach to eating depends entirely on the freshness and quality of the herbs — straight from the garden is best! Failing that, try to buy herbs in big, hearty bunches from the market or a good greengrocer.

This is hardly a recipe but, rather, a list of popular herbs that feature regularly on the Persian table, depending on the season. We've included two of the more unusual ones — costmary and summer savory — for those who are keen gardeners, as it's simple enough to grow them yourself. The idea is to choose four or five herbs that you fancy, and toss them together on a serving platter or in a basket. You'll need about a cup of herbs per person to be really Iranian — and you'll be surprised how quickly you want to eat more and more of them. At first it may seem strange to eat this sort of salad without a dressing, but doing so really allows the flavour of each herb to shine through.

SABZI KHORDAN

baby beetroot leaves | basil (all the varieties, including Asian) | chives (regular and garlic)
coriander | costmary | dill | flat-leaf parsley | French tarragon | mint (all the varieties)
radishes | spring onions | summer savory | turnip leaves | watercress
fresh white cheese and warm flatbread to serve

TO PREPARE THE HERBS, PICK THE leaves or sprigs from their stalks (discarding any wilted or discoloured leaves), then gently wash them and leave them to soak in a bowl of cold water for 20 minutes or so to allow any sand or dirt to sink to the bottom. Then drain and air-dry them in a colander, wrap them loosely in a clean tea towel and store in the fridge. Prepared this way, herbs should keep for about a week.

Serve a platter of herbs with your favourite fresh white cheese — a creamy feta is ideal — and a pile of warm flatbread, so that everyone can wrap or roll to their heart's content.

In Lebanon and Syria they have tabbouleh; in Turkey they have kisir. The ingredients in kisir vary from town to town, but in the south-east of the country it is usually enlivened with red pepper paste and pomegranate molasses. While Arabic tabbouleh is, in essence, a herb salad flecked with burgul, Turkish kisir is staunchly grain based. Both salads, though, make a great addition to a mezze table, and are best eaten scooped up in little lettuce leaves.

Don't be tempted to increase the amount of boiling water here: it doesn't look like a lot of liquid, but the burgul will soften further in the juice from the tomatoes and the dressing.

SPICY KISIR SALAD

200 g fine white burgul | 125 ml boiling water | 1 tablespoon tomato paste
1 teaspoon hot Turkish red pepper paste | juice of 1 lemon
1 teaspoon pomegranate molasses | 60 ml extra-virgin olive oil
1 long green chilli, seeded and finely chopped | 3 large vine-ripened tomatoes, chopped
5 spring onions, finely chopped | 1 cup chopped flat-leaf parsley leaves
1 cup chopped mint leaves | sea salt and freshly ground white pepper
baby lettuce leaves to serve

SOAK THE BURGUL IN THE BOILING water for 15 minutes, then tip into a large bowl.

Add the pastes, lemon juice, pomegranate molasses and oil to the burgul. Use clean hands to work the grains so that the pastes and liquid are evenly distributed and the burgul is tinted a pretty pale pink. Add the chilli, tomatoes, spring onions and herbs and mix well. Taste and adjust the seasoning by adding salt and pepper and more lemon juice or pomegranate molasses if required.

Mound the salad onto a serving platter and garnish with baby lettuce leaves. Alternatively, use wet hands to form the mixture into walnut-sized balls and serve them nestled in the lettuce leaves.

SERVES **6-8 as part of a mezze selection**

TABBOULEH WITH ROASTED HAZELNUTS

160 g hazelnuts | 2 bunches flat-leaf parsley, leaves only | 1/2 bunch mint, finely shredded
1 large purple onion, finely chopped | 4 medium tomatoes, finely diced
juice of 2 lemons | 1/2 teaspoon ground allspice | 1/3 teaspoon ground cinnamon
1/2 teaspoon sea salt | 1/2 teaspoon finely ground black pepper | 100–120 ml olive oil
1 tablespoon hazelnut oil

PREHEAT THE OVEN TO 160°C (GAS 3). Spread the hazelnuts out on a baking sheet and put it in the oven for 8–10 minutes. After 4 minutes, shake the tray around so that the nuts colour evenly. Remove the tray from the oven and tip the nuts into a tea towel. Rub them vigorously between your hands to remove as much of the papery brown skin as you can. Weigh out 60 g nuts, cut them in halves and reserve for garnish. Chop the remaining nuts finely to the texture of coarse breadcrumbs, then sieve them to remove the dust.

Put the parsley, mint, onion, tomatoes and hazelnut crumbs into a large bowl. Add the remaining ingredients and mix well with your hands. Taste and adjust the seasoning if necessary.

Mound the tabbouleh on a serving platter and arrange the reserved hazelnut halves around the base. Drizzle with hazelnut oil and serve.

SERVES **8–10 as part of a mezze selection**

LENTIL TABBOULEH

Put 100 g Puy lentils into a small saucepan and cover with twice their volume of cold water. Bring to the boil, then lower the heat and simmer for 25–30 minutes, or until the lentils are tender. Drain well and leave to cool. Tip the lentils into a large mixing bowl and add the juice of 1–2 lemons, 1/2 cup roughly shredded mint leaves, 2 cups roughly shredded flat-leaf parsley, 3 finely diced shallots, 2 seeded and diced tomatoes, 1 teaspoon ground allspice, 1 teaspoon ground cinnamon, sea salt and freshly ground black pepper and 60 ml extra-virgin olive oil. Toss well and leave for 10 minutes so the flavours mingle and intensify.

This tabbouleh is also the perfect accompaniment to grilled sardines, hot off a charcoal grill. Brush them with a little olive oil and season with salt, pepper and sumac. They'll only take a few minutes on each side.

SERVES **8 as part of a mezze selection**

One of our very favourite Turkish salads, this almost has the consistency of a gazpacho soup and definitely needs to be served with a spoon. The secret is to dice the ingredients individually first, then chop them together to very fine and even dice. This salad has a wonderful balance of heat from the chillies and sweetness from the molasses. Serve it as part of a mezze selection, or with kebabs. Offer lots of Turkish bread to mop up the juices.

TURKISH SPOON SALAD

2 very ripe vine-ripened tomatoes, skinned and finely diced
1 long red banana pepper, seeded and finely diced
2 long red chillies, seeded and finely diced
1 small Lebanese cucumber, peeled, seeded and finely diced
1 large shallot, peeled and finely diced
2 tablespoons finely chopped flat-leaf parsley leaves | 1/2 teaspoon dried mint
1 heaped teaspoon hot Turkish red pepper paste | 1/2 teaspoon pomegranate molasses
1 teaspoon red-wine vinegar | 60 ml extra-virgin olive oil
sea salt and freshly ground black pepper | pomegranate seeds to garnish (optional)

PLACE THE DICED TOMATOES, pepper, chillies, cucumber and shallot on a large chopping board. Use a very sharp, large knife to chop them all together. You are aiming for well-integrated, even and fine dice. Scrape into a large bowl and add the herbs, pepper paste, molasses, vinegar and 1 tablespoon of the oil, then season with salt and pepper. Stir thoroughly and leave for 20 minutes to macerate.

Just before serving, tip the salad into a colander and drain for a few moments to remove some of the excess liquid — you want the salad to be wet, but not swimming in liquid. Pour out onto a shallow serving platter, then drizzle on the remaining oil and scatter over the pomegranate seeds, if using. Serve straight away.

SERVES 4 as part of a mezze selection

We were surprised to see interpretations of this old-fashioned favourite on buffet tables at restaurants and hotels around Iran. Its success rests on the quality of the ingredients, so use young, tender, freshly cooked vegetables. It's also vital to use French tarragon, which has a much more intense flavour than the Russian variety.

For a heartier dish, add about 250 g of cooked chicken cut into small chunks — a peculiarly Iranian addition.

PERSIAN-STYLE RUSSIAN SALAD WITH TARRAGON MAYONNAISE

250 g peas in the pod or 100 g frozen peas | 400 g waxy potatoes
6 baby carrots, lightly scraped | 250 g cooked chicken, cut into small chunks (optional)
1/2 cup finely diced cornichons | 3 hard-boiled free-range eggs, finely chopped
2 tablespoons thick natural yoghurt or sour cream
3-4 tablespoons Mayonnaise (page 385) or good-quality bought mayonnaise
2 tablespoons chopped tarragon leaves, or to taste
sea salt and freshly ground black pepper

SHELL THE PEAS, IF USING FRESH ones. Cook the potatoes, carrots and peas, separately, until tender. Peel the potatoes and cut into 1 cm dice. Cut the carrots into 1 cm chunks. Toss the vegetables together in a large mixing bowl and allow to cool.

Add the chicken, if using, along with the cornichons and egg and toss gently.

In a separate bowl, mix the yoghurt with the mayonnaise. Stir in the chopped tarragon, adding more or less to taste, and season with salt and pepper. Add to the salad and toss so that everything is lightly coated. Add a little more mayonnaise if necessary. Taste and adjust the seasoning to your liking.

SERVES 6 as part of a mezze selection

Bronte and Tarkyn are my stepchildren, and since they came into my life I've had a wonderful time experimenting with child-friendly recipes, and getting them involved in the kitchen. Luckily they love cooking, and dreamt up this salad all by themselves. It's become a firm family favourite.

BRONTE AND TARKYN'S CUCUMBER BURGUL SALAD

60 g fine white burgul
1 Lebanese cucumber, peeled, seeded and cut into 2 mm dice
2 tablespoons chopped flat-leaf parsley leaves | 2 tablespoons chopped mint leaves
2 tablespoons snipped chives | 1 teaspoon dried mint
2 tablespoons thick natural yoghurt | 40 ml extra-virgin olive oil
juice of 1/2 lemon | sea salt and freshly ground black pepper
100 g soft, creamy feta, crumbled | edible rose petals to garnish (optional)

SOAK THE BURGUL FOR 5 MINUTES in just enough cold water to cover it. Drain it well through a sieve, then tip it into a tea towel and squeeze out as much water as you can. Tip into a mixing bowl.

Add the diced cucumber and the fresh and dried herbs, then pour in the yoghurt, olive oil and lemon juice and season with salt and pepper. Finally add the crumbled feta and gently mix. Spoon onto a plate and garnish with rose petals, if using.

SERVES 4 as part of a mezze selection

A stunning salad from south-east Turkey where all the ingredients grow in abundance. I love the balance of sweet, salty and chilli-hot, and the ruby-red pomegranate seeds look gorgeous against the muted khakis and greens of the other ingredients.

GREEN OLIVE, WALNUT AND POMEGRANATE SALAD

100 g walnuts | 100 g pitted green olives, washed and roughly chopped
40 g unsalted pistachio kernels, roughly chopped | 1/2 cup pomegranate seeds
2 small shallots, peeled and finely diced | 1 red bullet chilli, seeded and finely diced
1 tablespoon shredded flat-leaf parsley leaves | 1 tablespoon olive oil
1 tablespoon walnut oil | splash of pomegranate molasses | juice of 1/2 lemon
sea salt and freshly ground black pepper

PREHEAT THE OVEN TO 180°C (GAS 4). Scatter the walnuts onto a baking tray and roast for 5–10 minutes, or until a deep golden brown. Tip the nuts into a tea towel and rub well to remove as much skin as possible. Chop the walnuts roughly and toss in a sieve to remove any remaining skin and dust. Combine all the ingredients in a large bowl and toss gently. Leave to stand for 5 minutes or so before serving, to allow the flavours to meld.

SERVES 4 as part of a mezze selection

Olive salads are often found in Middle Eastern mezze selections. This one is particularly good, as the nuttiness of the toasted sesame seeds and creamy richness of the eggs make a lovely contrast to the salty olives. Serve as an accompaniment to grills — fish in particular — and with pickled or cured meats.

EGG AND OLIVE SALAD

1 small purple onion, peeled and finely sliced crosswise | 4 free-range eggs
65 g green olives, pitted and halved | 100 g pine nuts, toasted and roughly chopped
1/4 cup flat-leaf parsley leaves | 2 teaspoons sweet paprika
2 teaspoons ground sumac | 1/2 teaspoon cayenne pepper
3 tablespoons sesame seeds, toasted | juice of 1 lemon
1 clove garlic crushed with 1/2 teaspoon sea salt
100 ml extra-virgin olive oil | freshly ground white pepper | sweet paprika to serve

SOAK THE ONION IN COLD WATER for 10 minutes to reduce the sharpness.

Put the eggs into a bowl with hot tap water for 5 minutes to bring them to room temperature. Bring a pan of water to the boil. Carefully lower in the eggs and cook for 5 1/2 minutes. Remove from the water and refresh briefly under cold running water.

When the eggs are cool, peel and chop 3 of them roughly. Reserve the fourth egg for garnish. Put the chopped eggs in a large mixing bowl with three-quarters of the onion, the olives, pine nuts, parsley leaves, spices and sesame seeds. In another small bowl, whisk together the lemon juice, garlic paste and olive oil. Pour enough of the dressing onto the salad to moisten it, and toss lightly. Taste and season with pepper.

To serve, pile the salad into a small serving bowl and make a little well in the top. Fill with the remaining onion slices. Slice the top off the reserved egg to reveal the yolk and sit it on top of the onion. Sprinkle the egg and salad with a little paprika and serve at room temperature.

SERVES 4 as part of a mezze selection

Silverbeet (Swiss chard) is very popular in Lebanon and Syria, and both leaves and stems are used. The leaves are a little more robust than those of spinach, and have a unique, tangy flavour. In this classic mezze dish they are braised in flavoured oil and served with tahini sauce and topped with crisp fried onions.

BRAISED SILVERBEET WITH CRISP FRIED ONIONS AND TAHINI SAUCE

CRISP FRIED ONIONS **2½ onions, finely sliced | ½ teaspoon sea salt | 125 ml olive oil**

BRAISED SILVERBEET **1 large bunch silverbeet (Swiss chard) | 50 ml olive oil**
½ onion, finely diced | 1 clove garlic | 1 tablespoon coriander seeds, lightly roasted
juice of 1 lemon | 150 ml white wine | 100 ml good-quality chicken stock or water
sea salt and freshly ground black pepper

TAHINI SAUCE **1 clove garlic, crushed with ¼ teaspoon salt**
125 ml tahini, well stirred | 80 ml lemon juice | paprika

PUT THE ONIONS INTO A BOWL AND use your hands to break them up thoroughly. Sprinkle on the salt and toss through. Leave for 15 minutes. Rinse the onions well, then use your hands to squeeze out as much moisture as you can before drying the onions very thoroughly on paper towel. It is important that the onions are as dry as you can get them. Heat the oil in a large heavy-based frying pan. When it's nearly smoking, add the onions and fry for 8–10 minutes. You'll need to move them around the pan continuously, to ensure that they brown evenly and don't burn. The onions will darken and caramelise to a deep golden brown. Drain on paper towel and reserve.

Wash the silverbeet in several changes of water then slice out the stems, reserving them for another use. Shred the leaves roughly. Heat the oil in a large frying pan and sauté the onion and garlic until they start to soften. Meanwhile, use a mortar and pestle to crush the coriander seeds as finely as you can. Tip into a sieve to remove the husks.

Add the coriander seeds to the pan with the silverbeet, lemon juice, wine and stock. Season with salt and pepper, cover the pan and cook on a low heat for 20 minutes. Towards the end of the cooking time, remove the lid and increase the heat to allow some of the braising liquid to evaporate.

To make the tahini sauce, stir the garlic paste into the tahini, then gradually mix in the lemon juice and enough cold water to thin the sauce to the consistency of pouring cream. Serve the braised silverbeet with plenty of tahini sauce and the crisp onions. Sprinkle with paprika before serving.

SERVES **4–6 as part of a mezze selection**

This is such a versatile dish, equally happy as a mezze dish, on its own — perhaps with some Arabic flatbread or crusty bread and butter — or as an accompaniment to pink-roasted, garlicky lamb, grilled white fish or a humble roast chicken.

SWEET AND SOUR EGGPLANT SALAD

1 medium eggplant (aubergine), peeled | sea salt | 100 ml olive oil
1 purple onion, finely sliced | 1 tablespoon golden raisins, chopped
1 tablespoon pomegranate molasses | juice of 1/2 lemon | drizzle of honey
175 ml hot water | finely chopped flat-leaf parsley leaves

CUT THE EGGPLANT IN HALF lengthwise then cut each half into half-moons, 1 cm thick. Put them in a colander and sprinkle with salt. After 20 minutes, rinse the pieces under cold running water and pat dry with paper towel.

Heat the oil and fry the eggplant pieces, turning them from time to time, until they are coloured a light golden brown. Add the onion and raisins to the pan. Mix the pomegranate molasses with the lemon juice, honey and hot water and add to the pan. Toss well, so that everything is evenly coated. Continue to cook until the onion and eggplant are both meltingly soft. Leave to cool, then taste and adjust the seasoning, if necessary. Serve at room temperature, sprinkled with parsley.

SERVES 4 as part of a mezze selection

ARTICHOKES COOKED À LA NIÇOISE

20 small artichokes
a large bowl of cold water acidulated with the juice of 2 lemons
1 litre water | juice of 4 lemons | 500 ml white wine | 250 ml olive oil
4 shallots, peeled and quartered | 1 teaspoon coarsely ground black pepper
1 bay leaf | 2 sprigs thyme | 1 teaspoon fennel seeds | 2 cloves garlic
3 dried chillies | 8 strands saffron | 1 teaspoon salt

TRIM THE OUTER LEAVES FROM THE artichokes and place the artichokes in the acidulated water. Bring to the boil 1 litre of water with the remaining ingredients, and boil for 20 minutes. Drain the artichokes and add to the liquid — it should just cover them. Top up with boiling water if necessary. Bring back to a rolling boil and cook for 5–10 minutes, or until the artichokes are just tender. Remove from the heat and allow to cool in the marinade. Arrange the artichokes in a 4-litre jar and cover with the marinade. Seal tightly and sterilise by placing the whole jar in a pan of cold water, bringing to the boil and simmering for 10 minutes. These pickled artichokes will keep unopened for 5 months. Once opened, they will keep in the fridge for up to a month.

SERVES **6 as part of a mezze selection**

FRESH BROAD BEANS, ARTICHOKES AND PEAS

Blanch 100 g shelled fresh peas in boiling water for 2 minutes; drain and refresh in cold water. Blanch 150 g shelled fresh broad beans for 2 minutes; drain, refresh in cold water then peel. Peel 150 g shallots and place in a pan of cold, lightly salted water. Bring to the boil, lower the heat and simmer until just tender, about 6 minutes. Cut Artichokes Cooked à la Niçoise (above; or use bought artichokes in oil) in quarters. Cut 100 g bacon into batons and fry until golden. Add 1 teaspoon honey, cook for 1 minute, then strain the bacon through a sieve. In a clean pan melt 1 teaspoon butter and 60 ml extra-virgin olive oil and lightly sauté 1 finely chopped small clove of garlic. Add the whole shallots and mix well in the oil mixture. Add the broad beans and heat for a further minute or so, moving gently around in the oil. Finally, add the peas, artichokes, 1/2 cup whole mint leaves and 1/2 teaspoon sherry vinegar. Season with salt and pepper and serve.

SERVES **6 as part of a mezze selection**

You'll find cooked vegetable salads all around the Middle East and eastern Mediterranean, usually served at room temperature.

Beetroot are especially well suited to being served in this way. Dress them in the sharp, herby dressing while they're warm from the oven for maximum flavour. They are equally good as part of a mezze selection or as a vegetable accompaniment to roasts, barbecues or grills.

BABY BEETROOT IN A HERBED DRESSING

2 bunches baby red beetroot (about 600 g) | 4 cloves garlic, roughly smashed
sea salt | 1 tablespoon extra-virgin olive oil | 2 shallots, peeled and finely sliced
1/2 teaspoon freshly ground black pepper | 100 g feta, roughly crumbled

HERBED DRESSING **1 clove garlic crushed with 1 teaspoon sea salt | juice of 1 lemon**
30 ml olive oil | 30 ml walnut oil | 1 tablespoon dried oregano
1/4 cup chopped flat-leaf parsley leaves | baby soft herb leaves to garnish (optional)

PREHEAT THE OVEN TO 180°C (GAS 4). Wash the beetroot thoroughly to remove any grit, paying special attention to the area close to the stalks. Trim the roots and cut off the stalks, leaving about 3 cm attached. Place in a baking tray and scatter in the garlic cloves. Season lightly with salt, then add the oil and toss thoroughly. Cover the tray loosely with foil and roast for 30–45 minutes, until the beetroot are tender.

While the beetroot are cooking, whisk together the garlic paste, lemon juice and oils to make the dressing.

Remove the tray from the oven and discard the garlic. When the beetroot are just cool enough to handle, peel them and cut them in half lengthwise. Place in a large bowl with the shallots and season with salt and pepper. Add the herbs to the dressing, whisk, and pour onto the beetroot. Check the seasoning, then add the crumbled feta and toss gently. Garnish with baby herb leaves, if using. Serve warm or cold.

SERVES **4 as part of a mezze selection**

Although it's not terribly Middle Eastern to use wine in cooking, it adds a lovely dimension to this cooked vegetable salad. Here we also use orange, cardamom and coriander, which go particularly well with the carrots. You can strain, freeze and re-use the cooking liquor for other braised vegetable dishes.

Serve this versatile dish as part of a mezze selection. It also makes a good accompaniment to grilled chicken or lamb, or to baked fish.

BABY CARROTS AND LEEKS COOKED IN OLIVE OIL WITH ORANGE ZEST AND SPICES

10 baby carrots | 4 small leeks, white part only | 4 long red chillies | 4 cloves garlic, peeled long piece of zest from 1 orange | 2 bay leaves | few sprigs thyme | 1/2 teaspoon dried mint 5 cardamom pods | 1 teaspoon coriander seeds, lightly crushed 1/2 teaspoon black peppercorns, lightly crushed | juice of 3 lemons | 400 ml dry white wine 500 ml water | 400 ml extra-virgin olive oil | 1/2 teaspoon salt

SCRAPE THE CARROTS, THEN TRIM off the stalks and cut the carrots in half lengthwise. Split the leeks, keeping them attached at the root end, then carefully rinse under running water to remove any lingering dirt. Cut away the root end, then cut the leeks in half crosswise so they are about the same length as the carrots. Split each piece lengthwise. Split the chillies lengthwise, leaving them attached at the stalk. Use the point of a sharp knife to scrape out the seeds.

Put the carrots and leeks into a large, heavy-based, non-reactive saucepan. Add the remaining ingredients and stir well.

Press a piece of baking paper, cut to the size of the pan, down over the vegetables. Bring to the boil, covered, then lower the heat and simmer very gently for 25–30 minutes, or until the carrots are tender. Remove the pan from the heat and leave the vegetables to cool in the liquid.

When ready to serve, transfer the vegetables from the poaching liquor to a platter — you may want to discard the zest and other larger herbs and spices. Strain the poaching liquor and refrigerate or freeze it for later use.

SERVES **4 as part of a mezze selection**

Another of our favourite cooked vegetable salads. Serve as is, or with a dollop of creamy, garlicky Toum (page 386).

MONKS' SALAD WITH GARLICKY DRESSING

1 bunch baby turnips, peeled | 1/2 bunch baby carrots, scraped
1/2 bunch baby heirloom (purple) carrots, scraped | 8 baby leeks
8 shallots, peeled | 1/2 small cauliflower, broken into florets | 150 g baby green beans
olive oil | 60 ml sherry vinegar | 80 ml extra-virgin olive oil
1 small clove garlic crushed with 1/2 teaspoon salt
sea salt and lots of freshly ground black pepper

SPICE BAG 1 tablespoon coriander seeds | 1 tablespoon black peppercorns
1 tablespoon allspice berries | 1 red bullet chilli, split lengthwise

WASH, DRY AND TRIM ALL THE vegetables. Put them in a large, heavy-based casserole dish and pour on enough olive oil to cover them. Tuck the spice bag in among the vegetables and bring to the boil. Then lower the heat as far as possible — you just want to see the odd tiny bubble rising to the surface. Cook for about 10 minutes, by which time the vegetables should be just tender. Turn off the heat and leave the vegetables to cool in the oil.

Remove the vegetables from the oil and put them into a colander to drain. Discard the spice bag. Whisk together the vinegar, oil and garlic paste to make a dressing. Tip the vegetables into a large bowl, pour on the dressing, toss everything together, then taste and season with plenty of salt and pepper.

SERVES 4 as part of a mezze selection

This is the kind of dish that we love to knock up for an impromptu supper, using whatever leftovers we can find. This omelette is closer to an Italian frittata — thick and chunky, rather than semi-soft and folded like the French version. In Spain they'd be just as likely to colour the eggs with saffron to make a rich golden tortilla. We include it in the ingredients here, but feel free to vary the recipe as you choose. The real beauty of a meal like this is that you can throw in whatever goodies you find in the fridge.

This version, true to its Spanish roots, includes potatoes, thick chunks of spicy chorizo and the salty tang of large green olives. If you have any red peppers (capsicums) around, or tomatoes, throw them in for extra colour. This omelette is lovely eaten warm for supper or lunch, and is also delicious eaten cold. Cut it into wedges and include it in a mezze selection.

SPANISH OMELETTE WITH POTATO, GREEN OLIVES AND CHORIZO

100 ml olive oil | 1 onion, roughly chopped | 3 potatoes, cut into 1 cm cubes
2 cloves garlic, roughly chopped | 180 g semi-dried chorizo sausage, thickly sliced
a handful of large green olives, pitted | 1 tablespoon chopped flat-leaf parsley leaves
8 large free-range eggs | 15 strands saffron, lightly roasted and crushed
sea salt and freshly ground black pepper | green leaf salad, to serve

HEAT HALF THE OLIVE OIL IN A heavy-based frying pan. Use one that is fairly deep and not too large, or you'll end up with a flat pancake affair, rather than a dense, deep, eggy cake. Sauté the onion and potatoes on a medium heat for 10–15 minutes until they soften. You will need to stir them fairly often to make sure that they remain uncoloured. Add the garlic, chorizo, olives and parsley and mix everything together. Cook for a few more minutes over a medium heat, then transfer to a bowl.

Lightly whisk the eggs with the saffron and season with salt and pepper. Wipe out the pan, then pour in the remaining olive oil and heat it. Pour the eggs over the potato mixture, then tip everything into the pan. Cook on a high heat for a couple of minutes, until it starts to set on the underside and bubble and puff up around the edges. Lower the heat, cover the pan and cook for about 8 minutes or so, or until the eggs set.

Take the pan to the table, cut the omelette into wedges and serve with a green leaf salad.

SERVES **6 as part of a mezze selection**

Known as kuku-ye sabzi, this is the most famous of the Persian kukus — thick, tortilla-style egg dishes — and it is always served at Persian New Year to symbolise spring and new life. Kuku-ye sabzi is made with a startling quantity of soft herbs — you cut through the golden exterior to a soft, dense, green interior. The barberries are optional — they're usually reserved for special occasions (sometimes combined with chopped walnuts) — but we love the little bursts of zing they add. Use any combination of fresh herbs that you fancy, and add chopped spring onion or garlic, as you like. Omit the fenugreek if you don't like its slight curry flavour, but it is a traditional component of this particular kuku. A non-stick, ovenproof frying pan — no more than 24 centimetres in diameter — is ideal for making kuku.

SOFT HERB OMELETTE

2 tablespoons barberries, stems removed | 1 cup chopped flat-leaf parsley leaves
1 cup chopped coriander leaves | 1/2 cup chopped dill sprigs
1/2 cup snipped chives | 50 ml olive oil | 6 free-range eggs
2 tablespoons Saffron Liquid (page 218, optional) | 1 tablespoon self-raising flour
1/3 cup fenugreek leaves or 1/2 teaspoon fenugreek seeds, lightly crushed (optional)
1 teaspoon sea salt | 1 teaspoon freshly ground black pepper

PREHEAT THE OVEN TO 180°C (GAS 4). Soak the barberries in cold water for 2 minutes, then drain and dry. Toss the herbs together and use paper towel or a clean tea towel to pat out as much moisture as you can.

Pour the oil into a non-stick ovenproof frying pan and heat in the oven for 5–10 minutes.

Whisk the eggs and saffron liquid, if using, until frothy. Whisk in the flour, fenugreek, salt and pepper, followed by the herbs and barberries.

Pour the egg mixture into the hot oil. Cover the pan with a lid or foil and bake in the oven for 15 minutes, or until nearly set. Remove the cover and cook for a further 15 minutes to brown the surface.

Cut into wedges and serve hot from the pan. Alternatively, drain on paper towel and cut into wedges when cold. Cold omelette is particularly good as a sandwich filling.

SERVES 6 as part of a mezze selection

Although Kuku-ye Sabzi (opposite) is the most famous Iranian omelette, kukus can, of course, be made with almost any combination of fresh vegetables and herbs. Other popular fillings are lamb's brains or leftover cooked chicken, and there are even sweet kukus.

We love the pretty pale green zucchini (known as koussa in Arabic), which are more delicate and less bitter than the dark-green variety, but obviously either will do. Adding provolone is a deviation from the purist Iranian kuku, but hot from the oven, its melting softness is irresistible. A non-stick, ovenproof frying pan — no more than 24 centimetres in diameter — is ideal for this sort of kuku.

ZUCCHINI OMELETTE WITH MINT AND MELTING CHEESE

100 ml olive oil | 1 onion, finely diced
1 teaspoon freshly grated nutmeg | teaspoon dried mint
4 pale green oval zucchini (courgettes), about 350 g, coarsely grated | 6 free-range eggs
2 tablespoons self-raising flour | grated zest of 1 lemon | 1/2 teaspoon sea salt
1/2 teaspoon freshly ground black pepper
200 g provolone or any other melting cheese, grated | herbs to garnish (optional)
thick natural yoghurt to serve (optional)

PREHEAT THE OVEN TO 180°C (GAS 4).

Heat half the oil in a frying pan over a low heat and fry the onion until it softens. Stir in the nutmeg and mint and fry for another minute. Remove from the heat and leave to cool.

Pour the remaining oil into a non-stick ovenproof frying pan and heat in the oven for 5–10 minutes.

Squeeze the grated zucchini firmly to remove as much moisture as possible. Whisk the eggs until frothy. Whisk in the flour, lemon zest, salt and pepper, followed by the zucchini and cheese. The mixture will be quite sloppy.

Pour the mixture into the hot oil. Cover the pan with a lid or foil and bake in the oven for 15 minutes or until nearly set. Remove the lid and cook for a further 15 minutes to brown the surface.

Cut into wedges and serve hot from the pan with a sprinkling of herbs and thick yoghurt. Alternatively, drain on paper towel and cut into wedges when cold to serve with pickles or relish.

SERVES 6 as part of a mezze selection

The smooth, bland richness of soft-boiled eggs is a perfect foil to dukkah, the popular Egyptian blend of sesame seeds, roughly ground hazelnuts and heady cumin and coriander. Here, the eggs are coated in dukkah and deep-fried, which tastes delicious and looks stunning, but for for a simpler dish, just sprinkle dukkah onto soft-boiled eggs and eat with hot buttered toast.

EGYPTIAN EGGS WITH DUKKAH

4 free-range eggs | plain flour for dusting | vegetable oil for deep-frying
Dukkah (page 377) | dried shredded chilli to garnish (optional)

SOFT-BOIL THE EGGS FOR 3 MINUTES. Cool under running water and peel carefully. Dust them in plain flour and then deep-fry each egg for 1–1½ minutes, or until they are golden brown. Remove them from the oil and immediately roll them in dukkah.

Eat straight away as a snack or as a light lunch with hot buttered toast. They also make a good accompaniment to cured meats, or serve with a tangy goat's cheese salad or mixed green leaves as a starter.

SERVES **4 as a snack or part of a mezze selection**

These crisp little fritters can be served at room temperature as part of a mezze selection or as a starter — that's if you can resist eating them straight out of the pan! The grated zucchini is salted to help draw out as much moisture as possible. The fritters should be made as soon as the zucchini is thoroughly dried, or they will start to seep liquid. Mixing rice flour with the plain flour is a neat trick that helps make the fritters really crisp.

ZUCCHINI FRITTERS

600 g zucchini (courgettes), coarsely grated | sea salt | 1 small onion, grated
1 small clove garlic, finely chopped | 100 g Bulgarian feta, crumbled
2 tablespoons finely shredded flat-leaf parsley leaves
2 tablespoons finely shredded mint or dill | 1/2 teaspoon dried mint (omit if using dill)
2 free-range eggs, lightly beaten | 50 g plain flour | 30 g rice flour
freshly ground black pepper | olive oil for shallow-frying

PUT THE ZUCCHINI IN A COLANDER, sprinkle lightly with salt, toss and set aside for 20 minutes. Rinse briefly, squeeze well to extract as much excess liquid as you can and pat dry with paper towel. In a large bowl, mix the zucchini, onion, garlic, feta, herbs and eggs. Sift on the flours, then season with pepper and stir to combine.

Heat a little oil in a non-stick frying pan over medium heat until sizzling. Drop small tablespoons of batter into the hot oil and flatten gently. Cook for 2 minutes on each side, or until golden brown. Drain on paper towel and serve piping hot.

MAKES **about 16** SERVES **8 as part of a mezze selection**

Another variation on the Persian kuku theme, these potato patties are light, fluffy and incredibly tasty. You can also make the mix into one big thick pancake and serve it in wedges — although you have to be careful flipping it over when cooking. If you have two frying pans, then you can cook the patties all at the same time. Otherwise you'll have to cook them in batches and keep the cooked patties in a warm oven.

PERSIAN POTATO PATTIES WITH GARLIC CHIVES

2 desirée potatoes, peeled | sea salt | olive oil | 30 g unsalted butter | 1 large onion, diced
1 teaspoon ground turmeric | 2 teaspoons ground cumin
1/2 teaspoon freshly ground black pepper | 2 tablespoons self-raising flour
3/4 cup shredded coriander leaves | 3/4 cup snipped garlic chives | 5 free-range eggs
thick natural yoghurt and pickles, to serve

BOIL THE POTATOES IN GENEROUSLY salted water until tender, drain, then mash them roughly and allow to cool. It's nice to leave a bit of texture — you don't want the potato too smooth.

Heat 2 tablespoons oil with the butter in a frying pan over a low heat and fry the onion until it softens. Stir in the turmeric and cumin and fry for another minute. Remove from the heat and leave to cool.

Combine the potato and onion and mix in 1 teaspoon salt, the pepper, flour and herbs. Whisk the eggs until frothy, then stir them into the potato so that everything is well combined. The mixture will be quite sloppy.

Heat a shallow layer of oil in a large non-stick frying pan over a low-medium heat. Drop in large spoonfuls of the potato mixture and flatten gently. Cook for about 5 minutes, checking from time to time to make sure the patties are not burning. Turn them over and cook for another 5 minutes. Transfer to a warm oven while you cook more patties, adding more oil if needed. If you make one big pancake it will take about 8 minutes on each side.

Serve piping hot with thick yoghurt and your choice of pickles.

MAKES 12 SERVES 6 as part of a mezze selection

The inspiration for these little köfte comes from Yorem Mutfak, a lovely home-style restaurant in Gaziantep, Turkey. Rather unusually, the owner and chef is a woman, the charming and friendly Hatice Yildirim, who told us she'd been cooking for twenty-five years. We fell in love with these patties immediately; they are spicy with a lovely crunch from the burgul. Hatice served them on baby lettuce leaves with wedges of lemon and spring onions as part of a mezze selection.

CRUNCHY RED LENTIL KÖFTE WITH FRESH MINT

40 g butter | 1 small purple onion, finely chopped | 1 tablespoon tomato paste
1 tablespoon mild Turkish red pepper paste | 1 heaped teaspoon ground cumin
100 g red lentils | 350 ml water | 60 g fine white burgul | 2 tablespoons shredded mint leaves
1 heaped teaspoon dried mint | sea salt and freshly ground black pepper | juice of 1 lemon
100 ml extra-virgin olive oil | 1 baby cos lettuce, washed and leaves separated
6 baby salad onions

MELT THE BUTTER IN A HEAVY-BASED saucepan over a medium heat and add the onion, tomato paste, pepper paste and cumin. Sauté for a few minutes until the onion starts to soften, then add the lentils and water and bring to the boil. Lower the heat and simmer gently for 10 minutes, or until the lentils are tender and have absorbed two-thirds of the water. Stir in the burgul and fresh and dried mint and season to taste with salt and pepper. Remove the pan from the heat and leave to stand for 5 minutes, then stir in half the lemon juice and 2 tablespoons of the oil. Tip the mixture onto a tray to cool.

When ready to serve, whisk the remaining lemon juice and oil to make a dressing and season with salt and pepper. Form the cooled lentil mixture into little patties and use your thumb to make an indentation in the surface of each. Arrange the köfte on a platter with the lettuce leaves and onions, then drizzle over the dressing.

SERVES **8 as part of a mezze selection**

POTATO KIBBEH STUFFED WITH SPINACH, MOZZARELLA AND PINE NUTS

KIBBEH SHELL **600 g floury potatoes, washed but not peeled**
200 g fine white burgul, soaked in cold water for 5 minutes | **35 g plain flour**
1/2 teaspoon ground allspice | **1/2 teaspoon ground cinnamon** | **1/2 teaspoon ground cumin**
1/2 teaspoon ground coriander | **1/2 teaspoon salt** | **1/4 teaspoon freshly ground black pepper**

FILLING **1 tablespoon olive oil** | **1 small onion, finely diced**
1 bunch spinach, stalks removed, leaves blanched and chopped
80 g pine nuts, toasted | **1/2 teaspoon ground allspice**
sea salt and freshly ground black pepper | **150 g mozzarella, grated**
yoghurt to serve

TO MAKE THE KIBBEH SHELL, BRING a large pan of salted water to the boil. Cook the potatoes for 15–20 minutes, until they are tender. Remove from the heat and when they are cool enough to handle, peel them. Next, drain the burgul and, using your hands, squeeze out as much water as you can. Then tip into a tea towel and twist to extract even more. Tip the burgul into a large mixing bowl and add the potatoes. Mash the two together to form a smooth purée. Add the flour, spices, salt and pepper and knead with your hands until the mixture is thoroughly blended. Place the bowl in the refrigerator for 30 minutes, which will make the paste easier to work with.

While the shell mixture is chilling in the fridge, prepare the filling. Heat the oil in a frying pan and sauté the onion until it is soft. Add the chopped spinach, pine nuts and allspice and stir over the heat for a few more minutes. Remove the pan from the heat and leave it to cool, then season with salt and pepper and stir in the grated cheese.

To make the kibbeh, put a small lump of the potato paste into the palm of your left hand and roll it into a smooth, oval-shaped ball. Using the forefinger of your right hand, make an indentation in the ball and start to shape it into a hollow shell. Try to make it as thin and even as you can. Fill the shell with about a teaspoon of the filling, wet the edges of the opening with cold water and pinch it closed. You are aiming for a small torpedo-shaped dumpling, with slightly tapered ends. Leave the stuffed kibbeh on a tray in the refrigerator, covered, until you are ready to cook them.

You can either bake the kibbeh in a 190°C (Gas 5) oven for about 20 minutes, or deep- or shallow-fry them in 150 ml medium-hot vegetable oil, turning them to ensure that they're a deep golden brown all over. Drain them on paper towel and serve piping hot with a dollop of yoghurt.

MAKES **16** SERVES **8 as part of a mezze selection**

These spicy patties are a favourite snack all around the Middle East, and from Lebanese takeaway shops the world over. Different versions of falafel abound — in Egypt they are made using dried broad beans alone, whereas in Israel, Lebanon and Syria they are usually made with chickpeas. Others still, like the recipe below, use a combination of the two.

These homemade falafel are spicy and fragrant. It is better to use skinless split broad beans rather than the whole, unskinned variety. You can also use fresh yeast as a raising agent instead of the bicarbonate of soda. This will give you an even lighter, crisper falafel. Use 15 grams of yeast blended with a tablespoon of warm water.

FALAFEL

YOGHURT-TAHINI SAUCE **180 ml natural yoghurt | 60 ml tahini paste juice of up to 1 lemon | 1 clove garlic crushed with 1 teaspoon sea salt**

100 g skinless split broad beans, soaked overnight and drained
100 g chickpeas, soaked overnight and drained | sea salt
$1\frac{1}{2}$ cups fresh coriander, roots removed | 1 tablespoon ground coriander
1 tablespoon ground cumin | 1 teaspoon bicarbonate of soda | 1 small chilli, finely chopped
$\frac{1}{2}$ medium onion, finely chopped | 1 clove garlic, finely chopped
750 ml olive oil for frying | bread, salad, pickled turnips and lemon to serve

IN A FOOD PROCESSOR, WHIZ THE beans and chickpeas with a pinch of salt until they are the consistency of coarse, sticky breadcrumbs. Add all the other ingredients, except the oil, and whiz until they combine to form a bright-green paste which still has a fine crumb. Don't overwork the paste — it should not be smooth and wet. Refrigerate for half an hour before frying.

To make the yoghurt-tahini sauce, combine the yoghurt, tahini, lemon juice and garlic paste. Thin with a little water if necessary — the sauce should have the consistency of thin honey. Taste and adjust the flavours as necessary. What you are aiming for is a good balance of sharp yoghurt and lemon with garlic and nutty tahini. Refrigerate and use within 2–3 days.

Heat the oil to 180°C. It is ready when a cube of bread sizzles slowly to the top and turns a pale golden brown. Shape the falafel into little patties and fry for 6–7 minutes, or until they are a deep brown. Eat the falafel straight away, dipped into yoghurt-tahini sauce or stuffed into Arabic flatbread, with salad, pickled turnips and a squeeze of lemon.

MAKES **about 36** SERVES **8 as part of a mezze selection**

This is one of the most popular home-cooked Lebanese family meals. Ideally choose those pretty pale green, squat, bulbous zucchini (courgettes) stocked by European and Middle Eastern greengrocers in summer, as they are easy to hollow out. Baby marrows work well too. Regular, long zucchini require a little more patience and a long thin knife (like a fish filleting knife) to scrape out the insides, while maintaining the whole long shape of the vegetable. Koussa makes a simple supper dish, served with thick creamy yoghurt.

KOUSSA MAHSHI

8 pale green oval zucchini (courgettes) or baby marrows (at least 150 g each)

STUFFING 250 g minced lamb | 125 g long-grain rice | 3/4 teaspoon ground allspice
3/4 teaspoon ground cinnamon | 3/4 teaspoon freshly ground black pepper | 1/2 teaspoon salt
1 teaspoon extra-virgin olive oil | 1/3 cup water

SAUCE 1 tablespoon butter | 1 tablespoon olive oil | 1 medium onion, finely chopped
2 cloves garlic, finely chopped | 1/2 teaspoon dried mint | 400 g can crushed tomatoes
2 tablespoons tomato paste | 400 ml water | sea salt and freshly ground black pepper
1/4 teaspoon ground cinnamon

TRIM OFF THE ZUCCHINI AT THE narrow end. With a melon baller, apple corer or a long, thin knife, carefully hollow out the insides of each zucchini. The idea is to have as thin a shell as possible, but without piercing the skin. Reserve the pulp for the sauce.

To make the stuffing, use wet hands to mix the lamb, rice, spices, salt, extra-virgin olive oil and water. Divide the mixture into eight portions and loosely stuff each zucchini about three-quarters full, which leaves space for expansion during cooking.

To make the sauce, melt the butter with the oil and gently sauté the onion for about 5 minutes, until it is soft and translucent. Then add the garlic and mint. Cook for a few more minutes, then add the roughly chopped zucchini pulp, followed by the tomatoes, tomato paste and water. Season with salt, pepper and cinnamon. Stir well.

Place the zucchini in the sauce and bring to the boil. Then cover and simmer over a low heat for 40–45 minutes. About 10 minutes before the end of the cooking time, remove the lid and increase the heat to reduce the sauce by a quarter.

SERVES 6 as part of a mezze selection

There are numerous versions of stuffed vine leaves to be found all around the Middle East and Mediterranean. According to Claudia Roden, they were served at the court of King Khusrow II in Persia as early as the seventh century, subsequently spreading through the Muslim world and then the Ottoman Empire.

STUFFED VINE LEAVES, ISTANBUL-STYLE

500 g hand-sized vine leaves, fresh or preserved | 100 ml olive oil
40 g pine nuts | 1 large onion, finely chopped | 1 teaspoon ground allspice
1/2 teaspoon ground cinnamon | 1 teaspoon dried mint | 25 g currants
250 g short-grain rice | sea salt and freshly ground black pepper
250 ml good-quality chicken stock | 1 vine-ripened tomato, grated
2 tablespoons finely chopped dill | 2 tablespoons finely chopped flat-leaf parsley leaves
1 lemon, sliced | 200 ml hot water | juice of 1 lemon

IF USING FRESH VINE LEAVES, blanch them for 30 seconds and refresh in cold water. If using preserved vine leaves, soak them for 10 minutes, then rinse and pat dry.

To make the filling, heat half the oil in a heavy-based saucepan. Sauté the pine nuts for a few minutes over medium heat until golden brown. Add the onion and sauté until softened, then add the spices, dried mint, currants and rice and season with salt and pepper. Stir well and add half the chicken stock to the pan. Cook over a low heat for 5 minutes, stirring occasionally. Add the remaining stock and cook for a further 5 minutes, or until the stock has been absorbed. Remove the pan from the heat and stir in the grated tomato and fresh herbs.

Line the bottom of a heavy-based casserole dish with a few vine leaves and slices of lemon.

Arrange the remaining leaves over a work surface, vein side up, and slice away the stems. Place a spoonful of the filling across the base of the leaf. Roll it over once, then fold in the sides and continue to roll it into a neat sausage shape. The parcels should be about the size of your little finger — don't stuff them too tightly or they will burst during cooking. Continue stuffing and rolling until all the filling has been used.

Pack the stuffed vine leaves into the casserole dish, layering them with more lemon slices, then pour in the hot water, lemon juice and remaining oil. Place a small plate on top of the parcels to keep them submerged in the liquid, then simmer gently, covered, for 30 minutes. Check whether the vine leaves are ready — if there is still liquid, return the dish to the heat and simmer for another 15 minutes, then check again.

Leave the vine leaves to cool in the dish. When ready to serve, turn them out onto a large platter.

SERVES 6–8 as part of a mezze selection

Purists will have to forgive us for messing around with Turkey's most famous dish, but we think the goat's cheese adds an incomparable creamy tang to this luscious dish.

IMAM BAYILDI

6 medium eggplants (aubergines), up to 12 cm long | sea salt | olive oil
100 g soft goat's cheese

GARLIC PASTE **1 tablespoon olive oil | 5 cloves garlic, sliced | 2 teaspoons ground coriander**
1 teaspoon sea salt

SPICY TOMATO SAUCE **60 ml olive oil | 1 large onion, finely diced**
1 teaspoon sweet paprika | 1 teaspoon mild Turkish red pepper paste
6 vine-ripened tomatoes, skinned, seeded and chopped
1/4 cup finely chopped flat-leaf parsley leaves
1 tablespoon finely chopped French tarragon | zest of 1/2 lemon | 1 tablespoon pekmez
100 ml water | sea salt and freshly ground black pepper

SLIT THE EGGPLANTS IN HALF lengthwise from the base to 1 cm below the stalk. Ease each one open — keeping it joined at the stalk — and use the tip of a small sharp knife to score the flesh inside. Sprinkle one side generously with salt and squeeze the eggplant together, then leave to drain in a colander for 30 minutes.

Meanwhile, preheat the oven to 180°C (Gas 4).

Rinse the eggplants thoroughly, then sprinkle them inside and out with oil. Arrange in a baking tray and roast for 10 minutes. Transfer the eggplants to a container with a lid, then seal and leave to steam and cool down.

To prepare the garlic paste, heat the oil in a heavy-based frying pan. Add the garlic and sauté for a few minutes, taking care not to let it colour. Tip into a mortar with the coriander and salt and grind to a thick paste.

To make the sauce, heat the oil in a heavy-based frying pan and sauté the onion until soft and translucent. Stir in the paprika and pepper paste and sauté for another 2 minutes, then add the tomatoes, herbs, lemon zest, pekmez and water and season with salt and pepper. Bring to the boil, then lower the heat and simmer, uncovered, for an hour, stirring occasionally. It should reduce to a very thick, sticky sauce. Refrigerate until needed.

When ready to cook the imam bayıldı, preheat the oven to 180°C (Gas 4). Arrange the eggplants in a large baking dish. Carefully lift up the top half of each eggplant and smear a little garlic paste inside, pushing it down into the soft flesh. Smear a heaped spoonful of sauce inside each eggplant as well and dab in a little goat's cheese. Press the top down again to form a kind of sandwich. Drizzle with oil and bake for 10–12 minutes until the sauce is bubbling and the cheese oozing. Allow to cool and serve cold or at room temperature.

SERVES **6**

CRUNCHY ZUCCHINI FLOWERS STUFFED WITH HALOUMI, MINT AND GINGER

12 baby zucchini (courgettes) with flowers attached | vegetable oil | olive oil
plain flour for dusting | radish sprouts to garnish (optional)

HALOUMI STUFFING 100 g haloumi, washed | 50 g mozzarella
1 small clove garlic crushed with 1/2 teaspoon salt | generous pinch of ground cardamom
generous grind of black pepper | 1/4 teaspoon freshly grated ginger
2 tablespoons finely shredded flat-leaf parsley leaves
1 heaped teaspoon finely chopped mint leaves | 1/2 teaspoon dried mint

TEMPURA BATTER 120 g plain flour | 100 g cornflour | pinch salt
150 ml soda water | 2 tablespoons finely chopped Sugar-Dried Olives (page 399)

TO MAKE THE STUFFING, GRATE THE haloumi and mozzarella into a bowl. Stir in the remaining ingredients.

Carefully open each zucchini flower and pinch out the stamen. Roll a lump of the cheese stuffing into a thumb-sized sausage shape and gently stuff it into the flower. Twist the top of the flower to seal.

Heat equal quantities of the oils in a deep-fryer or saucepan to 180°C.

To make the tempura batter, combine the two flours and salt in a mixing bowl. Pour in the soda water and whisk briskly to combine, for up to 20 seconds. Don't worry if there are lumps. Mix in the chopped olives. Dust the stuffed flowers in plain flour, dip them into the batter then fry in the hot oil, no more than four at a time, until they turn turn crisp and golden. Remove and drain on paper towel, and repeat with the remaining flowers. Season lightly and serve straight away.

SERVES 4 as part of a mezze selection

HALOUMI IN VINE LEAVES

16 hand-sized vine leaves, fresh or preserved
2 blocks Cypriot haloumi, each about 200 g, soaked in cold water for 1 hour
1 teaspoon sweet paprika | 1/4 teaspoon chilli powder | 16 thin slices prosciutto
2 tablespoons extra-virgin olive oil | 2 tablespoons olive oil | lemon wedges

IF USING FRESH VINE LEAVES, blanch them in boiling water for 30 seconds and refresh in cold water. If using preserved vine leaves, soak them for 10 minutes, then rinse and pat dry.

After soaking the haloumi, pat dry and cut each block widthwise into 8 fat slices. Mix the paprika and chilli together and dust the cheese very lightly, then wrap with a slice of prosciutto. Lay the vine leaves, vein side up, on the work surface. Lay the prosciutto-wrapped cheese block across the base of the leaf and splash on a drop of extra-virgin olive oil. Roll the leaf over once, then fold in the sides and continue to roll into a neat little parcel. Brush each parcel with a little olive oil and cook under a preheated very hot griller for a few minutes on each side, or until the vine leaves start to colour and blister. Serve them straight from the grill with a squeeze of lemon.

SERVES **4 as part of a mezze selection**

GOAT'S CHEESE IN VINE LEAVES

8 large vine leaves, fresh or preserved | 200 g goat's cheese (25 g per person)
extra-virgin olive oil | pinch of dried mint | freshly ground black pepper

IF USING FRESH VINE LEAVES, blanch them in boiling water for 30 seconds and refresh in cold water. If using preserved vine leaves, soak them for 10 minutes, then rinse and pat dry.

Lay the vine leaf, vein side up (or two together if small) on a kitchen bench. Mould a portion of cheese into a small sausage shape and place across the base of the leaf. Drizzle a little oil over the cheese and add a pinch of mint and a grind of pepper. Roll the leaf over once, then fold the sides in and continue to roll it into a neat sausage shape. Brush it with a little oil and cook under a preheated hot griller for 4–5 minutes or until they start to colour and blister.

MAKES **8 little parcels to eat as a snack or quick and easy starter**

Add a Middle Eastern touch to a platter of oysters with one or all of the suggested accompaniments.

Bastourma is a Turkish air-dried beef which has first been rubbed with fenugreek, chilli and sugar. It combines beautifully with the briny tannin flavours of oysters and vital, metallic parsley. It's available from Turkish butchers and some delicatessens.

OYSTERS WITH PARSLEY–BASTOURMA SALAD

6 ripe tomatoes | 50 g sugar | 60 ml water | 30 ml olive oil for sautéing
200 g bastourma, thinly sliced then cut into 3 mm batons
1 1/2 cups shredded flat-leaf parsley leaves
2 small Artichokes à la Niçoise (page 67), or good-quality purchased artichokes in oil
100 ml red-wine vinegar | 1 clove garlic, finely minced | 100 ml extra-virgin olive oil
salt and freshly ground black pepper | 36 oysters, freshly opened

CUT THE TOMATOES IN HALF AND scoop out the flesh and seeds.

In a heavy pan, dissolve the sugar in 30 ml water. Once it is fully dissolved, simmer gently for 8 minutes, or until the syrup turns a deep golden colour. Add 30 ml warm water, stir and return to a simmer for 2 minutes more until the caramel thickens.

Put the tomatoes on a rack, skin side down, and drizzle the caramel over them. Leave to dry in a preheated 140°C (Gas 1) oven for 6–8 hours.

Heat the olive oil in a heavy-based pan and sauté the bastourma over a high heat until it is crisp, 3–4 minutes.

Cut the caramelised tomatoes into thick strips. In a large bowl, mix together the tomatoes, bastourma, parsley, artichoke leaves, red-wine vinegar, garlic and oil. Season lightly.

For each person, arrange six oysters in their shells on a plate, and place a heaped spoonful of the parsley salad on top of each oyster. Serve straight away.

SERVES **6 as a starter**

The combination of chilled briny oysters with tasty little plump pork sausages is a favourite in Northern France. Here we use chilli-hot, cinnamon-spiced Lebanese ma'ahani sausages. Make them yourself (see page 129) or go to a Middle Eastern butcher. If you can't find ma'ahani, then use North African merguez sausages instead.

OYSTERS WITH LEBANESE SAUSAGES

50 ml olive oil | 18 ma'ahani (page 129) or 12 merguez sausages | squeeze of lemon juice 36 oysters, freshly opened | À la Grecque Dressing (page 388)

HEAT THE OIL IN A HEAVY-BASED frying pan and sauté the sausages over a medium heat for about 4 minutes. Turn them from time to time so they colour evenly, but be careful not to overcook them. When they are ready, squeeze on the lemon juice and roll them around so that they are all coated with a little tangy acid.

Arrange six oysters on each plate. Cut the hot ma'ahani in half on the diagonal (or, if using merguez, cut them into thirds) and pop them on top of the oysters. Spoon over a little dressing and eat immediately.

SERVES **6 as a starter**

OYSTERS WITH TOMATO–POMEGRANATE DRESSING

Spoon a little Tomato–Pomegranate Dressing (page 388) onto each of 36 freshly opened oysters and serve.

SERVES **6 as a starter**

STUFFED MUSSELS, ISTANBUL STREET-STYLE

25 g currants | 150 g short-grain rice | 32 mussels, scrubbed and de-bearded
80 ml olive oil | 60 g pine nuts | 1 large onion, finely diced
2 cloves garlic, finely chopped | 1/4 teaspoon ground nutmeg
1 teaspoon ground cinnamon | 1 vine-ripened tomato, grated
pinch of sea salt | boiling water | 1/3 cup finely chopped dill
1/3 cup finely chopped flat-leaf parsley leaves | lemon wedges to serve

SOAK THE CURRANTS IN A LITTLE warm water for 10–15 minutes, then drain.

Meanwhile, put the rice into a large bowl and rinse well under cold running water, working your fingers through it to loosen the starch. Drain off the milky water and repeat until the water runs clear. Cover the rice with cold water and leave to soak for 10 minutes. Drain the rice and rinse a final time.

Soak the scrubbed mussels in a sink or large bowl of warm water for about 10 minutes.

Heat the oil in a saucepan. Fry the pine nuts, onion, garlic and spices on a medium–low heat for about 10 minutes, or until the pine nuts begin to colour a light golden brown. Stir in the drained rice, tomato and currants and cook for 2 minutes. Season lightly with salt, then pour on enough boiling water to just cover the rice. Stir, then bring to the boil and cover with a tight-fitting lid. Cook over a very low heat for 15 minutes, or until the liquid has been absorbed. Tip the rice into a shallow bowl, then fork through the herbs and leave to cool a little.

To prepare the mussels, use a small sharp knife and work over a large bowl to catch and reserve the juices. Hold each mussel by its narrow end, with the 'pointed' edge facing outwards. Insert the knife between the two shells near the large rounded top and cut through the mollusc where it is attached. You should then be able to prise the shells open, taking care not to break them — the idea is to open them slightly, not fully, and for the mussels to stay in their shells.

Strain the reserved mussel juice into a measuring jug and add water to make it up to about 500 ml if necessary, then tip this into a large, heavy-based saucepan. Stand a colander inside the pan. Spoon a generous amount of rice into each mussel, then squeeze the shells shut and wipe away any excess. Stack the mussels in the colander and cover with wet baking paper. Weight the mussels down with a plate to keep them from opening too wide as they cook. Cover the pan and bring to the boil, then lower the heat and simmer for about 20 minutes.

Remove from the heat and let the mussels cool in the pan. When cold, refrigerate for at least 1 hour before serving chilled or at room temperature.

Stack the mussels onto a serving platter when ready to serve. To eat, break off the top shell, squeeze on a little lemon juice, then use the loose shell to scoop out the contents.

SERVES **8 as part of a mezze selection**

Turkish pilaki are slow-braised dishes made with olive oil. They tend to be served cold with plenty of crusty bread to mop up the rich sauce. This wonderfully garlicky mussel pilaki is one of our favourites. Make sure you use good, tasty tomatoes.

MUSSEL PILAKI

36 mussels, scrubbed and de-bearded | 2 tablespoons olive oil | 1 large onion, finely diced
6 cloves garlic, cut in half | 1 carrot, scraped and cut into 1 cm dice
1 potato, peeled and cut into 1 cm dice | 2 sticks celery, cut into 1 cm dice
1 large vine-ripened tomato, skinned and chopped | 1 tablespoon tomato paste
250 ml Crab Stock (page 13), good-quality chicken stock or water | 2 sprigs thyme
1 teaspoon sugar | 1/2 teaspoon freshly ground black pepper | juice of 1/2 lemon
2 tablespoons chopped dill | 1/3 cup chopped flat-leaf parsley leaves
lemon wedges to serve

TO PREPARE THE MUSSELS, SOAK them in a sink or large bowl of warm water for about 10 minutes, then drain. To open the mussels, use a small sharp knife and work over a large bowl to catch and reserve the juices. Hold each mussel by its narrow end, with the 'pointed' edge facing outwards. Insert the knife between the two shells near the large rounded top and cut through the mollusc where it is attached. You should then be able to prise the shells open and slip the mussel meat into another bowl. When you've opened all the shells, strain the collected juices and set aside.

Heat the oil in a heavy-based saucepan, then sauté the onion and garlic for 5–10 minutes, until soft. Add the carrot, potato, celery, tomato and tomato paste and sauté for a few more minutes, then stir in the reserved mussel juices, stock, thyme, sugar and pepper. Cook over a low heat for 20–25 minutes, stirring occasionally, until the vegetables are tender and the sauce is thick.

Stir the mussels into the sauce gently. Squeeze on the lemon juice and cook for about 4 minutes, then stir in the dill and half the parsley. Remove from the heat and allow to cool. When cold, refrigerate until ready to serve. Eat within the day as part of a mezze selection, sprinkled with the remaining parsley and served with lemon wedges.

SERVES 6 as part of a mezze selection

Traditional güveç dishes are cooked in little earthenware pots buried in the ashes of an open fire or barbecue. Different herbs are used depending on the region, and along the shores of the Mediterranean the wild basil that grows in profusion adds a lovely spicy note. You could also use dill, parsley or oregano with success. The combination of prawns and melted cheese makes this dish rather rich. It would make a light supper or lunch for four people, with a salad of bitter green leaves and plenty of crusty bread to mop up the sauce and melted cheese. You could also serve it as part of a mezze selection for eight people.

PRAWNS BAKED WITH HALOUMI IN A CLAYPOT

8 raw king prawns, peeled (heads and tails removed) | 40 g unsalted butter
1 small purple onion, diced | 1 clove garlic, finely chopped
1 red banana pepper, seeded and cut into 1 cm dice
1 long red chilli, seeded and shredded
1 teaspoon coriander seeds, roasted and lightly crushed
1 teaspoon caraway seeds, roasted and lightly crushed | pinch of saffron threads
1/4 teaspoon freshly ground black pepper | few strips of lemon zest | sea salt
2 teaspoons pekmez | 2 large vine-ripened tomatoes, skinned, seeded and chopped
1/4 cup roughly torn basil leaves | extra-virgin olive oil
40 g haloumi, washed and finely grated | salad and crusty bread to serve

PREHEAT THE OVEN TO ITS HIGHEST setting. Use a sharp knife to butterfly the prawns and carefully pull away the intestinal tracts.

Melt the butter gently in a heavy-based frying pan. Add the onion, garlic, pepper, chilli, spices and zest and season lightly with salt. Sauté over a low heat for about 15 minutes, stirring frequently, until the vegetables are soft. Add the pekmez and cook for 5 minutes, then stir in the tomatoes and bring to a gentle boil. Gently add the prawns and basil to the sauce, then tip it all into a heavy-based casserole dish, or an earthenware pot if you have one. Sprinkle with oil, then scatter on the haloumi and bake in the oven for 3–5 minutes, or until the cheese is bubbling and brown.

SERVES **4 as a starter or 8 as part of a mezze selection**

It's important to use Arabic flatbread to make the crumbs for this recipe as they will be crunchier. Before you make the crumbs, dry the orange zest overnight or put it in a very low oven for 30 minutes. This will intensify the flavour.

SEARED SCALLOPS WITH ALMOND CRUMBS, HUMMUS AND CRISP ARMENIAN AIR-DRIED BEEF

ALMOND CRUMBS **40 ml olive oil | 80 g whole blanched almonds**
3 large cloves garlic, sliced | 25 g stale Arabic flatbread, diced
20 g sesame seeds, toasted | zest of 1/2 orange | sea salt

4 tablespoons olive oil | 8 slices bastourma, shredded
12 scallops | 1 cup watercress leaves | 1 cup frisée lettuce, roughly torn
1 small purple onion, very finely sliced | sea salt and freshly ground black pepper
60 ml Lemon-Garlic Dressing (page 387) | 200 g Hummus with Tahini (page 48)
extra-virgin olive oil for drizzling

PUT THE OIL IN A SMALL SAUCEPAN and when it is hot, fry the almonds for 1–2 minutes, until they just start to colour. Add the garlic and pieces of bread and continue to fry, tossing everything around in the pan, so the mixture colours evenly to a rich golden brown. Tip into a sieve to drain off any excess oil, then put into a food processor and blitz to smooth crumbs. Scrape the crumbs into a bowl and stir through the sesame seeds and orange zest. Season with a little salt.

Heat 2 tablespoons of the oil in a frying pan and fry the bastourma slices until crisp. Remove from the pan and drain on paper towel. Wipe the pan and add 2 more tablespoons of oil. When it's smoking hot, add the scallops and let them sit in the pan for 45 seconds without moving them. Turn them over and leave them for 30 seconds. Now add the crumbs to the pan and roll the scallops around to coat them in the mixture. Carefully remove the scallops from the pan and put them on paper towel.

In a large mixing bowl, toss together the watercress, lettuce, onion and bastourma. Season lightly with salt and pepper, pour on the dressing and toss well.

To serve, spoon three walnut-sized blobs of hummus on each plate and place a scallop on top of each blob. Divide the salad among the plates, creating a little mound in the centre of each plate. Drizzle with a little extra-virgin olive oil.

SERVES **4 as part of a mezze selection**

We find whitebait totally irresistible. Here, lightly seasoned with savoury cumin and deep-fried, they make a fantastically simple starter, served straight from the pan with lots of lemon wedges or a homemade preserved lemon mayonnaise.

CUMIN-FRIED WHITEBAIT

700 ml vegetable oil for deep-frying | 200 g plain flour | 1/2 teaspoon sea salt
3 tablespoons cumin seeds, lightly roasted, ground and sieved | 1 teaspoon ground ginger
1/2 teaspoon ground white pepper | 400 g whitebait
brown bread and butter, mayonnaise and lemon wedges to serve

HEAT THE OIL IN A DEEP-FRYER OR wok to 190°C, or until a cube of bread dropped in sizzles slowly to the top and turns golden brown in about 30 seconds.

Put the flour, salt, cumin, ginger and pepper into a large bowl and mix together well. Tip in the whitebait and toss them around in the seasoned flour until they are well coated. Then lift them out and shake off any excess flour.

Deep-fry the whitebait in batches for 2–3 minutes, until they are crisp and golden. Drain them briefly on paper towel, then tip into a large serving bowl and serve with fresh brown bread and butter, lots of lemon wedges and mayonnaise.

SERVES **6 as part of a mezze selection**

Ideally, you need fresh medium-sized squid tubes for this dish. Stuffed with a spicy pork-mince filling studded with pretty green pistachios, they make an attractive and very tasty starter. Serve with a handful of salad leaves and warm crusty bread.

CALAMARI STUFFED WITH PORK AND PISTACHIOS

4 medium calamari tubes, about 60 g each | 40 g pistachio kernels
320 g minced pork | 1 clove garlic, finely chopped | 1 shallot, finely chopped
1 teaspoon sweet paprika | 1/2 teaspoon ground ginger
1 long green chilli, seeded and finely shredded
1 tablespoon olive oil | 1 free-range egg | sea salt and freshly ground black pepper
1 tablespoon extra-virgin olive oil | 1 lemon, cut into 4 wedges
Preserved Lemon Mayonnaise (page 385) to serve

CLEAN THE CALAMARI TUBES WELL and pat them dry.

Soak the pistachios in cold water for 5 minutes to get rid of any extra salt. Mix the pork, nuts, garlic, shallot, spices, chilli, oil and egg until thoroughly combined. Preheat the oven to 200°C (Gas 6).

Stuff a quarter of the stuffing into each calamari tube, making sure you work it right down to the very bottom and that no air is trapped inside. Leave about 1 cm at the open end. If you like, use a piping bag for this bit. Close the ends with a toothpick. Lightly season the tubes with salt and pepper.

Heat the olive oil in an ovenproof pan and sear the calamari tubes on medium-high heat, rolling them around like sausages, until they are a nice golden colour all over. Transfer the pan to the middle shelf of the oven and cook for 12 minutes.

Remove the squid tubes from the oven and allow them to rest for a couple of minutes on a wire rack until ready to serve.

Slice each tube into 4 even pieces and arrange them on a plate. Drizzle a little extra-virgin olive oil over the top and serve with lemon wedges and a generous dollop of preserved lemon mayonnaise.

SERVES 4 as part of a mezze selection

Deep-fried calamari is a universally popular dish, and the golden spice mix is a nice way to liven it up a bit.

CRUNCHY FRIED CALAMARI WITH TAHINI RÉMOULADE

TAHINI RÉMOULADE **150 g thick natural yoghurt | 3 tablespoons tahini, well stirred**
1 clove garlic crushed with 1/4 teaspoon salt | juice of 1 lemon
1/2 teaspoon freshly ground black pepper | 1 tablespoon chopped flat-leaf parsley
1 tablespoon chopped gherkins | 1 teaspoon chopped capers

EGGPLANT CRISPS **1 small eggplant (aubergine), sliced 1 mm thick**
olive oil, for shallow-frying | sea salt and freshly ground black pepper

8 small calamari tubes, quartered | sea salt and freshly ground black pepper
vegetable oil for shallow-frying | chive flowers to garnish

CRUNCHY COATING **3 tablespoons cornflour | 3 tablespoons fine polenta**
3 tablespoons fine semolina | 1 tablespoon Golden Spice Mix (page 378)

TO MAKE THE TAHINI RÉMOULADE, combine the yoghurt, tahini, garlic paste and lemon juice in a bowl and whisk together thoroughly. Add the remaining ingredients and stir well.

To make the eggplant crisps, shallow-fry the eggplant slices in the olive oil until golden. Season lightly.

Split the calamari tubes lengthwise, then trim the sides neatly. Use a very sharp knife to score a fine diamond pattern on the inner surface.

Prepare the coating by sieving together the cornflour, polenta, semolina and spice mix. Season the calamari pieces lightly with salt and pepper, then dunk them into the crunchy coating mixture. Put the calamari pieces into the sieve to shake off any extra coating mix.

Heat the oil in a large frying pan until it is nearly smoking. If the oil isn't hot enough, the calamari will 'stew' rather than fry, and the result will be soggy rather than crunchy. Add the calamari pieces to the hot oil in batches, shaking the pan to coat them with the oil and to help them colour evenly. They should take less than a minute to cook. Remove from the pan and drain on paper towel. Serve them piping hot with eggplant crisps and chive flowers to garnish.

SERVES **4 as part of a mezze selection**

Locally caught calamari, octopus and cuttlefish are all popular in the villages and towns on the Persian Gulf. They are sometimes braised slowly in a tomato-based sauce, but frying is also common — usually in a light dusting of flour mixed with ground turmeric. This recipe uses a spice mix that's really popular in this part of Iran to jazz up the coating. The accompanying tomato sauce is light and fresh.

BANDARI-SPICED CALAMARI WITH TOMATO-CORIANDER SAUCE

6 x 120 g calamari tubes, cleaned (tentacles reserved) | 100 g fine semolina
2 teaspoons Bandari Spice Mix (page 380) | 1/2 teaspoon sea salt
vegetable oil for shallow-frying | 1 tablespoon pistachio slivers (optional)
rice and Arabic flatbread to serve

TOMATO-CORIANDER SAUCE **2 tablespoons olive oil | 1 large shallot, finely diced**
1 small clove garlic, finely chopped | 1 tablespoon Bandari Spice Mix (page 380)
1 teaspoon tomato paste | 300 ml crushed tomatoes | 250 ml water
juice of 1/2 lemon | 1 teaspoon sea salt | 1/3 cup shredded coriander leaves

TO MAKE THE TOMATO-CORIANDER sauce, heat the oil in a heavy-based saucepan over a low heat. Add the shallot and garlic and fry gently until soft and translucent. Stir in the spice mix and fry for another couple of minutes. Stir in the tomato paste, tomatoes and water and bring to a boil over a medium heat. Lower the heat and simmer gently for 30 minutes.

Split the calamari tubes lengthwise, then trim the sides neatly. Use a very sharp knife to score a fine diamond pattern on the inner surface.

Combine the semolina, spice mix and salt in a bowl. When the sauce is ready, heat a shallow layer of oil in a heavy-based frying pan over a high heat. Working in small batches, dust the calamari pieces (including the tentacles) with the spicy semolina and fry for about 30 seconds on each side. The scored calamari pieces will curl up into tight little cylinders as they cook. When evenly golden and crisp, transfer them to a plate lined with paper towel to drain.

Just before you serve, add the lemon juice and salt to the sauce and stir in the coriander. Top with the fried calamari, garnish with pistachio slivers if you wish and serve with your choice of rice and plenty of warm flatbread for mopping up the sauce.

SERVES **6 as part of a mezze selection**

Some people baulk at the thought of eating raw meat, which is what kibbeh nayeh is — a kind of Middle Eastern steak tartare, using lamb, burgul, onion and spices (page 112). However, most of us are familiar with sushi and sashimi, and are happy to eat raw fish — so this version of kibbeh nayeh uses fresh salmon or tuna, both of which work very well. The fish requires less mincing and pounding than the traditional lamb and results in a lighter dish which is delicious eaten with Arabic flatbread, white salad onions and a big blob of Yoghurt Cheese (page 44), or as below, with a fresh herb salad.

SALMON KIBBEH NAYEH WITH A SOFT HERB SALAD

300 g Atlantic salmon, finely minced and chilled | 2 purple shallots, finely chopped
150 g fine-grade white burgul, soaked for 8 minutes in 3/4 cup water, then squeezed dry
1/3 teaspoon ground allspice | 1 small red bullet chilli, seeded, scraped and finely chopped
1 teaspoon sea salt | freshly ground black pepper | 1 tablespoon extra-virgin olive oil
Yoghurt Cheese (page 44) | 1/2 clove garlic crushed with 1/3 teaspoon salt

SOFT HERB SALAD 1/3 cup coriander leaves | 1/3 cup mint leaves | 1/3 cup flat-leaf parsley
4 Artichokes à la Niçoise (page 67), or good-quality purchased artichokes preserved in oil
1 small purple onion, finely sliced | juice of 1/2 lemon | 100 ml extra-virgin olive oil
sea salt and freshly ground black pepper | 1 teaspoon ground sumac

IN A CHILLED STAINLESS STEEL OR glass bowl, mix the salmon, shallots, burgul, allspice, chilli, salt, pepper and oil. Refrigerate until ready to serve.

When ready to serve, blend the yoghurt cheese with the garlic paste. In another bowl mix the herbs, artichoke leaves, onion, lemon, 50 ml of the extra-virgin olive oil and salt and pepper to taste.

Smooth the salmon mixture out on a large plate to form a neat, flat circle. Use a sharp knife to mark the surface with the traditional crosshatch pattern, if you wish. Drizzle with the remaining extra-virgin olive oil. Put a generous dollop of yoghurt cheese on top and garnish with the soft herb salad and sumac.

SERVES 4 as part of a mezze selection

FRAGRANT CURED SALMON

1 x 1 kg side Atlantic salmon, skinned | olive oil for brushing | 1/3 cup flat-leaf parsley
1/2 cup frisée lettuce | 8 small radicchio leaves, torn
2 small fennel bulbs, cored and shaved | 1 tomato, seeded and cut into slivers
30 ml sherry vinegar | 80 ml extra-virgin olive oil
sea salt and freshly ground black pepper | edible flowers to garnish (optional)

FRAGRANT CURING SALT 1/2 teaspoon ground cumin seeds | 1/2 teaspoon ground coriander
1/2 teaspoon ground cardamom | 1/2 teaspoon ground fennel seeds
1/2 teaspoon ground nigella seeds | 1/2 teaspoon sesame seeds, toasted
2 tablespoons sea salt

TO MAKE THE FRAGRANT SALT, PUT the ground spices, toasted sesame seeds and salt in a frying pan and gently warm through so they merge into one fragrant powder.

To prepare the salmon, first trim off the tapering tail end of the salmon and square off the head end. Trim about 1.5 cm from the belly so you have a neat, even-sided rectangle. Remove all pin bones. Season the salmon all over with the fragrant salt. Cover and refrigerate for 1 hour.

Preheat the oven to 80°C (Gas 1/4). Remove the salmon from the fridge and allow it to come to room temperature. Rinse in cold water and dry it thoroughly. Brush both sides with olive oil then wrap in baking paper and place, skin side down, in a large baking tray. Bake for 10 minutes.

Remove from the oven and carefully turn the salmon skin side up. Return to the oven for a further 10 minutes.

Remove from the oven and leave to rest in the tray for 10 minutes. Unwrap and discard the paper and gently scrape away all the grey blood line from the fish. Set aside and leave to cool.

When ready to serve, combine the parsley, lettuce, radiccio, fennel and tomato in a mixing bowl. Whisk the vinegar with the oil and pour on enough to lightly dress the salad. Toss gently and season to taste. Cut the salmon into eight thick slices and cut each slice in half crosswise. Arrange on a serving platter with the salad and garnish with edible flowers, if using.

SERVES 6 as part of a mezze selection

You would be hard pressed to find a simpler dish than ceviche, the traditional Mexican technique of 'cooking' fish with the acids from citrus fruit — in particular, limes. You can use this method with pretty much any seafood — all white fish work well, as do oily fish such as salmon and mackerel, and even molluscs such as scallops.

Here we use red mullet, a lovely delicate fish that is enormously popular around the Mediterranean. Go to a good fishmonger to make sure that they are very fresh. If you feel up to the task, clean and fillet the fish yourself, otherwise ask the fishmonger to do it for you. Explain what you are preparing, and ask the fishmonger to be as gentle as possible so as not to crush the delicate flesh. If you cannot find red mullet, use any other good white fish — whiting or garfish would work well.

CEVICHE OF RED MULLET WITH RAS AL HANOUT

8 x 150 g red mullet | 2 tomatoes, seeded and very finely diced
2 mild green chillies, seeded, scraped and finely shredded
2 shallots, very finely chopped | 1 cup roughly chopped coriander leaves
1/3 cup chervil leaves | 1 clove garlic crushed with 1/2 teaspoon sea salt
juice of 3 limes | 85 ml good-quality extra-virgin olive oil
1 level teaspoon Ras al Hanout (page 378) | sea salt and freshly ground black pepper
pomegranate seeds to garnish (optional) | bread and salad to serve

FIRST, SCALE THE RED MULLET. HOLD it under running water and use your thumb to run against the scales from tail to head. They are delicate and come away very easily. Then use a really sharp knife and carefully slice away the two fillets from the bones. Use tweezers to remove any little bones, being as gentle as you can so as not to mush the flesh.

In a large mixing bowl, combine the tomatoes, chillies, shallots, coriander and chervil. Whisk the garlic paste with the lime juice, olive oil and ras al hanout. Pour the marinade into the bowl and mix everything together well. Taste and add a little extra salt if necessary.

Spoon half the marinade into the bottom of a shallow dish, spreading it out evenly, and lay the fish fillets on top, skin side up. Then spoon the rest of the marinade over the fish so they are completely covered. Lightly sprinkle with salt and pepper, then cover the dish with plastic wrap and refrigerate for an hour.

Garnish with pomegranate seeds and serve with plenty of warm crusty bread, and perhaps a tomato salad.

SERVES **4 as a starter or 8 as part of a mezze selection**

RED MULLET WITH GOLDEN SPICES AND A CITRUS SALAD

CITRUS SALAD **2 medium navel oranges | 2 medium lemons | 2 limes | 1 small purple onion, very finely sliced | 1/2 cup roughly shredded flat-leaf parsley leaves | 1/3 cup roughly shredded mint leaves | extra-virgin olive oil | freshly ground black pepper**

12 x 120–140 g red mullet | sea salt and freshly ground black pepper | olive oil for frying | 100 g plain flour | 30 g rice flour | 3 teaspoons Golden Spice Mix (page 378)

TO PREPARE THE SALAD, FIRST PEEL the skin and white membrane from the citrus fruit. Using a sharp knife, carefully cut the membrane between each segment and flip the fruit out of its skin casing, removing the seeds as you go. Toss the segments with the onion, parsley and mint.

To scale the red mullet, hold it under running water and use your thumb to run against the scales from tail to head — they come away very easily. Leave the fins and tail attached for presentation, but use a sharp knife to slice the fish along the underbelly. Hold the sides open and pull the intestines away. Insert your finger into the reddish-coloured gills and pull them out too. Rinse the insides of the fish under running water, paying special attention to rubbing away the dark blood line against the back bone. Pat dry.

Season the fish lightly inside and out. Heat the oil to 190°C or until a little sprinkle of flour sizzles. Mix the flours with the golden spice mix. Dust the fish all over with the seasoned flour. Fry the fish for 2–3 minutes on each side until they are golden brown.

To serve, tip the citrus salad onto a shallow serving platter, drizzle with extra-virgin olive oil and season with freshly ground black pepper. Arrange the fish on top and let everyone help themselves.

SERVES **6 as part of a mezze selection**

Kibbeh nayeh is a kind of Middle Eastern steak tartare and is a great favourite on the mezze table. It uses the best-quality lamb, pounded or minced to a fine paste with onion, burgul and spices, and served with a drizzle of fruity olive oil, salad onions, fresh mint and plenty of Arabic flatbread.

The traditional spice for kibbeh nayeh is allspice — although in Aleppo they like a touch of chilli heat (see opposite). This recipe is entirely my own creation, and we love the freshness that the herbs and green chilli add. You can prepare the mixture up to 2 hours ahead of time, keeping the meat separate from the other ingredients.

KIBBEH NAYEH WITH BASIL, MINT AND GREEN CHILLIES

100 g fine white burgul | 90 g white onion, roughly chopped
1 long green chilli, seeded and roughly chopped | 1/3 cup roughly chopped basil leaves
1/3 cup roughly chopped mint leaves | 1/3 cup roughly chopped flat-leaf parsley leaves
1/2–3/4 teaspoon salt | freshly ground black pepper | 1/4 teaspoon chilli powder
300 g lean lamb, roughly diced | 3 ice cubes
extra-virgin olive oil, Arabic flatbread, fresh onions and mint leaves to serve

SOAK THE BURGUL FOR 5 MINUTES in just enough cold water to cover it. Drain it well through a sieve, then tip it into a tea towel and squeeze out as much water as you can. Tip into a mixing bowl.

Put the onion, chilli and fresh herbs through a mincer — it will come through as a green slush. Add to the burgul. Stir in the salt, a few grinds of pepper and the chilli powder. Roughly chop the meat, then put it through a mincer twice.

When you're ready to eat, add the meat and ice cubes to the burgul mixture. Mix well with your hands. As the ice dissolves, it will bind everything together into a smooth, sticky paste. Tip onto a plate and spread into a smooth, shallow layer reaching right up to the rim. Use the back of a spoon or a knife to make dimples or lines in the surface to decorate, and drizzle with extra-virgin olive oil before serving. It is also delicious with yoghurt cheese, although most Lebanese would throw up their hands in horror at this unorthodox accompaniment.

SERVES 4 as part of a mezze selection

ALEPPO-STYLE LAMB TARTARE WITH SMOKY CHILLI AND PARSLEY

3 long red chillies | 1 tablespoon olive oil | 100 g fine white burgul
1/3 cup roughly chopped flat-leaf parsley leaves | 1/2–3/4 teaspoon salt
freshly ground black pepper | 1/2 teaspoon ground cinnamon | 1/4 teaspoon smoked paprika
1/4 teaspoon chilli powder | 90 g white onion, roughly chopped
300 g lean lamb, roughly diced | 3 ice cubes
extra-virgin olive oil, Arabic flatbread, fresh onions and mint leaves to serve

PREHEAT THE OVEN TO 200°C (GAS 6). Brush the chillies with a little olive oil and roast them for 5–10 minutes, turning them occasionally, until they start to blacken all over. Remove them from the oven and, when cool enough to handle, peel away all the charred skin. Split the chillies open and scrape out the seeds. Put the chillies into a mortar and pound to a smooth paste.

Soak the burgul for 5 minutes in just enough cold water to cover it. Drain it well through a sieve, then tip it into a tea towel and squeeze out as much water as you can. Tip into a mixing bowl with the chilli paste and add the chopped parsley and spices. Mix together well. Put the onion through a mincer and add to the burgul, mixing well.

Finally, put the lamb through the mincer twice, then add it to the other ingredients with the ice cubes. Mix well with your hands. As the ice dissolves, it will bind everything together into a smooth, sticky paste. Tip onto a plate and spread into a smooth, shallow layer reaching right up to the rim. Use the back of a soup spoon to make little crescent-shaped indentations on the surface and drizzle with extra-virgin olive oil before serving.

SERVES **4 as part of a mezze selection**

Not strictly kibbeh nayeh, as it is not made with burgul, this is really more of a steak tartare eaten in the Middle Eastern style.

BEEF TARTARE WITH MINCED PARSLEY, MINT AND HOT ENGLISH MUSTARD

350 g lean beef, roughly diced | 1/2 cup roughly chopped flat-leaf parsley leaves | 1/2 cup roughly chopped mint leaves | 1/4 teaspoon ground allspice | 1 teaspoon salt | 1/4 teaspoon freshly ground black pepper | 120 g white onion, very finely chopped | 1 tablespoon hot English mustard | 3 ice cubes | extra-virgin olive oil, Arabic flatbread, Pickled Onions in Rose Vinegar (page 391) and mint leaves to serve

ROUGHLY CHOP THE MEAT AND PUT it in a large mixing bowl with the herbs and spices. Toss well, then put it through a mincer twice to achieve a smooth paste. Add the onion, mustard and the ice cubes and mix well with your hands. As the ice dissolves, it will bind everything together into a smooth, sticky paste. Tip onto a plate and spread into a smooth, shallow oval. Use the back of a soup spoon to make little crescent-shaped indentations on the surface and drizzle with extra-virgin olive oil before serving.

SERVES **4 as part of a mezze selection**

Kibbeh are those little torpedo-shaped meat dumplings that were once the yardstick by which all Middle Eastern cooks were judged. Serve them as part of a mezze selection.

KIBBEH

250 g fine white burgul | 1 onion, very finely diced | 3/4 teaspoon ground allspice
1/2 teaspoon ground cinnamon | 1 teaspoon sweet paprika
1/4 teaspoon hot paprika | 1/2 teaspoon freshly ground black pepper | sea salt
600 g lean lamb (from the leg or shoulder), minced twice | 1 ice cube
250 ml vegetable oil | natural yoghurt to serve

PINE NUT AND LAMB STUFFING **80 ml olive oil | 1 small onion, finely diced**
1/4 teaspoon ground allspice | 80 g pine nuts
200 g lean lamb (from the leg or shoulder), minced | sea salt
freshly ground black pepper | 2 tablespoons chopped flat-leaf parsley leaves

PUT THE BURGUL INTO A SMALL BOWL and pour on just enough cold water to cover it. Leave for 5 minutes, then tip into a sieve and squeeze out as much water as you can using your hands. Tip the burgul into a large bowl with the onion and spices, season with salt and knead to a paste. Leave for about 5 minutes to allow the burgul to soften and absorb some of the flavours.

Add the lamb and ice cube to the bowl and knead them thoroughly into the burgul mixture. As the ice melts it will bind everything into a smooth, sticky paste. Refrigerate the mixture for 30 minutes.

Meanwhile, make the stuffing. Heat half the oil in a heavy-based frying pan. Sauté the onion and allspice over a low heat for 5 minutes until the onion has softened. Add the pine nuts and increase the heat. Sauté, stirring continuously, until the pine nuts are golden brown. Tip into a bowl and set aside.

Wipe out the pan, then add the remaining oil and heat over a medium-high heat. Add the lamb, then increase the heat and sauté for about 5 minutes, breaking up any lumps with a wooden spoon. When any liquid has evaporated, add the onion and pine nut mixture, then season with salt and pepper and stir through the parsley. Tip into a bowl and leave to cool.

To make the köfte, take a small lump of the chilled burgul and lamb paste in the palm of your left hand and roll it into a smooth ball. Use the forefinger of your right hand to make an indentation in the lump and start to shape it into a hollow shell (reverse hands if you're left-handed). Try to make the walls of the shell as thin and even as you can. Fill the shell with a teaspoon of the stuffing. Wet the edges of the opening with cold water and pinch shut. Use your fingers to shape the ends gently into the traditional torpedo shape. Arrange the stuffed köfte on a tray, then cover and refrigerate.

When ready to cook the köfte, heat the oil in a large, heavy-based frying pan or even a wok. Fry the köfte, a few at a time, turning them around in the oil until they are a deep golden brown all over. Drain on paper towel and serve hot, with plenty of yoghurt alongside.

SERVES **6 as part of a mezze selection**

These untraditional kibbeh are filled with gooey molten cheese. They are a little fiddly to make, but with a bit of practice you can achieve a passable, if not exceptional, result.

LAMB KIBBEH STUFFED WITH MOZZARELLA AND PINE NUTS

KIBBEH SHELL **200 g fine white burgul | 600 g lamb, minced twice | 1 onion, puréed in a food processor | 3/4 teaspoon allspice | 1/2 teaspoon ground cinnamon | 1/4 teaspoon chilli powder | sea salt and freshly ground black pepper | Toum (page 386) or Yoghurt Whipped with Tahini (page 150) to serve**

FILLING **150 g mozzarella | 80 g pine nuts | 1 tablespoon olive oil | 1/2 onion, finely diced | 1/4 teaspoon ground allspice | 2 tablespoons finely chopped parsley | 150 ml vegetable oil**

PUT THE BURGUL INTO A SMALL BOWL and pour on just enough cold water to cover it. Leave for 5 minutes, then tip into a sieve and squeeze out as much water as you can using your hands.

Put the lamb into a mixing bowl with the onion, burgul, spices and salt and pepper. Use your hands to mix everything to a soft, smooth paste. You may need to add a little cold water to help bind everything together. Place the bowl in the refrigerator for 30 minutes, which makes the paste easier to work with.

While the lamb mixture is chilling in the fridge, prepare the filling. First, grate the mozzarella. Fry the pine nuts in the olive oil until they are golden brown, then drain them on paper towel. Add the onion to the oil in the frying pan and sauté gently for a few minutes until softened. Tip the onion into a bowl and stir in the cheese, pine nuts, allspice, parsley and salt and pepper.

Take a small lump of the lamb paste in the palm of your left hand and roll it to a smooth ball. Using the forefinger of your right hand (reverse hands if you're left-handed), make an indentation in the lump and start to shape it into a hollow shell. Try to make it as thin and even as you can. Fill the shell with about a teaspoon of the stuffing, wet the edges of the opening with cold water, and pinch it closed. You are aiming for a small torpedo-shaped dumpling, with slightly tapered ends. Leave the stuffed kibbeh on a tray, covered, in the refrigerator until you are ready to cook them.

Bake them in a 190°C (Gas 5) oven for about 20 minutes (the more virtuous option) or deep-fry or shallow-fry them in medium-hot oil, turning to ensure a deep golden brown colour all over. Drain on paper towel and serve hot.

SERVES **4 as part of a mezze selection**

True kibbeh shaham — the speciality of Zghorta, a mountain village in northern Lebanon — are not terribly appealing to a Western palate as they are stuffed with sheep's tail fat. This version is a twist on the traditional and incorporates a lightly spiced butter filling which keeps the shell moist, as is the intent, but is slightly less threatening to the arteries.

ZGHORTA-STYLE KIBBEH PATTIES STUFFED WITH CINNAMON AND PINE NUT BUTTER

KIBBEH SHELL **230 g fine white burgul | 1 onion, puréed in a food processor | 3/4 teaspoon ground allspice | 1/2 teaspoon ground cinnamon | 1/4 teaspoon chilli powder | sea salt and freshly ground black pepper | 450 g lean lamb, roughly diced | natural yoghurt to serve**

CINNAMON AND PINE-NUT BUTTER **200 g unsalted butter, softened | 1 teaspoon ground cinnamon | 1/2 teaspoon salt | 80 g pine nuts, sautéed**

SOAK THE BURGUL IN PLENTY OF salted cold water for about 10 minutes. Use your hands to squeeze out as much water as you can, then tip into a tea towel and twist to extract even more. Tip into a mixing bowl. Add the puréed onion, spices, salt and pepper to the burgul and use your hands to squeeze and mix everything together.

Put the lamb through a mincer, then add it to the burgul. Mix well with your hands, then put it through the mincer again. Place the bowl in the refrigerator for 30 minutes, which will make the paste easier to work with. While the shell mixture is chilling in the fridge, prepare the filling. Put the softened butter into a mixing bowl with the cinnamon, salt and pine nuts and mash together well. Scrape the filling out onto a square of plastic wrap and shape into a log about 3 cm wide. Roll up tightly and refrigerate until it sets firm.

To make the patties, cut the butter into slices no more than 5 mm thick.

Divide the shell mixture into 16 pieces. Roll each piece into a smooth ball, and stick your thumb into the ball to create a cavity. Ideally, the shells should be as thin as you can make them. Slip in a piece of cinnamon and pine nut butter, then use a little water to moisten the open edges and seal them well. Cup your hands and smooth and shape the shells into thick, rounded patties. Leave the stuffed kibbeh on a tray in the refrigerator, covered, until you are ready to cook them.

Traditionally, these kibbeh are cooked on a charcoal grill or barbecue. Alternatively, bake them in a 190°C (Gas 5) oven for about 20 minutes or shallow-fry them in 150 ml medium-hot vegetable oil, turning them to ensure that they're a deep golden brown all over. Drain on paper towel and serve piping hot with yoghurt.

MAKES **16** SERVES **8 as part of a mezze selection**

The chicken and pistachios make these home-made dolmades more delicate than traditional lamb versions.

CHICKEN AND PISTACHIO DOLMADES

250 g hand-sized vine leaves, fresh or preserved | 100 g long-grain rice
200 g minced chicken | 1/4 teaspoon ground allspice | 1/4 teaspoon ground cinnamon
freshly ground black pepper | 60 g unsalted pistachio kernels
zest of 1 lemon, finely chopped | pinch of sea salt
4 tomatoes, sliced | 4 cloves garlic, cut in half | 1 bunch mint
1 litre good-quality chicken stock | juice of 1 lemon | natural yoghurt to serve

IF USING FRESH VINE LEAVES, blanch them in boiling water for 30 seconds and refresh in cold water. If using preserved vine leaves, soak them for 10 minutes, then rinse and pat dry.

Wash the rice and mix it with the chicken mince, allspice, cinnamon, pepper, nuts, zest and salt.

Line the bottom of a heavy-based casserole with a few vine leaves and a layer of sliced tomatoes.

Arrange the remaining leaves on a work surface, vein side up, and slice out the stems. Place a spoonful of filling across the base of a leaf. Roll it over once, fold in the sides and roll it into a neat sausage shape. The dolmades should be about the size of your little finger — don't roll them too tightly or they will burst during cooking. Continue stuffing and rolling until all the filling is used.

Pack the dolmades in tightly on top of the tomatoes, stuffing the halved garlic cloves in among them. Lay the bunch of mint over the top, then pour in the chicken stock and lemon juice and season with salt and pepper. Place a plate on top to keep the dolmades submerged in the liquid, and slowly bring to the boil. Once boiling, lower the heat and simmer gently for 45 minutes.

Allow to cool, then turn out into a serving dish and serve hot, warm or even cold, with plenty of yoghurt.

SERVES **8 as part of a mezze selection**

Ask any good Lebanese boy what his favourite home-cooked dish is, and the chances are that he will nominate his mum's dolma — stuffed vine leaves. This is my mother's recipe, which we both love, not just because it tastes delicious, but because of the neat way in which both the first course and meat course are prepared together in one large pot. The idea is simple: after filling the vine leaves with a traditional rice stuffing, they are placed on top of lamb chops in a large pot. During cooking, all the bubbling juices rise to impregnate the dolma. These you eat first, with plenty of creamy yoghurt, and then follow with the meat course.

MAY'S STUFFED VINE LEAVES

500 g hand-sized vine leaves, fresh or preserved | 300 g medium-grain rice
500 g minced lamb | 1 teaspoon ground allspice | 1/2 teaspoon ground cinnamon
sea salt and freshly ground black pepper | 4 lamb chops from the neck (or chump chops)
1 head garlic, cloves separated but not peeled | 750 ml water | juice of 2 lemons
Mint Labneh (page 45)

IF USING FRESH VINE LEAVES, blanch them in boiling water for 30 seconds and refresh in cold water. If using preserved vine leaves, soak them for 10 minutes, then rinse and pat dry.

Wash the rice and mix it with the minced lamb, spices, salt and pepper.

Lay the vine leaves out on a work surface, vein side up, and slice out the stems. Place a spoonful of filling across the base of the leaf. Roll it over once, fold in the sides and roll it into a neat sausage shape. The stuffed vine leaves should be about the size of your little finger — don't roll them too tightly or they will burst during cooking. Continue stuffing and rolling until the filling is all used.

Lay the lamb chops on the bottom of a heavy-based casserole dish, then pack the stuffed vine leaves in tightly on top, stuffing the garlic cloves in among them. Pour in the water and lemon juice, and place a plate on top to keep the rolls submerged in the liquid. Slowly bring to the boil, then lower the heat and simmer gently for an hour.

The vine leaves can be eaten hot, warm or even cold. If serving them hot, carefully take them out of the pot and arrange them in a pile on a serving dish. Lay the lamb alongside to be eaten with or after the vine leaves.

If you plan to eat the dish cold, cool everything completely in the casserole dish. The whole thing will solidify into a lump. When cold, run a knife around the side of the dish, then invert it, a bit like a cake, onto a serving dish and allow everyone to help themselves. Hot, cold or warm, serve the vine leaves and chops with plenty of mint labneh.

SERVES **8 as part of a mezze selection**

This slightly strange dish is a masterpiece of Ottoman cuisine. Serve it as a starter or as part of a mezze selection, on hot buttered Turkish bread, triangles of toasted flatbread or Lavosh Crackers (page 270) and accompany with Pickled Cucumbers with Fennel (page 392).

CIRCASSIAN CHICKEN

60 ml walnut oil | 2 teaspoons sweet paprika | 120 g Strained Yoghurt (page 44)
3/4 cup shredded coriander leaves

POACHED CHICKEN 1 large free-range chicken breast on the bone
1 small onion, cut into quarters | 1 stick celery | 1 sprig thyme | 2 bay leaves
1/2 lemon | 1/2 teaspoon white peppercorns | 1 red bullet chilli, split lengthwise

WALNUT SAUCE 30 g unsalted butter | 1 purple onion, finely diced | 4 cloves garlic
2 teaspoons sweet paprika | 1/2 teaspoon hot paprika
2 slices stale sourdough bread, crusts removed
chicken stock (reserved from the poached chicken) | 150 g walnuts
1 teaspoon sea salt | 1/4 teaspoon freshly ground black pepper
squeeze of lemon juice

PUT THE CHICKEN AND ALL THE aromatics into a large, heavy-based saucepan and cover with water. Bring to the boil, skimming away any fat and impurities that rise to the surface, then lower the heat immediately. Simmer very gently, covered, for 5 minutes. Turn off the heat and leave the chicken in the stock for 20 minutes. Pull the meat off the bone, shred it as finely as you can and reserve. Strain the stock and reserve.

Meanwhile, heat the walnut oil and paprika in a small saucepan until just warm. Remove from the heat and leave to infuse for at least 30 minutes.

To make the walnut sauce, melt the butter in a heavy-based frying pan. Add the onion, garlic and both paprikas and sweat over a low heat for 10 minutes, until the onion is very soft.

Soak the bread in a little of the reserved chicken poaching stock. Squeeze it to remove as much moisture as possible and set aside.

Pulse the walnuts to fine crumbs in a food processor. Add the onion mixture and pulse to a smooth purée. Crumble in the bread, then add the salt, pepper and lemon juice and blend. With the motor running, trickle in enough of the reserved poaching stock to produce a mayonnaise consistency.

Tip the walnut sauce into a large bowl. Add the shredded chicken, strained yoghurt and coriander and stir well to combine. Taste and adjust the seasoning. To serve, place scoops of the mixture onto each of four serving plates. Use the back of a teaspoon to make an indentation in the surface and drizzle in a little paprika oil.

SERVES 6 as part of a mezze selection

CONFIT CHICKEN TERRINE WITH DUKKAH

CONFIT CHICKEN **2.5 kg chicken wings | 150 g Fragrant Curing Salt (page 106) | 1 kg duck fat | 1 litre vegetable oil | 4 cloves garlic | 1 bay leaf | 2 sprigs thyme**

2 sheets gold-strength gelatine | 1 tablespoon extra-virgin olive oil, warmed | 1 tablespoon sesame oil | 1 tablespoon ground cumin seeds, toasted | 1 tablespoon sesame seeds | 1 teaspoon freshly ground black pepper | 12 pencil-sized leeks | 50 g assorted edible flower petals | bread or croutons to serve

TO CONFIT THE CHICKEN, FIRST wash the wings well and pat them thoroughly dry. Place in a large mixing bowl and toss well with the fragrant salt. Cover and refrigerate for 6 hours or, better still, overnight.

Preheat the oven to 140°C (Gas 1). Rinse the chicken wings well and pat them dry. Heat the duck fat and vegetable oil in a large, ovenproof saucepan or casserole. When the fat has melted, add the garlic, bay leaf and thyme. Tip in the chicken wings and stir them gently to coat in the oily mixture. Cover the pan and bake for 2 hours, or until the chicken is very tender, but not mushy.

Tip the wings into a colander to drain. (The oil can be kept in a sealed jar for 2 weeks and re-used for the same purpose.) Once the chicken wings are cool, remove the skin and bones and transfer the meat to a bowl — it should yield about 1 kg.

Soak the gelatine in cold water for 2 minutes then squeeze it dry. Mix with the warm olive oil until dissolved.

Add the two oils, ground cumin, sesame seeds and pepper to the chicken meat and mix well. Taste and adjust the flavours to your liking; you won't need to add salt, as there will be enough from the confit process. Divide the mixture in half.

Blanch the leeks in boiling water for 90 seconds, then refresh in iced water. Dry thoroughly on a clean tea towel.

Place a double layer of plastic wrap on your work surface, to create a 30 cm x 30 cm square. In the centre of this, spread out half of the petals in a layer to form a 20 cm x 10 cm rectangle. Spoon half of the chicken mixture on top of the flowers, to cover them entirely. Use your fingers or the back of a spoon to spread it evenly, taking care not to disturb the flowers too much — it's easier than it sounds. Now lay half of the leeks along the length of the rectangle.

Carefully roll the terrine up in the plastic wrap to form a neat long cylinder with the leeks at the centre. Roll it along your work surface to even the surface and to expel any air bubbles, then twist the ends tightly and secure with string. Repeat with the rest of the ingredients to create a second roll. Refrigerate for a minimum of 4 hours or, even better, overnight.

To serve, use a very sharp, thin-bladed knife to cut each log into eight slices. Carefully peel away the plastic from each slice and serve straight away with crusty bread or on croutons.

SERVES **8 as part of a mezze selection**

This is a Portuguese-inspired twice-marinated and twice-cooked quail dish. The birds are rubbed with a spicy paste and then cooked in a tangy, hot-sour beer marinade. They are left in the marinade for up to three days, and once cooked they require only a quick grilling or frying to turn their skin a delightful golden red.

PORTUGUESE-MARINATED QUAIL

4 whole quail | 2 cloves garlic | 1 teaspoon sea salt | 2 teaspoons sweet paprika
1 teaspoon crushed cumin seeds | 1 tablespoon olive oil | 200 ml beer
1 tablespoon balsamic vinegar | 1 tablespoon white-wine vinegar
2 long red chillies, cut into thirds | 4 small sprigs oregano
4 baby turnips, brushed and halved | 100 g cooked chickpeas
300 ml good-quality chicken stock | 150 ml olive oil for frying
sea salt and freshly ground black pepper | 1 purple salad onion, very finely sliced
oregano flowers to garnish (optional)

TRIM THE QUAIL OF NECKS AND wing tips. Split down the backbone with a heavy knife and clean the insides. Wash and pat dry.

Pound the garlic with the salt to a smooth light paste, then pound in the paprika and cumin seeds for a few more minutes so you have a thick, stiff paste. Loosen the paste with 1 tablespoon oil and rub thoroughly all over the quail.

In a bowl, mix together the beer and vinegars. Marinate the quail in this mixture overnight in the refrigerator.

Place the quail and marinade into a heavy pot and bring to the boil. Lower the heat, add the chillies and oregano and cook gently for 12 minutes. Remove the quail and drain it on paper towel.

Reduce the marinade by two-thirds until thick and syrupy, then pour it over the quail. Cover the quail and marinade with plastic wrap and allow to cool completely. Refrigerate until you are ready to cook. You can do this up to 3 days ahead of time.

When ready to cook, remove the quail from the marinade and set aside. Tip the marinade ingredients into a saucepan and add the baby turnips, chickpeas and chicken stock. Bring to a boil, then lower the heat and simmer for 12 minutes, or until the turnips are tender.

Grill the quails on a griddle or barbecue, or cook them under the griller for 1½–2 minutes on each side. Alternatively, pat them dry, dust in paprika flour (100 g flour to 1 teaspoon sweet paprika) and deep-fry until crisp (about 1 minute in 200°C oil). To shallow-fry, heat about 2 cm of oil in a frying pan and fry, skin side down, for about a minute on each side, or until golden brown. Season lightly. To serve, tip the simmering marinade into a warm serving bowl and arrange the quail on top. Garnish with purple onion rings and oregano flowers, if using.

SERVES 4 as part of a mezze selection

While the spices in this dish are a classic Lebanese combination, the technique is a Chinese method which I learnt during my time in Hong Kong. Dunking the birds quickly into boiling stock has the effect of tightening the skin, without cooking the flesh. Then when you fry or roast them, you get a wonderfully crisp, parchment-like skin. You can use this method with all poultry or game birds.

CRISP QUAIL WITH FRAGRANT SALT

2 litres water | 150 ml cider vinegar | 8 x 200 g jumbo quail
2 teaspoons Fragrant Salt (page 380) | 1 large thumb fresh ginger, peeled and sliced
4 star anise | 400 ml vegetable oil

PUT THE WATER AND VINEGAR INTO a large non-reactive pan and bring to the boil. When bubbling away, drop in a quail and leave it for 10–15 seconds. Remove and refresh the bird in cold water before patting dry. Repeat with the remaining birds, then put them in the refrigerator, uncovered, for at least 6 hours, to dry completely.

When you are ready to fry the quail, season them all over with the fragrant salt. Heat a medium-sized heavy-based pot. Add the ginger and star anise to the dry pot and move them around over the heat to release the aromatic oils. Carefully pour in the vegetable oil and heat to 180°C, or until a cube of bread sizzles to the surface. Drop in four of the quails, breast side down, and fry for 2–3 minutes. The quails won't be fully immersed in oil, so you'll need to gently shake the pan so the bubbling oil swirls around them. Once they start to turn golden, turn them over and fry for another few minutes.

Remove the birds from the oil and sit them on paper towel for a few minutes to absorb any excess oil. Repeat with the remaining 4 birds. Serve them straight away as a starter, perhaps with a little watercress salad.

SERVES **4 as part of a mezze selection**

Many Middle Eastern butchers make their own version of these wonderful spicy sausages known as ma-ahani, and they are a popular addition to the mezze table. If you are unable to find them ready-made, the good news is that they are simple to make at home as you don't need to use casings: simply roll the mixture into skinless sausages.

Try not to use ready-minced lamb as it can sometimes be too fatty. Instead, buy a piece of lamb shoulder or round and mince it yourself at home. Just make sure you ask your butcher for meat that isn't too lean — you do need some fat. Make the sausages the day before you plan to cook them to let the flavours develop.

SPICY LEBANESE SAUSAGES WITH PINE NUTS

1 teaspoon ground cinnamon | 1 teaspoon ground ginger | 1 teaspoon sweet paprika
1 teaspoon freshly grated nutmeg | 1 teaspoon ground black pepper
1/2 teaspoon ground cloves | 1/2 teaspoon mahlab (crushed cherry seeds)
500 g minced lamb shoulder | splash of red wine | sea salt | 40 g pine nuts
olive oil for frying | squeeze of lemon juice | Arabic flatbread and lemon wedges to serve

STIR ALL THE SPICES TOGETHER. ADD to the minced lamb with a good splash of red wine. Mix thoroughly and season with a little salt. Pinch off a small piece of meat and fry. Taste it and adjust the seasoning if need be. Stir in the pine nuts so they are evenly distributed through the sausage mixture. Cover and refrigerate overnight.

To make the ma'ahani, wet your hands and roll the mixture into small, even-sized chipolata sausage shapes.

To cook, fry in oil until coloured. Add a good squeeze of lemon juice to the pan and toss the sausages briefly. Serve with fresh Arabic flatbread and lemon wedges.

MAKES about 20 sausages SERVES 6 as part of a mezze selection

LARGE DISHES

Fish markets around the shores of the Eastern Mediterranean are mounded high with pretty little red mullet and this method of wrapping them in tangy vine leaves and grilling — a dish known as sultan ibrahim — is one of our favourites. It also works very well using sardines.

RED MULLET GRILLED IN VINE LEAVES

CHOPPED EGG, CORIANDER AND LEMON DRESSING **125 ml Lemon-Garlic Dressing (page 387) | 2 soft-boiled eggs, chopped | 1/2 cup roughly chopped coriander leaves**

12 x 120-140 g red mullet | 12 vine leaves, fresh or preserved | olive oil for frying

TO MAKE THE DRESSING, TOSS THE ingredients together and keep at room temperature until ready to serve.

To scale the red mullet, hold it under running water and use your thumb to run against the scales from tail to head — they come away very easily. Leave the fins and tail attached for presentation, but use a sharp knife to slice the fish open along the underbelly. Hold the sides open and pull the intestines away. Insert your finger into the reddish-coloured gills and pull them out too. Rinse the insides of the fish under running water, paying special attention to rubbing away the dark blood line against the backbone. Pat dry.

If you are using preserved vine leaves, soak them well, then rinse and pat them dry. Fresh vine leaves should be blanched in boiling water for 30 seconds and then refreshed in cold water.

Arrange the vine leaves on a work surface, vein side up. Trim off the stalks and cut each leaf into a rectangle. Place a red mullet in the middle of each vine leaf and wrap the leaf around the fish.

Heat the oil in a large non-stick frying pan and fry the fish in batches, for 2–3 minutes on each side. The vine leaves should be slightly blackened, but the fish will be tender, white and juicy. Serve straight away with the dressing.

SERVES **4**

Dried herbs can often look rather unappealing, but they scrub up well as a coating for this quick tuna dish. You could serve it as part of a Persian-themed dinner, perhaps with polow rice (pages 219–225) and a Shaved Cucumber and Pomegranate Salad (page 259).

TUNA STEAKS WITH DRIED MINT, OREGANO AND SUMAC

6 x 180 g tuna steaks | 1 tablespoon dried oregano | 1 tablespoon dried mint
1 teaspoon freshly ground black pepper | 1 teaspoon ground sumac | sea salt
80 ml olive oil | rice or salad and lime wedges, to serve

TRIM ANY VISIBLE BLOOD LINE FROM the tuna steaks, if necessary.

Combine the dried herbs, pepper and sumac in a mortar and pound to an even, fairly fine consistency.

Season the tuna steaks with salt, then sprinkle on a generous layer of the herb-spice mixture so they are evenly coated on both sides.

Heat the oil in a heavy-based frying pan over a high heat. Fry the tuna steaks in two batches for 1–2 minutes, which will cook them rare. Turn them every 30 seconds to make sure they don't burn. Serve straight away with rice or salad.

SERVES **6**

As salmon is a dense, oily fish, it benefits from being matched with robust flavours. Baking salmon medallions in this tangy spice mix is surprisingly simple and effective.

SALMON GRILLED WITH FENNEL, LIME AND SUMAC

SPICE MIX **1 tablespoon fennel seeds**
finely grated zest of 1 lime | 1 teaspoon ground sumac

SALMON **4 x 160 g salmon fillets, skinned | 1/4 teaspoon sea salt**
freshly ground black pepper | 40 ml olive oil | 1 teaspoon Dijon mustard

FENNEL-MINT SALAD **1 medium fennel bulb, cored and very finely sliced**
2 shallots, very finely sliced | 1/2 cup baby red and green shiso leaves
1/2 cup watercress leaves | 100 g creamy feta, roughly crumbled | 1/2 teaspoon dried mint
juice of 1/2 lemon | 75 ml extra-virgin olive oil | 1/2 teaspoon ground sumac
sea salt and freshly ground black pepper | fennel pollen to garnish (optional)

PREHEAT THE OVEN TO 120°C (GAS 1/2). Scatter the fennel seeds and lime zest on a small baking tray and dry in the oven for 15–20 minutes. Allow to cool briefly, then tip into a mortar and pound to an even, fairly fine consistency. Combine with the sumac and set aside.

Increase the oven to maximum heat. Lightly season the salmon fillets with salt and pepper. In a heavy-based ovenproof pan, heat the olive oil and sauté the salmon pieces (skin side up) for 30–40 seconds, moving constantly so they don't stick. Turn and sauté for a further 30 seconds. Remove the pan from the heat, brush each fillet with the mustard and sprinkle generously with the spice mix. Place the pan on the top shelf of the oven and cook for 2 minutes for medium–rare, or longer as desired. Remove from the oven and allow to rest in a warm spot for 4–5 minutes.

To make the salad, put all the ingredients in a large mixing bowl and toss together. Divide the salad among four plates, garnish with fennel pollen, if using, and serve the salmon alongside.

SERVES **4**

Freshwater fish, such as trout, are popular in the north of Iran, and the proximity to Turkey and Azerbaijan adds a touch of chilli heat to some dishes from the region. It would be in keeping with the Iranian custom of balancing 'hot' and 'cold' dishes to serve cooling herbs alongside this spicy recipe.

PAN-FRIED TROUT WITH ORANGE ZEST, CAYENNE PEPPER AND SUMAC

finely grated zest of 1 orange | 1 tablespoon freshly ground black pepper
1 teaspoon cayenne pepper | 2 teaspoons ground sumac | 1 teaspoon sea salt
6 x 350 g rainbow trout | 80 ml vegetable oil | rice, lemon wedges and fresh herbs to serve

PREHEAT THE OVEN TO 120°C (GAS 1/2). Scatter the orange zest on a small baking tray and dry in the oven for 30 minutes. Mix the dried zest with the spices and salt.

Snip the fins from each trout and trim the tails neatly. Pat dry inside and out. Heat the oil in a heavy-based frying pan over a high heat. Sprinkle the spice mix over the trout, inside and out. Fry in batches, for about 4–5 minutes on each side, until the skin is golden and the flesh cooked through. Serve straight away.

SERVES 6

MARINATED FRIED WHITING WITH BABY FENNEL BRAISE

MARINADE **2 cloves garlic | 1 teaspoon sea salt | finely grated zest of 1/2 lemon**
2 tablespoons chopped fennel fronds | 1 tablespoon extra-virgin olive oil

8 x 100–120 g whiting fillets | 4 baby fennel bulbs, long stalks attached | 30 ml olive oil
1 small purple onion, finely sliced | 1 teaspoon ground cumin | 1/4 teaspoon hot paprika
10 kalamata olives, pitted and roughly chopped
1 vine-ripened tomato, skinned, seeded and diced | 80 ml water
sea salt and freshly ground black pepper

COMBINE ALL INGREDIENTS FOR THE marinade in a shallow dish. Add the whiting fillets and turn them in the marinade so they are evenly coated. Cover and refrigerate for 30 minutes, basting from time to time.

Preheat the oven to 200°C (Gas 6). Trim the ends of the fennel stalks neatly. Cut each bulb into quarters lengthwise. Heat the oil in an ovenproof frying pan or small, heavy-based baking pan. Add the fennel, onion, cumin and paprika and sauté over medium heat for 3 minutes. Add the olives, tomato and water to the pan and season with salt and pepper. Transfer the pan to the oven and cook for 8–10 minutes, until the fennel is just tender. Return the pan to the stove top and cook on a high heat until the liquid has reduced and you have a thick braise.

Heat a heavy-based frying pan over a very high heat. Fry the fish, four pieces at a time, for a minute per side until lightly coloured. Serve immediately on top of the fennel braise.

SERVES **4**

For fish kebabs you need a firm, meaty fish, such as monkfish, rockling, hapuka or blue-eye, or an oily fish, such as swordfish, marlin or even tuna. Dried limes are available from Middle Eastern food stores and are worth hunting down.

SKEWERED TAMARIND FISH WITH DRIED-LIME BUTTER AND CHIVES

1.2 kg firm fish fillets, skin removed | 2 tablespoons tamarind paste | 50 ml hot water 1/2 teaspoon ground turmeric | 120 ml olive oil | 1 onion, grated | 12 bay leaves rice, lemon wedges, fresh herbs and Arabic flatbread to serve

DRIED-LIME BUTTER **1 dried lime, cracked with a rolling pin | 100 ml water | 50 ml verjuice juice of 1/2 lime | 3 sprigs thyme | 160 g unsalted butter, diced and chilled 2 tablespoons finely snipped chives**

SHAVED CUCUMBER SALAD **2 Lebanese cucumbers | 1/2 cup black basil leaves 1/3 cup tarragon sprigs | edible flowers | juice of up to 1 lime | 60 ml extra-virgin olive oil sea salt and freshly ground black pepper**

REMOVE ANY STRAY BONES FROM the fish, cut it into 24 large chunks, and transfer to a shallow dish. Whisk the tamarind paste with the hot water until dissolved, then whisk in the turmeric and oil. Stir in the grated onion and pour the mixture over the fish. Cover and refrigerate for 20 minutes.

While the fish is marinating, make the dried-lime butter. Put the cracked dried lime into a small saucepan with the water, verjuice, lime juice and thyme and simmer vigorously over a high heat until the liquid has reduced by half. Strain, discard the solids, then return the liquid to the pan. Add half the chilled butter, then reduce the heat to very low and whisk vigorously until the mixture comes together as a creamy emulsion. Slowly drop in the remaining butter, whisking all the time, until it has all been incorporated. Remove from the heat and keep in a warm place until ready to use.

To make the salad, use a vegetable peeler to shave the cucumber flesh into long strips, being careful not to include any seeds. Discard the seedy core. Tip the shavings into a colander set on a plate and refrigerate for 10 minutes.

When ready to cook, preheat a barbecue or griller to high. Thread the fish chunks onto six metal skewers, interspersing two bay leaves on each. Grill for 4–5 minutes, turning a few times to prevent them from burning, and brush with the marinade as they cook.

To finish the salad, combine the shaved cucumber, herbs and flowers in a large mixing bowl. Whisk the lime juice and oil together and pour over the salad. Season with salt and pepper and toss gently.

Pile the skewers onto a warm platter. Stir the chives into the dried-lime butter and spoon over the fish.

SERVES 6

GARFISH IN DUKKAH CRUMBS WITH LEBANESE-STYLE CABBAGE SALAD

6 x 200 g garfish | sea salt and freshly ground black pepper
2 heaped tablespoons Dukkah (page 377) | 2 cups coarse fresh breadcrumbs
2 free-range eggs | 250 ml milk | 120 g plain flour | 100 ml olive oil | 25 g butter

LEBANESE-STYLE CABBAGE SALAD **300 g Savoy cabbage, cored and very finely shredded**
1/4 cup shredded mint leaves | 1 small purple onion, thinly sliced and rinsed in cold water
juice of 1–2 lemons | 1 small clove garlic crushed with 1/2 teaspoon salt
80 ml extra-virgin olive oil | 1 teaspoon dried mint | sea salt and freshly ground white pepper

CLEAN THE GARFISH AND FILLET them into butterflies, so the two halves remain attached to each other. Season the fish with salt and pepper. Mix the dukkah with the breadcumbs. Whisk the eggs with the milk. Working with one piece of fish at a time, dust lightly with flour then dip into the egg mixture and then into the breadcrumb mixture until evenly coated.

Heat the oil and butter in a large non-stick frying pan and fry the garfish fillets in batches for 1 minute on each side, or until a deep golden brown. Drain on paper towel and serve with cabbage salad.

To make the cabbage salad, mix the cabbage with the mint leaves and sliced onion. In a separate bowl, blend the lemon juice with the garlic paste, extra-virgin olive oil and dried mint. Season to taste. Pour the dressing over the salad ingredients and toss lightly.

SERVES **6**

ABOVE SKEWERED TAMARIND FISH WITH DRIED-LIME BUTTER (PAGE 138)
OPPOSITE GARFISH IN DUKKAH CRUMBS WITH LEBANESE-STYLE CABBAGE SALAD (PAGE 139)

We like to use rock flathead tails for this dish, but you can use any firm white-fleshed fish. Ask your fishmonger for three large tails and to prepare them so you end up with six fillets. Make sure the skin is left on.

PERSIAN GULF-STYLE FISH WITH SAFFRON-LEMON POTATOES

80 ml olive oil | 1 onion, finely chopped | 1 clove garlic, finely chopped
1/2 teaspoon ground cinnamon | 1/2 teaspoon ground cumin | 1/2 teaspoon ground coriander
1/4 teaspoon ground turmeric | 1/4 teaspoon crushed saffron threads
1/4 teaspoon freshly ground black pepper | 500 ml good-quality chicken stock
2 long red chillies, seeded and finely shredded
4 medium waxy potatoes, peeled and diced
6 rock flathead tail fillets, skin on, but neatly trimmed | 2 tablespoons extra-virgin olive oil
2 tablespoons currants, soaked in warm water for 10 minutes
juice of 1/2 lemon | 2 tablespoons verjuice

PREHEAT THE OVEN TO 180°C (GAS 4). Heat half the olive oil in a heavy-based ovenproof pan. Add the onion, garlic and spices and fry for a few minutes over a high heat. Add the stock and bring to the boil, then lower the heat and simmer for 5 minutes. Add the chillies and potatoes. Return to a simmer and cook a further 20 minutes, or until the potatoes are tender and the stock is reduced.

Use a sharp knife to score the skin of the fish in a neat cross-hatch pattern and season lightly. Heat the remaining oil in a frying pan, and sear the fish pieces on both sides. Remove from the pan and sit the fish on top of the potato stew. Drizzle on the 2 tablespoons olive oil. Drain the currants and sprinkle them over the fish and potatoes. Bake in the oven for 8 minutes.

Take the pan to the table to serve, or divide the potatoes among six warm plates and sit the fish on top, drizzled with lemon juice and verjuice.

SERVES 6

There's something irresistible about battered, deep-fried fish — especially if the batter is light and crisp and flavoured with heady spices. If you want a more pronounced tangy, yeasty flavour. Use beer in the batter instead of soda water,

If you're serving this as part of a generous banquet spread, you'll only need one whiting fillet per person, otherwise serve two per person for a main course.

WHITING IN SPICY CHICKPEA BATTER

SPICY CHICKPEA BATTER **500 ml soda water or beer | 150 g chickpea flour**
250 g self-raising flour | 50 g cornflour | 1 teaspoon ground turmeric
1 teaspoon cumin seeds, roasted and lightly crushed
1 teaspoon coriander seeds, roasted and lightly crushed
1/2 teaspoon freshly ground black pepper | 1 dried red chilli, seeded and finely chopped
1 shallot, grated | 1 clove garlic, grated | pinch of sea salt | pinch of bicarbonate of soda

12 whiting fillets | vegetable oil, for deep-frying | plain flour, for dusting
salad and lime wedges to serve

TO MAKE THE BATTER, POUR THE soda water or beer into a bowl and whisk in the flours, spices, chilli, shallot and garlic. Add the salt and bicarbonate of soda and leave to rest for 30 minutes before using.

When ready to cook, cut the fins away from the whiting fillets and remove any stray bones. Heat the oil in a deep-fryer or large saucepan to 185°C. Test by dropping in a little batter. If it sizzles slowly to the top, turning golden brown in 10–15 seconds, the oil is hot enough.

Working in batches, dust the whiting fillets lightly with flour, then dip into the batter, allow the excess to drip off, and gently lower into the oil. Fry for 1–2 minutes, or until the batter is golden brown.

Drain briefly on paper towel before serving with salad and lime wedges.

SERVES 6 as a main course or 12 as part of a banquet

Cooking prawns in their shells intensifies the flavour and stops them drying out as quickly. Tiger prawns are robust enough to serve with this highly spiced dressing and warm burgul salad. You can also sprinkle them with a little of the spice mix before cooking. The salad should be served as soon as possible after it's made or it will start to go soggy.

GRILLED TIGER PRAWN SHISH KEBABS WITH SPICY CRACKED WHEAT SALAD AND TOMATO DRESSING

16 tiger prawns | sea salt and freshly ground black pepper | olive oil
450 ml Spicy Tomato Dressing (page 388)

SPICY CRACKED WHEAT SALAD **200 g fine white burgul, rinsed in cold water**
1 tablespoon golden raisins, roughly chopped | 360 ml water
1 teaspoon Golden Spice Mix (page 378) | sea salt and freshly ground black pepper
1 long red chilli, seeded and finely diced | 1 medium tomato, seeded and finely diced
1/3 cup finely shredded flat-leaf parsley leaves | 1 small clove garlic, finely chopped
60 ml extra-virgin olive oil | juice of 1 lemon

CUT THE HEADS OFF THE PRAWNS and use a pair of scissors to trim off their legs. To split the prawns open, use a small, sharp knife to cut each prawn in half lengthwise, through the underbelly, to the shell. Pull away the intestinal tract, open the two halves out and then fold them back on themselves. Cut each prawn in half crosswise, and slide the pieces onto soaked wooden skewers. You should have two whole prawns (four halves) on each skewer.

Put the burgul and raisins into a small saucepan and add the water. Sprinkle on the spice mix, season lightly and stir well. Bring to the boil, then cover and simmer gently for 6–8 minutes, or until all the water has been absorbed. Tip into a mixing bowl and add the remaining ingredients. Use a fork to break up the burgul and mix everything together well.

Heat a griller or barbecue, or heat some oil in a large non-stick frying pan. Sprinkle the prawns lightly with salt and pepper. Cook the prawns until they just turn pinkish-red, turning once. To serve, mound the cracked-wheat salad onto a large serving platter and stack the prawns around it. Serve a jug of the spicy tomato dressing on the side for people to help themselves.

SERVES 4

Matching prawns with anise is a rather French thing to do — although the French would be more likely to use Pernod, of course. The flavours blend nicely with the black basil salad.

ARAK PRAWNS WITH GARLIC SAUCE AND BLACK BASIL SALAD

BLACK BASIL SALAD **1 cup black basil leaves | 1 cup watercress leaves | 1 bunch French radishes, topped but tails left on | drizzle of extra-virgin olive oil | squeeze of lemon juice | sea salt and freshly ground black pepper | edible flower petals (optional)**

12 king prawns | sea salt and freshly ground black pepper | 60 ml arak | 100 ml white wine | 1 shallot, finely diced | 2 cloves garlic, finely chopped | 75 g butter, cubed | squeeze of lemon juice

TO MAKE THE SALAD, COMBINE THE black basil, watercress and radishes in a mixing bowl and set aside until the last moment.

Cut the heads off the prawns and use a pair of scissors to trim off their legs. Alternatively, peel the prawns completely if you prefer. To butterfly them, use a small, sharp knife to cut each prawn in half lengthwise, through the underbelly, to the shell. Remove the intestinal tract and open out the halves.

Preheat a heavy-based frying pan to high. Season the prawns with salt and pepper and cook for 2–3 minutes, until the shells turn pink and the flesh is cooked through. At the last minute, turn the heat up to high and splash in half the arak. Allow to bubble for a moment then remove the prawns from the pan and keep them warm while you finish the sauce. Add the wine and the rest of the arak with the shallot and garlic, and let it bubble away until the liquid has reduced by three quarters. Remove the pan from the heat and drop in the cubes of butter, whisking to make a smooth butter sauce. Season and add the lemon juice.

When ready to serve, add the oil and lemon juice to the salad, season lightly and toss everything together. Divide the salad among four plates, arranging it in a mound. Tuck three prawns into each serve of salad and pour the warm sauce around the plate. Garnish with flower petals, if using, and serve straight away.

SERVES **4**

Baked whole fish or fillets, served at room temperature as part of a buffet spread, are hugely popular in the Middle East. Generally, a firm-fleshed white fish is used, although the technique works equally well with salmon.

WHOLE SALMON FILLET IN FRAGRANT SALT, TARATOR-STYLE

1 x 1 kg side Atlantic salmon, cut from the centre, skin on, pin bones removed
1 tablespoon Fragrant Curing Salt (page 106) | olive oil for brushing

YOUGHURT WHIPPED WITH TAHINI **150 g natural yoghurt | 3 tablespoons tahini, well stirred**
1 clove garlic crushed with 1/4 teaspoon sea salt | juice of 1 lemon
1/2 teaspoon freshly ground black pepper

TARATOR **60 g walnuts | 1 cup finely shredded coriander leaves**
1 small purple onion, very finely diced | 1 long red chilli, seeded and finely diced
1/2 teaspoon ground sumac | juice of 1 lemon | 60 ml extra-virgin olive oil
sea salt and freshly ground black pepper

TO PREPARE THE SALMON, FIRST TRIM off the tapering tail end of the fish and square off the head end. Trim about 1.5 cm from the belly so you have a neat, even-sided rectangle. Remove all pin bones. Season the salmon all over with the fragrant salt. Cover and refrigerate for 1 hour.

Preheat the oven to 80°C (Gas 1/4). Remove the salmon from the fridge and allow it to come to room temperature. Rinse in cold water and dry it thoroughly. Brush both sides with olive oil then wrap in baking paper and place, skin side down, in a large baking tray. Bake for 12 minutes. Remove from the oven and carefully turn the salmon skin side up. Return to the oven for a further 12 minutes.

Remove from the oven and leave to rest in the tray for 10 minutes. Unwrap and discard the paper. Peel away the skin, then gently scrape away all of the grey blood line from the fish. Set aside.

To make the yoghurt whipped with tahini, whisk all the ingredients together until smooth and creamy.

To make the tarator, preheat the oven to 160°C (Gas 3). Spread the walnuts out on a baking tray and roast for 8–10 minutes, shaking them around from time to time so they colour evenly. Tip the nuts into a tea towel and rub vigorously to remove as much of their papery brown skin as possible. Chop the walnuts finely and put in a mixing bowl with the coriander, onion, chilli and sumac. Pour on the lemon juice and oil, season with salt and pepper and mix together well.

To serve the salmon, smear the exposed surface with a little yoghurt-tahini sauce, then pack on the tarator topping neatly and evenly so it completely coats the fish. Serve at room temperature, with some extra sauce on the side.

SERVES **6**

FLOUNDER ROASTED ON THE BONE WITH TAKLIA, FENNEL, SHALLOTS AND WILD OREGANO

4 x 300 g flounder, skin on | 8 shallots | 2 small fennel bulbs, quartered
2 tablespoons Taklia (page 384) | 60 ml olive oil | sea salt and freshly ground black pepper
splash of sweet sherry | 250 ml good-quality chicken stock | 2 tablespoons butter
4 generous twigs dried wild oregano | Goat's Cheese Mashed Potatoes (page 242) to serve

TO PREPARE THE FLOUNDER, REMOVE the heads just below the gills. Snip off the side fins and cut each fish into three pieces, crosswise through the bone.

Peel the shallots and poach them in simmering water until tender. Blanch the fennel in boiling water for 2 minutes, then refresh in iced water.

Preheat the oven to 180°C (Gas 4). Season the flounder pieces, shallots and fennel with salt and pepper and rub the fish all over with the taklia. Heat the oil in a large heavy-based ovenproof frying pan. Fry the flounder pieces on both sides until lightly coloured then add the shallots and fennel to the pan. Add the sherry, chicken stock, butter and the twigs of oregano. (Don't worry if the oregano leaves burn as this looks quite dramatic!)

Transfer to the oven and roast for 6 minutes, or until the fish is just cooked and the fennel is tender. Serve with mashed potato.

SERVES 4

Although it might at first seem a little strange to bake fish in yoghurt, we guarantee that this wonderful dish from the north of Iran, with its crunchy walnut and herb topping, will surprise and delight you. You'll need to select a firm white fish that becomes succulent and tender as it cooks — rockling or monkfish are ideal. Chelow rice (pages 217-218) or broad bean, borlotti and dill rice (page 219) is good with this.

YOGHURT-BAKED FISH WITH WALNUT-HERB CRUMBS

unsalted butter, for greasing | 1 x 1 kg firm white fish fillet, skin removed
sea salt and freshly ground black pepper | rice and fresh herbs to serve

WALNUT-HERB CRUMBS **150 g fresh breadcrumbs**
150 g shelled walnuts, coarsely chopped and sieved
1/4 cup shredded flat-leaf parsley leaves | 1/4 cup shredded tarragon leaves or dill sprigs
90 g unsalted butter, melted

YOGHURT SAUCE **250 g thick natural yoghurt | 1/2 teaspoon cornflour**
1 large free-range egg | 1 small shallot, finely diced | 2 tablespoons finely snipped chives
juice of 1/2 lime | 1 tablespoon extra-virgin olive oil | sea salt and ground black pepper

PREHEAT THE OVEN TO 180°C (GAS 4). Lightly grease a baking dish just large enough to fit the fish comfortably.

To make the walnut-herb crumbs, combine the ingredients thoroughly in a bowl.

To make the yoghurt sauce, whisk the yoghurt with the cornflour and egg. Stir in the shallot, chives, lime juice and oil and season lightly with salt and pepper.

Remove any stray bones from the fish, then cut the fillet into six even pieces. Season the fish lightly all over with salt and pepper and arrange in the baking dish. Pour the yoghurt sauce over the fish. Pack a generous layer of the walnut-herb crumbs on top of each piece of fish. Season lightly again and bake for 15–20 minutes, or until the topping is golden and crunchy and the fish is cooked through. Serve straight away.

SERVES **6**

This dish was inspired by a wonderful meal that we enjoyed at Doğa Balik, a seafood restaurant in Istanbul. The original version included turbot and sea bass, but you could also choose a selection of baby snapper, John Dory, whiting or black bream. Cooking the fish on the bone adds incomparably to the flavour of the finished dish.

THE FISH DOCTOR'S STEW — WITH BLACK PEPPER, LEMON ZEST AND MINT

2 x 400-500 g whole baby snapper, cleaned | 2 x 300 g whole whiting, cleaned
sea salt and freshly ground black pepper | 50 ml extra-virgin olive oil
2 large onions, very finely diced | 2 cloves garlic, very finely diced
1/2 teaspoon dried oregano | 1 teaspoon dried mint | 3 bay leaves
long piece of zest from 1 lemon | few sprigs thyme | 1/2 teaspoon red chilli flakes
250 ml good-quality chicken stock | snipped baby chives to serve

PREHEAT THE OVEN TO ITS HIGHEST temperature.

To prepare each snapper, cut away the head just below the gills. Snip off the side fins and cut the fish in half crosswise through the bone. To prepare each whiting, cut away the head, then cut the body into three pieces crosswise through the bone. Season the fish well with salt and pepper.

Heat the oil gently in a heavy-based casserole dish. Add the onion and garlic and sweat very gently for a few minutes until they start to soften. Add the oregano, mint and bay leaves, zest and 1/2 teaspoon freshly ground black pepper, then cook over a low heat for another 5 minutes. Lay the pieces of fish on top of the onion mixture, then sprinkle on the thyme and red chilli flakes. Add the stock and transfer to the very hot oven. Cook for 8 minutes, which should be long enough to colour the fish and just cook it through. Remove the pan from the oven, sprinkle with baby chives and take it to the table straight away.

SERVES 4

ROASTED MONKFISH IN GREEN CHERMOULA WITH KATAIFI WAFERS

GREEN CHERMOULA **2 tablespoons cumin seeds, lightly roasted and finely ground**
1 tablespoon coriander seeds, lightly roasted and finely ground
$1\frac{1}{2}$ tablespoons sweet paprika | 1 tablespoon ground ginger
2 cloves garlic, roughly chopped | 4 long green chillies, seeded, scraped and chopped
100 g spring onions | 1 cup coriander leaves
1 cup flat-leaf parsley leaves | juice of 1 lemon

KATAIFI WAFERS WITH PARMESAN CHEESE **100 g kataifi pastry | 60 g clarified butter**
50 g grated parmesan cheese | 1 tablespoon sesame seeds
sea salt and freshly ground white pepper

2 x 500 g monkfish tails, skinned and filleted | sea salt and freshly ground black pepper
60 ml olive oil | 1 tablespoon unsalted butter
Braised Baby Beetroot with Chickpeas (page 249) to serve

TO MAKE THE GREEN CHERMOULA, combine all the ingredients in a food processor and whiz to a smooth paste. Tip into a clean jar and cover the surface with olive oil to prevent it from discolouring. It will keep in the refrigerator for up to 1 week. Top up with a little oil each time you use it.

To make the kataifi wafers, preheat the oven to 180°C (Gas 4) and lightly grease a baking tray. Unfold and loosen the kataifi pastry and place it in a large bowl. Tip on the clarified butter, parmesan cheese and sesame seeds and season lightly with salt and white pepper. Use your hands to gently mix everything together. Spread the pastry out evenly over a corrugated (or flat) baking tray. Place another corrugated (or flat) tray on top and press gently until there is a snug fit. Bake for 15 minutes, or until golden brown. Remove from the oven and leave to cool until ready to use.

Season the monkfish fillets with salt and pepper and brush them liberally all over with green chermoula. Refrigerate for 2 hours.

When ready to cook, preheat the oven to 180°C (Gas 4). Heat the olive oil in a large ovenproof frying pan over a medium heat and sear the fillets on all sides until lightly coloured. Add the butter to the pan and transfer it to the oven. Roast for 4 minutes then turn and roast for a further 4 minutes. Remove from the oven and allow to rest for 2 minutes.

While the fish is resting, transfer the kataifi wafers onto a flat baking tray and warm through in the oven for 1 minute. To serve, cut the monkfish fillets into large pieces. Break the kataifi wafers into pieces and use as a garnish.

SERVES 4

This couscous is thick, rich and intensely spicy — perfect with simply grilled calamari. It is also delicious served cold. Zhoug is a fiercely hot coriander relish, and is the ideal condiment for many seafood dishes.

COUSCOUS STEW WITH GRILLED CALAMARI AND ZHOUG

COUSCOUS STEW **60 ml olive oil | 1 medium onion, finely chopped**
2 cloves garlic crushed with 1 teaspoon sea salt | 1 teaspoon ground coriander
1 teaspoon ground cumin | 1/2 teaspoon ground allspice | 1 teaspoon chilli powder
1/2 teaspoon sweet paprika | 400 g can chopped tomatoes
1 long green chilli, seeded, scraped and finely shredded | 1 teaspoon honey
sea salt and freshly ground black pepper | 100 g couscous
100 g chickpeas, soaked and cooked | 6 kalamata olives, pitted and sliced
1 tablespoon finely chopped flat-leaf parsley leaves
1 tablespoon finely chopped mint leaves

12 medium calamari tubes, split and scored on the inner surface | 80 ml olive oil
1/2 cup Zhoug (page 384) | juice of 1 lemon | warm Arabic flatbead to serve

TO MAKE THE COUSCOUS STEW, heat the olive oil in a heavy-based saucepan, add the onion and cook over a gentle heat until soft. Add the garlic paste, coriander, cumin, allspice, chilli powder and paprika, and mix well. Cook for a further 2 minutes, then add the tomatoes, green chilli and honey. Cook for another 10 minutes, then taste for seasoning.

Add the couscous, chickpeas and olives, cover the pan and cook over a low heat until the couscous swells and softens. This will take 5–10 minutes.

When you are ready to eat, heat the griller or barbecue to its highest temperature. Brush the calamari with olive oil and season, then place the calamari, scored side down, on the hotplate. After 40 seconds, turn them over. In a few moments, they will curl into a tight cylinder. Cook for no more than a minute, then remove from the heat.

To serve, stir the parsley and mint through the couscous. Place the calamari on top and dot with tiny blobs of zhoug (be careful, it is very hot!). Sprinkle with lemon juice and serve with bread.

SERVES **6**

This is definitely a special occasion dish, with its glorious golden tones, luscious, velvety cream sauce and strong, heady flavours. This is a modern-day fricassee, without the traditional egg yolks for enriching. Instead, the sauce is reduced to an intensely sticky richness, and only needs some egg noodles or plain steamed rice to accompany it.

PRAWN, SAFFRON AND LEEK FRICASSEE

12 king prawns, about 1 kg | 1 tablespoon Ras al Hanout (page 378)
60 ml olive oil | 3 small leeks, white part only, cut into medium dice
1 clove garlic, finely chopped | 2 small bulbs fennel, cored and thinly sliced
generous splash of white wine | 15 saffron threads, lightly roasted and ground
500 ml chicken or vegetable stock | 1 teaspoon Dijon mustard
100 ml cream (35% fat) | sea salt and freshly ground black pepper
juice of 1/2 lemon | 2 tomatoes, skinned, seeded and cut into medium dice
1 tablespoon chopped flat-leaf parsley leaves
buttered noodles or plain rice and a soft green-leaf salad to serve

PEEL THE PRAWNS AND REMOVE THE heads, but leave the tails intact. With a sharp knife, split them along the back and carefully pull away the intestinal tract. Rub the prawns all over with the ras al hanout and allow them to sit for an hour to marinate.

Heat the oil in a frying pan until sizzling hot. Sear the prawns very quickly on both sides, and then remove from the pan. Keep the heat high and add the leeks, garlic and fennel and toss them around the pan for a minute. Add the white wine to deglaze the pan, then add the saffron. Pour in the stock, reduce the heat a little and allow to bubble away until the liquid reduces by two-thirds and the vegetables soften. This will take about 8 minutes.

When reduced, add the mustard and cream and stir in well. Bring the sauce back to the boil, taste and season with salt, pepper and lemon juice. Put the prawns back into the pan with the tomatoes and cook for another minute, just so that the prawns cook through. Sprinkle with parsley before serving.

SERVES 4

In traditional bouillabaisse recipes the fish are cooked in the broth as a fish stew. Here they are grilled separately and placed in the soup as it is served. This means that oily fish like salmon may be included, and each fish retains its colour and texture. You can use any white reef fish, such as garfish, snapper or black bream.

GRILLED SEAFOOD BOUILLABAISSE

**1.2 litres Crab Stock (page 13) | 3 large waxy potatoes, peeled and sliced thickly
3 leeks, sliced 2 cm thick | 80 g double-peeled broad beans
2 medium fennel bulbs, cored and cut into 8 wedges | 4 tomatoes, seeded and diced
sea salt and freshly ground black pepper | 1.5 kg black mussels
6 blue swimmer crab claws | 750 g salmon fillet, skinned and cut into thick slices
750 g white fish fillets | 12 king prawns (2 per person) | fennel pollen to garnish (optional)
Cumin Rouille (page 386) and crusty bread to serve**

HEAT THE STOCK IN A SAUCEPAN. Add the potato slices and parboil them for about 10 minutes, then add the leek, broad beans and fennel and cook for a further 4 minutes. Add the tomatoes, taste, then season lightly. Remove the pan from the heat and set aside.

Steam the mussels and crab claws in 250 ml of the crab stock, until all the mussels have opened. Grill the salmon, white fish and prawns. Ladle the broth into six bowls and divide the seafood evenly among them. Garnish with fennel pollen and serve straight away with cumin rouille and bread.

SERVES **6**

Marinated chicken wings are irresistible whether grilled on the barbecue or baked in the oven to sticky golden goodness. And we love the Persian way of spearing them onto skewers, instead of just scattering them randomly over the flames. The yoghurt in this marinade helps to tenderise the meat, and it adds a faint but delectable tang. It's best to grill the tomatoes separately, rather than spearing them with the wings, as they cook at different rates and the tomatoes are easier to handle if they can maintain some shape.

If you don't feel like firing up the barbecue, the chicken wings can also be baked at 180°C (Gas 4) for about 20 minutes, in which case you should add the tomatoes halfway through the cooking time.

MARINATED CHICKEN WING KEBABS WITH SKEWERED TOMATOES

12 free-range chicken wings, tips removed | 1 clove garlic crushed with 1 teaspoon sea salt
3 tablespoons olive oil | 120 g thick natural yoghurt | 2 tablespoons Saffron Liquid (page 218)
juice of 1 lime | grated zest of 1/2 orange | 1/2 teaspoon freshly ground black pepper
6 small vine-ripened tomatoes | splash of pomegranate molasses
1 teaspoon chopped thyme leaves | rice, lemon wedges, fresh herbs and flatbread to serve

CUT THE CHICKEN WINGS IN HALF through the joint and put them in a shallow dish.

In a bowl, combine the garlic paste, 1 tablespoon of the oil, the yoghurt, saffron liquid, lime juice, orange zest and pepper, and mix well. Pour the marinade onto the chicken wings and turn them around in it so they are evenly coated. Cover and refrigerate overnight, or for at least 6 hours. Allow to come to room temperature before cooking.

When ready to cook, preheat your barbecue or griller to high. Thread the wing pieces onto metal skewers (any width will do here), and grill, turning so they colour evenly. As they begin to colour, move them away from the direct heat to prevent them from burning. They will take 15–20 minutes to cook through.

Halfway through the cooking time, thread the tomatoes onto a skewer. Whisk the remaining oil with the pomegranate molasses and thyme and baste the tomatoes as they cook, turning them continuously so they char evenly.

Pile all the skewers onto a warm platter and serve straight away, with rice, lemon wedges, herbs and flatbread.

MAKES **6**

Eating liver kebabs for breakfast is a regional eccentricity of south-eastern Turkey, especially of Şanliurfa and Gaziantep, so we rose with the birds one morning to sample ciğer kebaps for ourselves. Following our noses and the intense blue smoke from the grill, we joined a surprisingly large crowd of men outside Ciğerici Haydar. Threaded on a long, flat skewer with chunks of solid lamb's tail fat to keep the liver moist, the kebabs proved to be spicy and delicious. We ate them wrapped in flatbread with parsley, onion and an extra sprinkling of chilli.

SPICY LIVER KEBABS WITH ONION AND SUMAC SALAD

1 lamb's liver (about 450 g) | 1 tablespoon ground sumac | 1 tablespoon ground cumin
1 teaspoon freshly ground black pepper | 1/4 teaspoon hot paprika
1 teaspoon hot Turkish red pepper paste | 80 ml extra-virgin olive oil | sea salt
Arabic flatbread and lemon wedges to serve

ONION AND SUMAC SALAD **1/2 cup shredded flat-leaf parsley leaves**
1 small purple onion, finely sliced | 1 baby cos lettuce, shredded
juice of 1/2 lemon | sea salt | 1 teaspoon ground sumac

USE YOUR FINGERS TO REMOVE THE membrane from the liver, then cut out any little tubes with a small sharp knife. Cut the trimmed liver into even 2 cm cubes. Combine the spices, pepper paste and oil in a bowl, then add the liver and toss gently to coat. Leave for 30 minutes to marinate.

To make the salad, toss all the ingredients in a large bowl.

When ready to cook, heat a ridged chargrill pan or barbecue to maximum heat. Thread eight cubes of liver onto each of eight flat skewers, packing the liver close together; this way the liver will cook brown and crisp on the outside, but remain a little pink inside. Cook for 15–20 seconds on each side — no more than a minute in total — and season with salt as you go.

Remove the skewers from the grill and serve them on flatbread. The idea is for everyone to wrap their own kebabs in flatbread, garnish with salad and add a squeeze of lemon.

SERVES **4**

'ŞIŞ' (pronounced shish) is the Turkish word for skewer, and this method of spearing meat — on any kind of makeshift skewer — and cooking it over an open fire is one of the very earliest cooking methods. Its popularity throughout Turkey dates back to the nomadic Turkic tribes, who migrated out of the eastern and central Steppes and into Anatolia from the seventh century onwards. ŞIŞ kebabs can be made from almost any meat or poultry, cubed or minced, and are often interspersed on the skewer with tomato, capsicum (pepper), onion and eggplant (aubergine). However, as the meat and vegetables take different lengths of time to cook, we prefer to keep them separate. Here the kebabs are served the traditional way, with warmed flatbread, salad and a yoghurt dressing.

ŞIŞ KEBABS

**500 g lamb (from the leg or shoulder) | 1 heaped teaspoon ground cinnamon
1 heaped teaspoon ground allspice | 1 teaspoon hot paprika
1 teaspoon ground nutmeg | 1/2 teaspoon freshly ground black pepper
80 ml extra-virgin olive oil | sea salt | warmed flatbread, Baby Iceberg Salad (page 164) and 300 ml Basil Tzatziki (page 43) to serve**

TRIM THE LAMB OF ANY FAT AND connective tissue, then cut it into 2 cm cubes. Combine the spices and oil in a bowl, then add the lamb and toss gently to coat. Leave for 45 minutes to marinate.

When ready to cook, heat a ridged chargrill pan or or barbecue to maximum heat. Thread six cubes of lamb onto each of eight flat skewers, packing the meat close together; this way the meat will cook brown and crisp on the outside, but remain a little pink inside. Cook for 4–5 minutes, turning frequently and seasoning with salt as you go.

Remove the skewers from the grill. The idea is for everyone to wrap their own kebabs in flatbread with salad and a drizzle of basil tzatziki.

SERVES **4**

These Persian favourites are definitely a cut above your average kebab. Kabab-e barg are traditionally made from lamb fillet, which is cleverly sliced into long, wafer-thin strips that are woven onto skewers for grilling. The word 'barg' means 'leaf', which tells you how thin the meat should be. They are just as succulent and exquisitely tender when made using beef fillet — we suggest that you ask your butcher for a centre-cut piece of fillet, to ensure you have a piece of uniform thickness. Whether you use beef or lamb, the fillet is an expensive cut and in Iran kabab-e barg are usually served sparingly as part of a wider kebab selection.

Although Iranian kebabs are often marinated to tenderise the meat, in this instance the yoghurt is purely to add flavour, as the cut is already so tender.

SKEWERED BEEF 'LEAVES' MARINATED IN YOGHURT, CARDAMOM AND BLACK PEPPER

100 g thick natural yoghurt | juice of 1 lemon | 1 tablespoon olive oil
1 teaspoon dried oregano | 1 teaspoon ground cardamom | 1/2 teaspoon sea salt
1/2 teaspoon freshly ground black pepper | 1 x 1 kg centre-cut beef fillet
warm flatbread, ground sumac and rice to serve

PUT THE YOGHURT, LEMON JUICE, oil, oregano, cardamom, salt and pepper in a bowl and whisk together well.

With a very sharp knife, carefully cut the beef fillet in half lengthwise. Cut each half into 3 portions. Working with a portion at a time, cut it through the centre horizontally, but not all the way through — it should still be attached at one short end. Open it out to form one longer strip. Repeat with the remaining portions of beef so you have six long, thin strips. Carefully weave a medium-width metal skewer through each strip of meat and arrange in a shallow dish. Brush the marinade over the meat, then cover and refrigerate for 2–2 1/2 hours.

When ready to cook, preheat your barbecue or griller to high. Grill the kebabs for 1–2 minutes on each side, or to your liking. Because they are so thin, they will cook in a flash.

Pile the skewers onto a warm platter and cover with a piece of flatbread. Serve with sumac to sprinkle, a rice dish, and lots more warm flatbread.

SERVES **6**

In Turkey when spiced minced meat is shaped into long sausages around skewers for grilling, it becomes ŞIŞ köfte (ŞIŞ is the Turkish word for skewer). Almost every town in Turkey has its own version of köfte kebabs, flavoured with different combinations of spices and herbs, and many butchers will even sell their own homemade köfte mixture. The following is a simple and tasty version that everyone will adore. If you can, try to find the long flat skewers — the meat is far less likely to fall off these than the regular round ones.

BUTCHER'S KÖFTE KEBABS

500 g lamb (from the leg or shoulder) | 1 clove garlic, minced
1 vine-ripened tomato, diced | 1 teaspoon pomegranate molasses
1 heaped tablespoon Köfte Spice Mix (page 377) | sea salt and freshly ground black pepper warm flatbread to serve

BABY ICEBERG SALAD **4 baby iceberg lettuces, outer leaves removed**
200 g Whipped Feta Dip (page 43) | 2 teaspoons chopped dill
2 teaspoons finely snipped chives

TRIM THE LAMB OF ANY CONNECTIVE tissue and sinew, but leave the fat. Cut the meat into manageable chunks and mince it twice. Knead the minced lamb with the garlic, tomato, pomegranate molasses and spice mix for 2–3 minutes to combine thoroughly, then season with salt and pepper. Cover and refrigerate for 20 minutes to allow the flavours to develop.

Cut the iceberg lettuces in half and wash gently to remove any dirt, but keep the leaves intact. Combine the whipped feta dip and chopped dill and loosen with a little water, if necessary, to make a thick dressing consistency. Set aside with the lettuce cups until ready to serve.

When ready to cook, heat a ridged chargrill pan or barbecue to maximum heat. With wet hands, divide the seasoned mince into four equal portions and mould each one around a flat metal skewer into a long sausage shape.

Cook the köfte for 2–3 minutes on each side, or until golden brown and cooked through. Just before serving, sprinkle the chives onto the dressing. Serve the köfte with warm flatbread, the lettuce cups and dressing alongside for everyone to help themselves.

SERVES **4**

This is a slightly spiced-up version of a Persian favourite. To the standard saffron-lemon combination we've added a rather un-Persian touch of chilli and a mixture of dried and fresh mint. It's a brilliant way to liven up what can sometimes be a bland white meat. Serve with a rice or couscous dish and creamy yoghurt dressing to take the edge off the chilli heat.

GRILLED SAFFRON CHICKEN WITH LEMON, CHILLI AND MINT

800 g boneless free-range chicken thighs, trimmed of excess fat
sprigs of watercress and wafer-thin slices of French radish to serve (optional)
rice or couscous, flatbread and lemon wedges to serve

LEMON, CHILLI AND MINT MARINADE **1 cup loosely packed mint leaves | 2 long red chillies, finely chopped | 1 dried red chilli, finely chopped | 3 cloves garlic, finely chopped | 50 ml olive oil | 2 tablespoons Saffron Liquid (page 218) | grated zest and juice of 2 lemons | 1 teaspoon ground cardamom | generous pinch of dried mint**

YOGHURT DRESSING **1 tablespoon olive oil | 1 clove garlic crushed with 1/2 teaspoon sea salt | 1/4 teaspoon ground turmeric | 200 ml thick natural yoghurt | squeeze lime juice**

CUT THE CHICKEN THIGHS INTO large chunks and put in a large bowl.

Combine the marinade ingredients in the bowl of a food processor and whiz to a paste. If you prefer, you could, of course, do this by hand using a mortar and pestle. Pour the marinade over the chicken pieces and toss to coat thoroughly. Cover and refrigerate for at least 1 hour.

To prepare the yoghurt dressing, heat the oil in a small frying pan and fry the garlic paste gently until soft but not browned. Stir in the turmeric and fry for 5 minutes then remove from the heat and cool briefly. Stir into the yoghurt with a squeeze of lime juice. Set aside until ready to serve.

When ready to cook, preheat your barbecue or griller to high. Grill the chicken for 2–3 minutes on each side, or until lightly charred and good and sticky. Alternatively, you can cook it in a stove-top chargrill pan.

Arrange the chicken pieces on a serving platter, garnish with watercress sprigs and radish wafers, if using, and serve with lots of yoghurt dressing.

SERVES **6**

BARBECUED YOUNG CHICKEN SCENTED WITH CARDAMOM AND THYME

18 cardamom pods | 3 cloves garlic, roughly chopped | 1/2 tablespoon sea salt
2 tablespoons chopped fresh thyme or 2 teaspoons dried thyme
1/2 teaspoon ground sumac | 80 ml olive oil
1 x 1.2 kg free-range chicken, jointed, or 4 Marylands
freshly ground black pepper | 4 teaspoons Toum (page 386)
2 pieces Arabic flatbread | 1 cup coarsely chopped flat-leaf parsley leaves
4 tomatoes, roughly chopped | 1 small purple onion, finely diced
1 Lebanese cucumber, roughly chopped

USING A MORTAR AND PESTLE, pound the cardamom pods to loosen the husks. Remove the husks and continue pounding to bruise the seeds and release their flavour. Add the garlic, salt, thyme and sumac. Pound for a few minutes, mixing all the ingredients together well. Add 3 tablespoons of the olive oil and stir in well. Continue to crush until you have a thick, smooth paste.

Rub three-quarters of the paste over the chicken, making sure you get into all the little creases and corners. Mix the remaining paste with the remaining oil and pour over the chicken pieces. Cover and leave to marinate in the fridge for 4–8 hours, turning from time to time.

When ready to cook, heat your barbecue or griller to its highest temperature. Season the chicken with plenty of black pepper and cook for a few minutes, until golden all over. Lower the heat and cook slowly for a further 10–15 minutes, until the chicken is cooked through. Turn the chicken pieces constantly to prevent them from burning. Towards the end of the cooking, brush the chicken pieces all over with the remaining marinade and a little toum. Cook for a few more minutes.

Split each piece of bread in half. Arrange half a piece of bread on each plate and scatter on some parsley, tomato, onion and cucumber. Top with chicken and serve with extra toum if you're game!

SERVES **4**

This flattened chicken dish is cooked under the griller and served smeared with the earthy and spicy broad bean crush. The crush is also delicious on toasted bread, served as a canapé with drinks before dinner.

GRILLED FLAT CHICKEN WITH BROAD BEAN CRUSH

2 x 500 g free-range chickens or poussins | sea salt and freshly ground black pepper
Arabic flatbread, lemon wedges and soft-leaf salad to serve

BROAD BEAN CRUSH 1 clove garlic | 1/2 teaspoon sea salt
125 g double-peeled broad beans | 1 shallot, very finely diced
1/4 cup finely chopped coriander leaves | 50 ml extra-virgin olive oil
pinch of cayenne pepper | freshly ground black pepper | juice of 1 lemon

PREHEAT THE GRILLER TO ITS highest temperature and line the griller tray with foil to make cleaning up easier.

To prepare the chickens, cut them down the back and splay them open. Season them with salt and pepper and place them under the griller, skin side down, making sure they are about 3 cm from the heat source. Cook for 5 minutes, then turn and cook for a further 5 minutes, or until the skin starts to blister.

While the chickens are grilling, prepare the broad bean crush. First, pound the garlic and salt to a smooth paste. Next, add the remaining ingredients one by one to the mortar and pound them, or tip everything into a food processor. Either way, what you are aiming for is a sludgy, rough texture.

When the chickens are cooked, smear on the broad bean crush and cook for a few more minutes. Serve with flatbread, lemon wedges and salad.

SERVES 4

We spent a lot of time in the souks of Aleppo following our noses towards the smell of grilling chicken. As well as chickens roasting on spits, we also found stalls where chickens were split, squashed between metal holders and barbecued over glowing coals. A Weber barbecue (or another solid-fuel barbecue) is ideal for cooking this recipe, and it will seem more authentic if you are cooking outdoors. Otherwise, use a ridged chargrill pan in your kitchen. Be warned, though — it will create quite a lot of smoke! If you have a hinged metal barbecue grill you'll find it's ideal for keeping the chicken flat. Otherwise, spear each chicken crosswise with a couple of long metal skewers. This will keep them flat.

CHICKEN COOKED ON COALS, ALEPPO-STYLE, WITH CRUSHED WALNUTS, LEMON ZEST AND MINT

2 x 500 g free-range chickens or poussins
2 cloves garlic crushed with 1/2 teaspoon sea salt
50 g walnuts, lightly toasted and chopped | zest and juice of 1 lemon
1 red bullet chilli, seeded, scraped and finely chopped
1/4 cup finely chopped mint leaves | 1/4 cup finely chopped coriander leaves
50 ml olive oil | sea salt and freshly ground black pepper
lemon wedges, Arabic flatbread and chopped-leaf salad to serve

TO PREPARE THE CHICKENS, CUT them down the back and splay them open. Mix the garlic paste with the walnuts, lemon zest and juice, chilli, mint, coriander and olive oil. Mix briefly, then pour onto the chicken and rub well all over. Set aside for 30 minutes or so.

When your barbecue is glowing, or your ridged chargrill pan is smoking hot, cook the chicken for 10 minutes or so, turning it from time to time so it doesn't burn. When the chicken is cooked, season with salt and pepper and remove from the heat. Cut into pieces and serve straight away with lemon wedges, flatbread and salad.

SERVES 4

These are a Malouf family favourite, as cooked by my mother, May. They are easy to prepare and bursting with tangy flavours.

MAY'S MARINATED QUAIL

8 quail, or 1 large jointed chicken | 2 cups coriander, roots removed, finely chopped
4 shallots, finely chopped | 2 cloves garlic, finely chopped | zest and juice of 1 lemon
2 red bullet chillies (optional), finely chopped
1 teaspoon coriander seeds, roasted and crushed | 200 ml olive oil
sea salt and freshly ground black pepper
risotto or Lebanese Nut Rice (page 225) and mixed-leaf salad to serve

TRIM THE QUAIL OF NECKS AND wingtips. Split down the backbone with a heavy knife and clean inside. Wash and pat dry.

Combine the coriander, shallots, garlic, lemon zest and juice, coriander seeds and oil in a very large mixing bowl. Place the quail in the marinade and rub it all over, thoroughly working into the cracks and crevices of the birds. Cover and marinate in the fridge for at least 6 hours, or overnight.

To cook, season the birds first with salt and pepper before grilling them straight from the marinade on a chargrill pan or barbecue or under the griller. Cook for 4 minutes, skin side down, then turn and cook for a further 4 minutes. Serve with rice and salad.

SERVES **4 (2 quail each)**

The Chinese are true masters of cooking birds such as pigeon and duck. While I was cooking in Hong Kong in the 1980s I learnt the trick of rubbing salt into the birds' skins the day before cooking, so that it permeates the skin and helps make the final result even more fragrant and crisp.

The poaching stock used for the pigeon in this recipe is a real joy — deliciously aromatic and a glorious golden colour, it can be strained, frozen and reused almost indefinitely.

CRISP EGYPTIAN PIGEON WITH CORIANDER SALT

4 x size 5 (or larger) pigeons | 2 tablespoons Fragrant Salt (page 380)
280 ml vegetable oil for frying
Shredded Carrot Salad (page 258), soft-herb salad or Toum (page 386) to serve

POACHING STOCK **2 large onions, quartered | 2 cloves garlic, crushed**
2 sticks celery, diced | 1/2 teaspoon ground cinnamon | 1 cinnamon stick
15 saffron threads | 1 red bullet chilli, split | 3 pods cardamom, cracked
1 small bunch coriander, including stems | 5 tablespoons honey
3 litres chicken stock or water | 3/4 teaspoon sea salt

USE A HEAVY KNIFE TO TRIM AWAY the claws and wing tips of the pigeons. Pull away any feathers that are still clinging to the skin. Rub half the fragrant salt into the pigeons, making sure you get into every little crack and crevice. Cover the birds and refrigerate them for at least 24 hours.

To make the poaching stock, put the onions and garlic into a saucepan with the celery, cinnamon powder and stick, saffron, chilli, cardamom, coriander and honey. Pour on the stock or water, bring it to the boil and reduce by a third. Now add the pigeon and salt and return to the boil. Cover the pan and lower the heat, then simmer gently for 20 minutes. When testing to see if the meat is tender, pierce the leg rather than the breast. If there is a little resistance and the juices are a faint pink, then the birds are done.

When the pigeons are cooked, remove them from the poaching stock and allow them to steam dry in the open air for 60 minutes, or even better, overnight.

Dust the birds with the remaining fragrant salt. Heat the oil until moderately hot in a wok and cook the pigeons, no more than two at a time, turning them around in the oil as they colour. After about 5 minutes they should have turned a glossy mahogany. Remove the birds from the oil and sit them on paper towel for a couple of minutes to drain off excess oil. Serve one bird per person as a main meal, with more fragrant salt for dipping.

SERVES **4**

This subtly scented glaze works beautifully with the richness of the duck meat and also brings out the underlying sweetness of the accompanying baby root vegetables.

CARDAMOM AND HONEY-GLAZED DUCK BREASTS WITH BABY ROOT VEGETABLES

12 baby red beetroot, washed and trimmed | 12 baby golden beetroot, washed and trimmed
8 baby leeks, washed and cut into 4 cm lengths | 4 x 200 g duck breasts
sea salt and freshly ground black pepper | 60 ml olive oil
12 baby turnips, brushed, trimmed and quartered | 600 ml good-quality chicken stock
1/2 teaspoon cardamom seeds, crushed | 1 teaspoon dried wild oregano, lightly crushed
2 tablespoons butter | edible flowers (optional)

GLAZE **2 tablespoons honey | 1 teaspoon dry sherry | 3 tablespoons water**
1/2 teaspoon cardamom seeds, crushed | 1/2 teaspoon black peppercorns, crushed
1 teaspoon orange-flower water

COOK EACH TYPE OF BEETROOT IN a separate pans of simmering salted water until tender. When cool enough to handle, peel them, cut into quarters and set aside. Blanch the baby leek pieces in boiling water for 2 minutes, then refresh in cold water, drain and dry.

To make the glaze, warm the honey gently with the sherry and water to dissolve, then stir in the cardamom seeds and crushed pepper. As the glaze cools, add the orange-flower water.

Preheat the oven to 200°C (Gas 6). Use a sharp knife to score the skin of the duck breasts in a neat criss-cross pattern and season lightly. Heat the oil in a heavy-based roasting pan over a medium–high heat until hot. Add the duck breasts, skin-side down, then lower the heat and cook for about 5 minutes, or until the skin turns golden brown and the fat starts to render. Turn the breasts over and cook for a further 3 minutes. Remove the duck breasts from the pan and tip away the rendered fat.

Add the golden beetroot and baby turnips to the pan, along with the blanched leeks, chicken stock, cardamom and oregano. Stir gently, then sit the duck breasts on top of the vegetables and brush the skin generously with the glaze. Cook in the oven for 6 minutes, then transfer the duck breasts to a warm plate.

Return the pan to the stove over a high heat and simmer vigorously until the stock has reduced by half. Add the butter, swirling the pan until it emulsifies with the sauce. Add the reserved red beetroot and heat through gently (without stirring, as the beetroot will discolour the sauce). Check and adjust the seasoning if need be.

Trim the ends of the duck breasts then slice them in half lengthwise, place on a baking tray and reheat in the hot oven for a minute. Divide the vegetables among four serving plates and top with the duck breast halves. Garnish with edible flowers, if using, just before serving.

SERVES **4**

There's little to beat tender young lamb cooked on the barbecue to pink perfection. As a rule, Turks don't really like complicated marinades or sauces, preferring to keep the sweet flavour of the meat unadulterated. But brushing the meat with this fresh herb dressing towards the end of the cooking time adds just the right amount of complementary seasoning. Ask your butcher to cut double-thick cutlets to ensure a rosy-pink centre after grilling.

GRILLED LAMB CUTLETS WITH MOUNTAIN HERBS

1 clove garlic crushed with 1/2 teaspoon sea salt | 1/2 teaspoon freshly ground black pepper
1 small shallot, finely chopped | 1 teaspoon finely chopped rosemary
4 twigs dried oregano | 1/2 teaspoon ground sumac | juice of 1 lemon
60 ml extra-virgin olive oil | 8 double lamb cutlets
Spicy Eggplant Relish (page 393) to serve
Tomato Salad with Tarragon, Shankleish Cheese and Sumac Dressing (page 262) to serve

COMBINE THE GARLIC PASTE, pepper, shallot, herbs, sumac and lemon juice in a bowl. Whisk in the oil to make a thick, pungent dressing. (This may not look like a lot, but don't worry as a little goes a long way.)

Heat a ridged chargrill pan or barbecue to maximum heat. Brush the cutlets very lightly with a little of the dressing, then cook for 2 minutes on each side for medium-rare. Towards the end of the cooking time, brush on a little more of the dressing.

Serve the cutlets hot from the grill with the remaining dressing on the side, accompanied with the relish and salad.

SERVES **4**

In spring, the northern part of Syria is covered with the white blossom of sour cherry trees. The fruit often features in dishes from this part of the world, and a meatball dish served in a sour cherry sauce is particularly renowned. This recipe is our interpretation, but it uses thick double lamb cutlets instead of minced lamb, which can be quite fatty. The addition of cream is unconventional, but it creates a delicately sweet-sour sauce that is delicious.

DOUBLE LAMB CUTLETS WITH ALEPPO-STYLE SOUR CHERRY SAUCE

1/2 teaspoon ground cumin | 1/2 teaspoon ground cinnamon
1/4 teaspoon ground white pepper | 4 double lamb cutlets
sea salt | 50 ml olive oil | buttered rice to serve

SOUR CHERRY SAUCE **1 tablespoon olive oil | 3 shallots, finely sliced**
1 clove garlic, finely chopped | 8 sour cherries, soaked in a little water for 1 hour
200 ml good-quality chicken stock | 60 ml cream (35% fat)
juice of 1/2 lemon | 1/3 cup finely shredded mint leaves

TO MAKE THE SAUCE, HEAT THE OIL in a small non-stick frying pan and sauté the shallots and garlic until they soften. Add the cherries and their soaking water to the pan with the chicken stock. Cover the pan and simmer very gently for 30–45 minutes, until the cherries begin to break down in the liquid. Once the cherries are very soft, remove the lid and raise the temperature. Bubble vigorously until most of the stock has evaporated and you are left with a thick sauce.

Mix the spices together. Season the lamb cutlets with salt, then dust them lightly with the spice mix. Heat the oil in a large heavy-based frying pan and cook the cutlets for 2 minutes on each side for medium-rare. Remove the lamb from the pan and leave it in a warm place to rest while you finish the sauce. Add the cherry sauce to the pan with the cream and lemon juice. Simmer gently for a few moments, then stir through the mint leaves and pour over the cutlets as you serve them.

SERVES **4**

Instead of the more usual Café de Paris butter, we like to make this equally delicious Middle Eastern version that we named with tongues firmly in cheeks. The butter recipe makes enough for twelve thick slices (you'll need four for this recipe). It will keep in the freezer for 3–4 weeks. Cut off discs and use as required.

BEEF RIB-EYE WITH 'BAGHDAD CAFÉ' BUTTER

4 x 300 g grass-fed beef rib-eye steaks
sea salt and freshly ground white pepper | 40 ml olive oil
Green Beans with Hazelnuts (page 248) to serve

BAGHDAD CAFÉ BUTTER **250 g softened unsalted butter, plus 1 tablespoon | olive oil**
1 shallot, finely diced | 2 long red chillies, seeded and shredded
1 small clove garlic, finely chopped | 1 level teaspoon Baharat (page 376) | 60 g pine nuts
1/2 teaspoon sea salt | freshly ground white pepper

TO MAKE THE BAGHDAD CAFÉ butter, place the 250 g butter into a mixing bowl. Melt the additional tablespoon in a small pan with a splash of olive oil and fry the shallot, chilli, garlic and baharat over a gentle heat until the shallots begin to soften and the spices release their fragrant oils. Remove from the heat and leave to cool.

Add the shallot mixture to the butter, together with the pine nuts, salt and pepper. Beat vigorously until smooth and well incorporated. Spoon onto a sheet of plastic wrap and shape into a log. Roll neatly, twist the ends, tie securely and chill until required.

Preheat the oven to 200°C (Gas 6). Season the steaks with salt and pepper. Add the oil to a heavy-based frying pan and heat until almost smoking. Add the steaks and sear for about 4 minutes on each side until they develop a dark crust. Lower the heat to medium and cook for a further 3 minutes on each side (for medium-rare) then remove from the heat and leave to rest for at least 5 minutes.

To serve, arrange a neat bundle of beans on each of four serving plates and spoon on the hazelnuts. Top with a few rings of onion. Place the steaks next to the beans and top each with a thick slice of Baghdad Café butter. Serve straight away.

SERVES **4**

DUCK BREAST WITH 'FESENJUN' SAUCE

6 x 200 g duck breasts | sea salt and freshly ground black pepper | 1 tablespoon honey
generous splash of boiling water | 1/2 teaspoon pomegranate molasses
1/4 teaspoon freshly ground black pepper | 1/4 teaspoon cardamom seeds, crushed
2 tablespoons olive oil | seeds of 1 pomegranate, to garnish
Persian Chelow (page 217) and peppery herbs to serve

FESENJUN SAUCE 200 g shelled walnuts | 3 tablespoons olive oil
1 onion, finely diced | 1 teaspoon ground cinnamon
1/2 teaspoon ground turmeric | 1/2 teaspoon freshly ground black pepper
1 tablespoon tomato paste | 1 tablespoon pomegranate molasses
250 ml pomegranate juice (freshly squeezed, if available) | 55 g sugar
1 bay leaf | 400 ml good-quality chicken stock | 1 teaspoon sea salt | juice of 1/2 lemon

PREHEAT THE OVEN TO 180°C (GAS 4). To make the sauce, roast the walnuts on a baking tray for 5–10 minutes until a deep golden brown. Tip the nuts into a tea towel and rub well to remove as much skin as possible, then set aside until cool. Pulse the cooled nuts in a food processor until coarsely ground — you want to maintain some texture and a few chunky bits, so don't overdo it.

Heat the oil in a large, heavy-based saucepan over a low heat. Add the onion and fry gently until soft and translucent. Stir in the spices and tomato paste and fry for about 2 minutes. Add the walnuts to the pan with the pomegranate molasses and juice, sugar, bay leaf and stock. Bring to the boil, add the salt, lower the heat and simmer gently for 1 hour, stirring regularly, until rich, thick and a little oily.

Meanwhile, score the duck skin in a criss-cross pattern with a sharp knife and season generously with salt and pepper. In a small saucepan, warm the honey over a gentle heat with the water and the pomegranate molasses, then stir in the pepper and cardamom seeds to make a glaze.

Heat the oil in a heavy-based roasting pan over a medium–high heat until hot. Add the duck breasts, skin side down, then lower the heat and cook for about 5 minutes until the skin turns golden brown and the fat starts to render. Turn the breasts over and cook for a further 4 minutes. Tip the rendered fat from the pan and brush the skin with the glaze. Turn the breasts, skin-side down again, and cook over a low–medium heat for a final 4 minutes; at this stage it's really important not to have the heat too high or the glaze will burn. Remove from the heat and rest in a warm place for several minutes; when carved the duck should be medium–rare.

When ready to serve, add the lemon juice to the sauce, then taste and adjust the seasoning to achieve a good sweet–sour–earthy balance. Spoon a generous amount of sauce onto each plate. Slice each duck breast into chunks and stack on top. Scatter on the pomegranate seeds and serve straight away with rice and herbs.

SERVES 6

CHICKEN STUFFED UNDER THE SKIN WITH FLAVOURED BUTTER

2 x 1.4 kg free-range chickens | flavoured butter of your choice (below) | 2 limes, quartered | 8 sprigs thyme | 8 cloves garlic, peeled | 2 long red chillies, split and seeded | sea salt and freshly ground black pepper | olive oil | rice and salad to serve

PREHEAT THE OVEN TO 180°C (GAS 4). Wipe the cavities of the chickens with paper towel, and pat dry all over. Working from the neck end, insert your fingers underneath the skin that covers the breast meat. Ease it gently away from the flesh to create a pocket, being careful not to tear it. Work back as far as you dare. Push knobs of flavoured butter deep into the pocket, then smooth it evenly over the surface with your fingers. Gently pull the breast skin forward again, to cover the meat.

Divide the limes, thyme, garlic and chillies into two portions, and stuff into the cavity of each bird. Sprinkle in a generous amount of salt and pepper.

Tie the chicken legs to the parson's nose as firmly as you can, then sit the birds side by side on a rack set inside a large roasting pan. Rub the skin with the oil and season generously with salt and pepper. Roast for 20 minutes, then lower the temperature to 160°C (Gas 3) and roast for a further 30 minutes, turning the chickens around and basting them every 15 minutes or so to ensure the skin colours evenly. After 50 minutes, turn off the oven and leave to rest for 10 minutes. Remove from the oven and pierce the thighs with a skewer to check that the juices run clear. If not, return to the oven, turn the heat up to 180°C (Gas 4) and cook for 10 minutes more. Serve with your favourite accompaniments.

SERVES **6**

BUTTER VARIATIONS

BARBERRY BUTTER Soak ½ cup dried barberries (stems removed) in cold water for 2 minutes; drain and pat dry. Heat a knob of unsalted butter in a small frying pan over a low heat. Crush 1 clove garlic with 1 teaspoon sea salt. Fry the barberries and garlic paste for 4–5 minutes, stirring constantly. Stir in the finely grated zest of ½ lime and 1 tablespoon icing sugar. Allow to cool, then add 200 g unsalted butter, ⅓ cup roughly chopped chervil or tarragon leaves and ½ teaspoon black pepper. Beat vigorously. Spoon onto a sheet of plastic wrap and shape into a log. Roll neatly, twist the ends, tie securely and chill or freeze until needed.

PRESERVED LEMON BUTTER Combine 175 g softened unsalted butter, the finely chopped rind only of 1 preserved lemon (page 394), 2 finely chopped shallots, 1/2 clove finely chopped garlic, 1 tablespoon finely chopped parsley, 1 teaspoon finely chopped thyme leaves and 1/2 teaspoon ground sumac. Beat vigorously. Roll into a log as above and chill or freeze until needed.

This is a dauntingly long list of ingredients, but they are nearly all spices. Otherwise it is pretty simple to make. Serve this spicy fried chicken with wedges of lemon or lime and a shredded cucumber salad. It is also delicious with creamy Harissa Potato Salad (page 258).

SOUTHERN-FRIED CHICKEN WITH EASTERN SPICES

1 corn-fed or free-range chicken (or 4 Marylands) | 6 pods cardamom, roasted and crushed
1/2 teaspoon black peppercorns, roasted and crushed
1/2 teaspoon fennel seeds, roasted and crushed | 1 teaspoon sea salt
1/2 teaspoon sugar | 2 teaspoons sweet paprika | 1 teaspoon ground coriander
1/2 teaspoon ground turmeric | 1/2 teaspoon cayenne pepper | 1/2 teaspoon ground cumin
1/2 teaspoon ground cinnamon | 1/4 teaspoon ground allspice | 100 g cornflour
50 g maize flour or very fine semolina | 2 free-range eggs | 200 ml buttermilk
vegetable oil for shallow-frying | lemon wedges, potatoes and green salad to serve

SHREDDED CUCUMBER SALAD 1 long cucumber, seeded and shredded
2 shallots, very finely sliced | 1/2 cup mixed herbs or micro-herbs (tarragon, chives, chervil and parsley are all good choices) | 1/2 teaspoon dried mint
2–3 tablespoons Mayonnaise (page 385) or good quality bought mayonnaise
sea salt and freshly ground black pepper

JOINT THE CHICKEN INTO EIGHT pieces (or cut each of the Marylands in half). Remove the skin and discard.

Roast the whole spices separately, then crush them. Combine them with the other spices, the salt and sugar, then mix with the flours. Whisk the eggs into the buttermilk.

Dip the chicken pieces in the flour, then into the egg mixture and then back in the flour again. Shallow-fry them in vegetable oil until each piece is golden brown all over.

Place them on a baking tray and cook in a preheated 200°C (Gas 6) oven for 20 minutes.

Remove from the oven and allow to rest in a warm place for 5 minutes.

To make the shredded cucumber salad, combine the ingredients in a mixing bowl and toss with enough mayonnaise to coat lightly. Season.

Sprinkle the chicken with salt and serve straight away with lemon or lime wedges and the shredded cucumber salad.

SERVES 4

ROAST CHICKEN WITH PINE NUT AND BARBERRY RICE STUFFING

1 x 1.5 kg free-range chicken | sea salt and freshly ground black pepper | 2 tablespoons olive oil | 250 ml good-quality chicken stock | watercress to garnish (optional) | 500 ml natural yoghurt | 1 tablespoon Red Harissa (page 381)

PINE NUT AND BARBERRY RICE STUFFING **280 g short-grain rice | 600 ml good-quality chicken stock | 55 g unsalted butter | 1 large purple onion, finely diced 2 cloves garlic, finely diced | 60 g pine nuts | 1/2 teaspoon ground allspice | 1/2 teaspoon ground cinnamon | 1/3 cup barberries | sea salt | squeeze of lemon juice | 1/3 cup unsalted pistachio kernels, roughly chopped | 1/2 cup shredded flat-leaf parsley leaves**

TO MAKE THE STUFFING, PUT THE rice into a large bowl and rinse well under cold running water, working your fingers through it to loosen the starch. Drain off the milky water and repeat until the water runs clear. Cover the rice with cold water and leave to soak for 10 minutes. Drain the rice and rinse a final time, then drain again.

Bring the stock to the boil, then lower the heat and keep at a simmer.

Melt the butter in a heavy-based saucepan. Add the onion and garlic and sauté over a low–medium heat, stirring continuously, until the onion starts to soften. Add the pine nuts and spices, then increase the heat and sauté until the nuts start to colour. Add the barberries to the pan, followed by the rice and simmering stock. Season with salt, then return to the boil, stir briefly, and cover with a tight-fitting lid. Cook over a very low heat for 15 minutes.

Tip the cooked rice mixture onto a shallow tray and sprinkle on the lemon juice, pistachios and parsley. Use a fork to fluff up the grains and leave to cool.

Meanwhile, preheat the oven to 200°C (Gas 6). Clean the chicken, removing any excess fat from around the cavity. Stand the chicken upright and season lightly inside with salt and pepper. Spoon about half the stuffing into the cavity, being careful not to overfill it, and secure the skin at the opening with a small skewer. Set the remaining rice mixture aside. Season the skin of the chicken lightly with salt and pepper and rub with oil, then transfer it to a heavy-based baking tray. Pour in half the stock and roast for 20 minutes. Lower the oven to 180°C (Gas 4) and roast for a further 40 minutes. Remove the chicken from the oven and leave in a warm place for 10 minutes to rest.

Swirl the harissa through the yoghurt.

While the chicken is resting, reheat the remaining stock and rice in a saucepan over a gentle heat. Spoon out the stuffing from the chicken and add it to the pan. Mound the rice onto the centre of a warm serving platter. Cut the chicken into quarters, stack it around the rice, garnish with watercress, if using, and serve with the yoghurt.

SERVES **4**

These pretty quail with their fragrant, exotic stuffing won 'Dish of the Year' in the 2010 *Age Good Food Guide*. Serve them as the centrepiece of a banquet spread on a special occasion. Otherwise, serve one each as a dinner party starter, or two for a main course.

VEILED QUAIL WITH RICE, DATE AND ROSE PETAL STUFFING

8 x 200 g jumbo quail | 2 tablespoons olive oil | 2 bushy sprigs rosemary
sea salt and freshly ground black pepper | yoghurt sauce or dip to serve

RICE, DATE AND ROSE PETAL STUFFING 120 ml olive oil
1 shallot, finely diced | 150 g medium-grain rice, rinsed in cold water
3 Medjool dates, pitted and cut into 1 cm dice | 200 ml good-quality chicken stock
1/2 teaspoon ground allspice | 1/4 teaspoon ground cinnamon | 1 teaspoon sea salt
2 bay leaves | 40 g flaked almonds | 80 ml extra-virgin olive oil | 2 tablespoons rose petals
rosewater | freshly ground black pepper | 8 vine leaves | assorted edible flowers (optional)

TO MAKE THE STUFFING, HEAT A third of the oil in a medium saucepan and gently fry the shallot until soft, about 3 minutes. Add the rice to the pan and stir well. Add the dates and pour on enough of the stock to cover the rice by two fingers' width. Add the spices, salt and bay leaves, cover the pan and cook on a very low heat for 20 minutes, or until all the water has been absorbed and the rice is tender.

While the rice is cooking, fry the almonds in the remaining olive oil until they turn golden brown. The almonds burn very easily, so stir them constantly.

When the rice is cooked, tip it into a mixing bowl, remove the bay leaves, and fork it through with 1 tablespoon extra-virgin olive oil. Mix in the almonds and rose petals and leave to cool completely, then sprinkle with 1 tablespoon rosewater.

When you are ready to cook the quail, preheat the oven to 180°C (Gas 4). Stuff each bird fairly tightly with 2–3 tablespoons of the stuffing. Secure the skin at the opening with a toothpick and tie the legs together over the parson's nose.

Pour a little more extra-virgin olive oil into a large roasting tin. Brush a little more over the quails and sprinkle with salt and pepper. Drape a vine leaf over each bird and tuck them underneath so they almost wrap around entirely. Sprinkle with a little more oil and roast in the centre of the oven for 10 minutes. Baste with the pan juices, lower the temperature to 160°C (Gas 3) and cook for a further 2 minutes. Just before serving, sprinkle on a little rosewater and scatter on edible flowers, if using. Serve with your favourite yoghurt dip or sauce.

SERVES 8 as a starter, 4 as a main course

Cook the poussins slowly on a barbecue or charcoal grill, taking care not to burn or char them, or you will overpower the fragrant spices. For four people you need four poussins, or you could use two smallish chickens (about 1 kg each).

POUSSIN ROASTED WITH CARDAMOM AND OREGANO

18 cardamom pods | 3 cloves garlic, roughly chopped | 1 tablespoon sea salt
2 tablespoons fresh oregano or 2 teaspoons dried oregano | 80 ml olive oil
4 whole poussins (400 g each), cut down the back and splayed open
freshly ground black pepper | mountain bread and vegetables or salad to serve

USING A MORTAR AND PESTLE, pound the cardamoms to loosen the husks. Remove these and continue to pound the seeds to bruise them and release their flavour. Add the garlic, salt and oregano. Pound for a few minutes, mixing all the ingredients together well. Then add 3 tablespoons of the olive oil and stir in well. Keep crushing until you have a thick, smooth paste.

Rub three-quarters of the paste over the poussins, ensuring that you get in all the little cracks and crevices. Mix the remaining paste with the remaining olive oil and then pour over the poussins. Cover and marinate the poussins in the fridge for 4–8 hours, turning occasionally.

When ready to cook, preheat a barbecue or griller to high heat. Season the birds with plenty of black pepper. Place them on the barbecue and cook on high for a few minutes until they are golden all over. Then reduce the heat and cook slowly for a further 10–15 minutes, until they are cooked through. Towards the end of cooking, brush the birds all over with the remaining marinade.

Serve with plenty of mountain bread and a braise of Fresh Broad Beans, Artichokes and Peas (page 67). Alternatively, serve with a robust salad, such as a traditional Greek salad, Harissa Potato Salad (page 258) or Bronte and Tarkyn's Cucumber Burgul Salad (page 61).

SERVES **4**

Roast pork is undoubtedly a firm family favourite, especially when it comes with its golden armour of tasty crackling. If you can buy a free-range or organically reared product you will get a better result. The rather sweet flavour of the lean pork is really zipped up by a mouth-tingling hit of aromatic pepper and comfortingly sweet cinnamon. For this dish we use a cut of pork called scotch fillet, which is the extension of the loin, and often comes oven-ready: trimmed, rolled and tied neatly with string. But do look for a piece that still has a thin layer of white fat — you don't want it stripped completely of its fatty layer as this creates important lubrication during the cooking process.

Slow-cooking allows the flavours of the marinade to meld into the meat. The moisture from the olive oil and water helps create some steam in the oven, which prevents it from becoming stringy and dry.

PORK ROASTED WITH BLACK PEPPER AND CINNAMON

1 tablespoon black peppercorns | 1/2 teaspoon ground cinnamon | 2 cloves garlic
2 teaspoons sea salt | 50 ml olive oil | 1.2 kg loin of pork | 400 ml water
mashed potato, creamed spinach or Green Beans with Hazelnuts (page 248) to serve

ROUGHLY CRUSH THE PEPPERCORNS using a mortar and pestle. Set aside. Put the cinnamon into the mortar with the garlic and 1 teaspoon sea salt and pound to a smooth paste, then mix in the pepper and half the olive oil.

Preheat the oven to 220°C (Gas 7).

Rub the paste all over the pork and allow it to sit while preheating the oven. Then sprinkle with the remaining sea salt, which adds a lovely salty crunchiness to the crust.

Put the remaining olive oil and the water into a roasting pan with 200 ml of the water. Put a roasting rack in the pan and sit the pork on top. Cook for 20 minutes, then lower the temperature to 160°C (Gas 3). Add another 200 ml water to the pan and cook slowly for a further hour.

When ready, remove from the oven, cover with foil and leave in a warm place to rest for 8 minutes. Reduce the pan juices with a few knobs of butter and drizzle over the meat. Serve with vegetable accompaniments.

SERVES **4**

There is something wonderfully impressive about pork rib-eye, which makes it a terrific option for a dinner party or celebration. Its flavour is good, for today's low-fat porkers, and you can cook it with or without its crackling. In this dish, the meat is rubbed with a spice mix and glazed during the cooking process, so ask your butcher to remove the crackling for you (you can always cook it separately), but to leave an even layer of fat. While you're at it, make sure you ask for a piece from a smallish animal, with six ribs attached, and neatly tied.

PORK RIB-EYE WITH CARAWAY, HONEY AND LIME

3 cloves garlic crushed with 1 heaped teaspoon sea salt
1/2 teaspoon cracked black pepper | 1 teaspoon caraway seeds
1 x 1.5 kg pork rib-eye (you want 6 ribs) | 50 ml olive oil | 1 litre water
a few knobs of butter | roast vegetables or soft-herb and flower salad to serve
Goat's Cheese Mashed Potatoes (page 242) to serve

GLAZE **zest and juice of 1 small lime | 3 tablespoons honey**

MIX THE GARLIC PASTE WITH THE pepper and caraway seeds and use your hands to rub it all over the exposed fat and meat. Cover and leave it in a cool place for an hour or so to allow the flavours to permeate.

Preheat the oven to 220°C (Gas 7). Sit a roasting rack in a large roasting pan and put the pork on top. Wrap the sticking-up bones with foil to stop them charring in the heat. Pour the oil and water into the pan to create some steam and provide extra moisture during the cooking process.

Put the pan into the oven and cook for 20 minutes, then lower the heat to 160°C (Gas 3) and cook for a further 1 hour 20 minutes. Check every 30 minutes or so and splash in more water if necessary. While the joint is cooking, make the glaze by heating the lime juice, zest and honey in a small pan, until it all melts together.

About 5 minutes before the end of the cooking time, take the joint out of the oven and turn the heat back up to 220°C (Gas 7). Brush the joint with the glaze and return it to the oven for the remaining 5 minutes or until it starts to caramelise and turn a lovely bubbly brown.

To serve, cut into thick chops with a very sharp knife. Reduce the pan juices with a few knobs of butter and drizzle over the meat. Serve with roasted vegetables or a soft-herb and flower salad and mashed potatoes.

SERVES 6

This is a great way of jazzing up lamb rumps or lamb rounds. To serve, slice each rump into two thick slices and accompany with a bowl of Goat's Cheese Mashed Potatoes (page 242), garlicky Parsnip Skordalia (page 248) or Harissa Potato Salad (page 258).

LAMB RUMP WITH PISTACHIOS AND PEPPERCORNS

50 g unsalted pistachio kernels | 30 g white peppercorns
10 g whole allspice berries | 2 tablespoons grated parmesan cheese
100 g fresh breadcrumbs | 4 lamb rumps (250 g portions)
1 tablespoon Dijon mustard | sea salt and freshly ground black pepper

SHALLOT, SAGE AND PARMESAN BRIK WAFER 2 sheets brik pastry
40 ml clarified butter or ghee | 2 large shallots, finely sliced into circles
10 sage leaves | 40 g grated parmesan cheese

PREHEAT THE OVEN TO 180°C (GAS 4). Lightly oil a heavy, flat baking sheet with baking paper. Arrange a sheet of brik pastry on top and brush with melted clarified butter. Arrange the shallot rings and sage leaves over the surface and sprinkle with parmesan cheese. Brush the remaining butter onto the second brik sheet and place it, buttered side down, on top of the first. Place a sheet of baking paper on top and weight with another heavy baking tray. Bake in the oven for 14 minutes, or until the pastry is crisp and golden brown. Remove from the oven and allow to cool before cutting into 6 long strips.

In a spice grinder or mortar and pestle, grind the pistachios, then the peppercorns and the allspice berries, then mix them together with the parmesan and breadcrumbs.

Brush each lamb rump evenly with a little mustard, season with salt and pepper, then roll in the crumbing mixture.

Preheat the oven to 200°C (Gas 6) and roast the lamb rumps for 12 minutes for medium-rare or a little longer for medium. Remove them from the oven and allow them to rest for another 12 minutes in a warm place.

When ready to serve, return the lamb rumps to a hot oven for 1–2 minutes. Cut into thick slices and serve with the brik wafers and your choice of accompaniment.

SERVES 4

A superb special occasion dish. Serve with Fried Potatoes with Garlic, Green Chilli and Coriander (page 244) and a simple green salad.

WHOLE BEEF FILLET IN CORIANDER-PEPPERCORN RUB

80 ml olive oil | 2 cloves garlic, finely chopped
50 g coriander seeds, roasted and lightly crushed
1 teaspoon black peppercorns, freshly cracked
1 teaspoon Turkish chilli flakes | sea salt
1 x 800 g grass-fed beef fillet, cut from the centre

PREHEAT THE OVEN TO 200°C (GAS 6).

Heat half the olive oil in a small saucepan over a low heat. Add the garlic and sweat gently for 5 minutes, until soft and translucent. Add the crushed coriander and black peppercorns and cook for 2 minutes. Stir in the chilli flakes, then remove from the heat and spread the spice mix out in a tray large enough to fit the fillet.

Season the beef fillet with salt. Roll the fillet in the spices until evenly coated.

Heat the rest of the oil in a large, heavy-based, ovenproof frying pan over a medium heat. Sear the beef all over until evenly coloured. Transfer to the oven and cook for 6 minutes. Turn the fillet over and cook for a further 4 minutes.

Remove from the oven and allow to rest for at least 10 minutes. Slice thickly and serve on a warm platter with salad and crunchy potatoes.

SERVES **6–8**

SLOW-COOKED SHOULDER OF LAMB WITH JEWELLED-RICE STUFFING

1 x 1.8 kg boned lamb shoulder | sea salt and freshly ground black pepper
olive oil | 2 teaspoons cumin seeds, roasted and ground
salad or vegetables, thick natural yoghurt and Arabic flatbread, to serve

JEWELLED-RICE STUFFING 60 g basmati rice | 50 g dried sour cherries, cut in half
50 g dried apricots, diced | 20 g unsalted butter | 1 shallot, finely diced
225 ml good-quality chicken stock, boiling | sea salt and freshly ground black pepper
80 g shelled walnuts | 2 tablespoons unsalted pistachio kernels
8 dried edible rosebuds, petals separated | 2 teaspoons cumin seeds, roasted and crushed
splash of rosewater | squeeze of lime or lemon juice

TO MAKE THE STUFFING, SOAK THE rice, sour cherries and dried apricots in separate bowls of cold water for 20 minutes, then drain. Melt the butter in a small saucepan over a low heat and fry the shallot gently until soft and translucent. Stir in the drained rice, then cover with the boiling stock. Season lightly with salt and pepper and simmer over a very low heat, covered, for 12 minutes, or until the rice is just tender and the liquid has been absorbed. Tip the rice into a large bowl and leave to cool. When cold, stir in the remaining ingredients and toss gently to combine. Season with a little more salt and pepper and set aside.

Open out the lamb shoulder on your work surface, skin side down. Season with salt and pepper, then cover the meat with an even layer of stuffing. Roll it up fairly tightly into a sausage shape, securing with kitchen string at intervals. Wrap the rolled shoulder tightly in several layers of plastic wrap, squeezing gently to ensure there are no bubbles. Twist and tie the ends to make the whole package air- and watertight (remember, the wrapped parcel is to be poached).

Fill a fish kettle or large, deep roasting pan with water and bring to the boil. Carefully lower in the plastic-wrapped lamb shoulder and simmer, covered, for 2 hours. If using a roasting pan, cover it loosely with a sheet of foil. You won't be able to submerge the meat completely, so turn it around in the water after 1 hour. Remove the poached lamb from the water and set it aside to rest, still in its plastic wrap, for at least 30 minutes or up to 2 hours.

Preheat the oven to 200°C (Gas 6). Carefully unwrap the rolled lamb and transfer it to a roasting pan, then brush it liberally with oil. Sprinkle on the cumin and season lightly with salt and pepper. Roast for 20 minutes, rolling the meat around in the pan so it browns evenly.

Rest in a warm place for 15–20 minutes, then serve with your choice or salad or vegetables as well as plenty of yoghurt and warm flatbread.

SERVES 6

Güveç are a style of Turkish dish which take their name from the earthenware pot in which they are cooked — in the same way that the tagine does in Morocco. In rural Anatolia the cooking pots may be sealed and buried in the ashes of a fire to cook slowly overnight — or, only slightly less romantically, in the local baker's oven. A claypot holds enough for two people, but you can easily double the quantities. If you don't have a claypot, or are increasing the recipe, a heavy-based cast-iron casserole dish will serve almost as well.

This güveç is spicy with a lingering sweetness, and a hint of non-traditional aniseed flavour. Serve it with a light salad or braised wild greens. A dollop of yoghurt on the side would also be delicious.

CLAYPOT CHICKEN WITH DATES, SUJUK AND BURGUL

45 g unsalted butter | 1 tablespoon extra-virgin olive oil
2 purple onions, cut into thick rings | 1 clove garlic, sliced
2 red banana peppers, seeded and cut into rings
2 green banana peppers, seeded and cut into rings
2 long green chillies, seeded and diced | 1 heaped teaspoon ground cumin
1 level teaspoon ground cinnamon | generous splash of dry sherry
2 large vine-ripened tomatoes, skinned, seeded and diced
50 g burgul, washed | 350 ml good-quality chicken stock | 1 stick cinnamon | 2 star anise
few sprigs thyme | 2 x 400 g poussins | sea salt and freshly ground black pepper
1 tablespoon olive oil | 50 g sujuk, sliced | 4 Medjool dates, seeded and cut into quarters

PREHEAT THE OVEN TO 200°C (GAS 6). Heat the butter and extra-virgin olive oil in a heavy-based casserole dish. Gently sweat the onions, garlic, peppers and chillies with the cumin and cinnamon for about 5 minutes, or until the vegetables soften. Add the sherry, tomatoes, burgul, chicken stock, cinnamon, star anise and thyme and bring to the boil. Lower the heat, then cover and simmer gently for 5 minutes.

Meanwhile, cut the poussins into quarters and season lightly with salt and pepper.

In another heavy-based frying pan, heat the olive oil over a medium heat and brown the poussins lightly all over. Add the sujuk and fry until golden brown on both sides. Transfer the poussins and sujuk to the casserole dish and tuck in the dates. Cover the pan and cook in the preheated oven for 20 minutes. Taste and adjust the seasoning and serve straight away.

SERVES 2

This dish, known as Musukhan, is based on a Syrian Bedouin recipe, in which chickens are cooked on bread with lots of sumac and bitter wild greens. This version is a little more refined in its presentation. Serve with a big dollop of thick natural yoghurt.

SPICY CHICKEN BAKED IN MOUNTAIN BREAD WITH SPINACH, CHICKPEAS AND PINE NUTS

SPICY CHICKEN 4 chicken Marylands, skin removed
2 cloves garlic crushed with 1/2 teaspoon salt
1/2 teaspoon ground cinnamon | 1/2 teaspoon ground cumin
1/2 teaspoon freshly ground black pepper | 2 tablespoons olive oil

40 ml olive oil | 2 onions, finely grated | 2 cloves garlic, finely chopped
1 teaspoon ground cinnamon | 1 teaspoon ground nutmeg | 1 1/2 teaspoons ground sumac
3 bunches spinach, leaves blanched, squeezed and chopped
150 g cooked chickpeas | 300 ml good-quality chicken stock | juice of 1/2 lemon
150 g toasted pine nuts, roughly crushed | 4 large square pieces of mountain bread
extra-virgin olive oil | sea salt and freshly ground black pepper | edible violets to garnish

CUT THROUGH THE MEAT OF THE Marylands to expose the bones. This will help them cook more quickly. Mix together the garlic paste, spices and olive oil and rub all over the chicken. Leave in a cool place to marinate for 1–2 hours.

Heat the oil in a large non-stick frying pan and sauté the onions and garlic until they are soft and the liquid has evaporated. Stir in the spices. Add the chopped spinach, then the chickpeas. Use a fork to lightly crush the chickpeas, then add half of the stock. Turn up the heat and boil until the stock has evaporated, about 5 minutes. Remove from the heat and add the lemon juice and pine nuts. Leave to cool, then refrigerate until needed.

When ready to cook, preheat the oven to 180°C (Gas 4) and line a large baking tray with baking paper. Lay the pieces of mountain bread out on a work surface. Spoon a dollop of spinach mixture onto the centre of each and place a chicken Maryland on top, flesh-side down. Fold in the sides and ends of the bread to create a neat rectangular parcel. Carefully turn the parcels upside down and arrange them on the baking tray. Transfer to the oven and bake for 30 minutes.

Meanwhile, tip the remaining spinach mixture into a pot with the remaining chicken stock. Add a splash of extra-virgin olive oil and season with salt and pepper. Cook for 10 minutes on a gentle heat.

When ready to serve, divide the extra spinach between 4 serving plates. Sit a chicken parcel on top, seam side up, and serve straight away, garnished with violets.

SERVES 4

In the Middle East they get their pigeons live from the souks, and grill them over a hot barbecue. Elsewhere we have to make do with farmed variety — usually sold as squab, which are tender baby birds weighing 250–400 grams. Their rich, dark meat is delicious in this spicy sauce. The combination of pigeon and dates is a Persian and Moroccan favourite, although traditional recipes, which use large amounts of fruit, can be too sweet for western palates. Here, the sauce is spiced with pungent saffron and ginger, which help cut the sweetness and richness of the dish.

PIGEON TAGINE WITH DATES AND GINGER

PIGEON STOCK **4 squab carcasses and trimmings | 20 ml olive oil | 1 carrot, chopped | 1 celery stick, chopped | 1 onion, chopped | 1 clove garlic, roughly bashed | 1 bay leaf | few sprigs thyme | 2 tablespoons dry sherry | 1.5 litres water**

TAGINE **4 squab pigeons | 100 g butter | 20 ml olive oil | 2 medium onions, finely chopped | 2 cloves garlic, finely chopped | 1 tablespoon fresh black pepper | 1/4 teaspoon powdered saffron (or 10 strands, roasted and crushed to a powder) | 2 teaspoons ground cinnamon | 1 teaspoon ground ginger | 1/2 teaspoon sea salt | 500 ml water or pigeon stock | 200 g fresh dates, pitted and chopped**

edible rose petals, fresh or dried (optional) and couscous or buttered rice to serve

PREPARE THE PIGEONS BY CUTTING off heads, necks and claws, trimming the wings and then neatly slicing away the breasts and Marylands (thigh and drumstick) from each bird. If you don't feel confident about preparing the pigeons yourself, ask your butcher to prepare them for you, and to keep the carcasses so you can make a stock.

To make the stock, briefly sauté the carcasses in the oil to add colour, then add the vegetables, bay leaf and thyme and sauté for a few more minutes. Add the sherry and scrape any bits from the bottom of the pan. Pour the water over the top and bring to the boil. Skim off any surface fat, then lower the heat and simmer for 1 hour, skimming off any additional fat from time to time.

To make the tagine, melt the butter and oil and fry the onions and garlic over a medium heat until softened. Add the pepper, saffron, cinnamon and ginger and stir well. Season the pigeon breast and Maryland pieces with salt and sauté in the spicy mixture for about 2 minutes, until they are well coated. Add the stock and bring to the boil. Lower the heat, cover and simmer for 15 minutes. Then add the chopped dates and stir in well. Cover again and simmer for a further 20–30 minutes, or until the pigeon pieces are nice and tender.

Sprinkle over the rose petals, if using, taste and adjust the seasoning if necessary. Serve with plain buttered couscous or a simple rice pilaf.

SERVES **4**

This rabbit hotpot is rich and smoky, similar to a French cassoulet. It needs only a big green salad and maybe a bowl of Goat's Cheese Mashed Potatoes (page 242) to make the perfect meal on a cold winter's evening.

RABBIT HOTPOT WITH WHITE BEANS AND SPANISH SAUSAGE

100 g white beans, soaked overnight in 2–3 times their volume of cold water | 1 kg rabbit hind legs cut in half, or rabbit pieces | sea salt and freshly ground black pepper 60 ml olive oil | 1 tablespoon honey diluted with 1 tablespoon hot water | 10 shallots | 120 g small button mushrooms, stalks trimmed flush | 6 cloves garlic | 200 g semi-dried chorizo sausage, cut into 1 cm discs | 100 ml white wine | 2 large ripe tomatoes (or 1 x 400 g can), skinned, seeded and chopped | 12 fresh sage leaves | 1/2 teaspoon juniper berries, lightly cracked | zest of 1/2 orange | 500 ml good-quality chicken stock | freshly ground black pepper

BREADCRUMB TOPPING 1 tablespoon ground sumac | 1 tablespoon fennel seeds, roasted and crushed | zest of 1/2 lemon | 1/2 cup fresh breadcrumbs | 6 Kalamata olives, stoned and finely chopped

COOK THE BEANS IN BOILING WATER until they are just tender, then drain and reserve. Preheat the oven to 180°C (Gas 4).

Pat the rabbit legs dry and lightly season with salt and pepper. In a large ovenproof casserole dish, sauté the rabbit pieces in olive oil until they colour. Towards the end of the cooking time, turn up the heat and pour in the honey glaze. Sauté for a further 30 seconds until the mixture gently caramelises, turning the rabbit pieces so that they are coated with the glaze. Add the whole shallots, mushrooms, garlic and chorizo pieces and sauté for 2 minutes, turning everything in the glaze. Add the white wine and stir to lift all the golden bits stuck to the bottom of the pan. Add the beans, chopped tomatoes, sage leaves, juniper berries, orange zest and chicken stock. Season with pepper.

Bring to the boil, then cover the surface of the casserole with a circle of baking paper and cover the dish with a lid. Cook on the middle shelf of the oven for 30 minutes. Remove from the oven and check that the rabbit is tender and the meat is beginning to fall from the bones. Return to the oven and cook for a further 20 minutes.

We usually serve this dish with a breadcrumb coating (not photographed). To prepare the breadcrumb topping, combine the sumac, fennel seeds and lemon zest with the breadcrumbs and chopped olives and set aside.

Preheat the griller to its highest temperature. Remove the baking paper and sprinkle the surface with the crumbing mix. Grill until golden brown and serve immediately.

SERVES 4

Greek in inspiration, this is one of the tastiest and easiest supper dishes you could imagine. It is full of lemony, tomatoey flavours and has the added virtue of being just the kind of one-pot cooking that suits most people's busy schedules. The addition of grated haloumi at the end of the cooking time gives a lovely gooey finish.

LAMB BAKED WITH ORZO PASTA, TOMATOES AND LEMON

60 ml olive oil | 1.5 kg lamb leg, cut into 4 cm pieces | sea salt and ground black pepper
2 large onions, diced | 1 tablespoon Taklia (page 384) | 1 teaspoon sweet paprika
1 preserved lemon (page 394), rind only, roughly chopped | 1 tablespoon honey
2 long red chillies, seeded, scraped and roughly chopped | 2 x 400 g cans tomatoes
2 cinnamon sticks | juice of 1 lemon | 1-1.5 litres chicken stock or water | 500 g orzo pasta
150 g haloumi cheese, grated | hot bread, butter and salad to serve

HEAT THE OIL IN A FRYING PAN. Season the lamb pieces with salt and pepper and sauté them, a few at a time, until lightly brown all over. Tip them into a large, heavy-based casserole dish as you go. Add the onions and taklia to the frying pan and cook gently until the onions soften. Add the paprika, lemon, honey and chillies and continue to stir over the heat.

Preheat the oven to 180°C (Gas 4).

Tip the spicy onion mixture on top of the lamb in the casserole dish and stir well. Pour in the tomatoes, then add the cinnamon, lemon juice and 500 ml of the stock. Raise the heat and when the liquid is bubbling, put the casserole dish into the centre of the oven, cover and cook for 40 minutes.

Remove from the oven and add the orzo and an additional 500 ml stock, mixing everything together well. Put the dish back into oven, uncovered this time, for a further 25 minutes. Stir occasionally to make sure it doesn't stick to the bottom of the pan. At the end of that time, check that the pasta is cooked and the lamb tender. If necessary, add a little more stock and cook for a further 10 minutes.

Remove the dish from the oven and turn the griller to its highest setting. When it is really hot, sprinkle the casserole with the haloumi and pop under the grill until it melts. Serve immediately with some hot crusty bread and butter, and a fresh green salad.

SERVES 6

We spent a wonderful afternoon and evening with Ayfer Unsal, the legendary Turkish food writer. Ayfer is a wonderful cook and she prepared this superb dish for us, explaining that her mother and grandmother used to brown the lamb over a charcoal fire before slow-cooking it with the quinces. It's not necessary to peel the quinces as the skins disintegrate into the thick, cinnamon-spiced sauce. Accompany this dish with rice or boiled new potatoes.

SLOW-COOKED LAMB WITH QUINCES

1.5 kg lamb shoulder chops | 2 tablespoons olive oil | 500 g onions, very finely chopped | 2 tablespoons tomato paste | 2 tablespoons mild Turkish red pepper paste | 1 tablespoon ground cinnamon | 1 tablespoon ground allspice | 1 tablespoon freshly ground black pepper | 8 cloves | boiling water | 1 teaspoon sea salt | 1½ tablespoons pomegranate molasses | 3 small quinces | shredded flat-leaf parsley leaves to garnish

TRIM THE LAMB CHOPS OF ANY excess fat. Heat the oil in a large, heavy-based casserole dish over a medium heat. Brown the lamb chops all over, then remove from the pan and set aside.

Add the onion to the pan, lower the heat and gently sweat for 15–20 minutes, until very soft and lightly coloured. Add the tomato and pepper pastes and all the spices to the pan and stir well. Return the lamb chops to the pan and pour on enough boiling water to cover everything generously. Stir in the salt and pomegranate molasses, then bring to the boil. Cover the pan, lower the heat and simmer gently for 30 minutes.

Cut the quinces in half and peel and core them. Cut each half into four slices and add to the pan. Cover the pan and cook for a further 30–40 minutes, until the sauce is thick and fragrant and the lamb and quinces are both meltingly tender. Taste and adjust the seasonings as required.

When ready to serve, garnish with parsley.

SERVES **4**

Meatballs with a difference! This makes a tasty supper dish, and with its spicy tomato sauce and rich runny eggs is bound to become a firm favourite.

LAMB KIFTA TAGINE WITH EGGS

MEATBALLS **500 g lamb, finely minced | 1 medium onion, finely chopped | 3 tablespoons finely chopped flat-leaf parsley leaves | 1/4 teaspoon cayenne pepper | sea salt and freshly ground black pepper | 2 tablespoons olive oil for frying**

SAUCE **2 tablespoons olive oil | 2 medium onions, finely chopped | 1 clove garlic, finely chopped | 2 x 400 g cans tomatoes, drained and chopped | 1 teaspoon ground cumin | 1 teaspoon ground cinnamon | 1/2 teaspoon cayenne pepper | sea salt and freshly ground black pepper | 500 ml water | 1/4 cup finely chopped flat-leaf parsley leaves | 1/4 cup finely chopped coriander leaves | 6 free-range eggs | baby radish leaves and sage flowers to garnish (optional) | Arabic flatbread or Buttered Couscous (page 234) and natural yoghurt to serve**

TO MAKE THE MEATBALLS, thoroughly mix all the ingredients, except for the oil, and with wet hands, form into walnut-sized balls. Heat the oil and brown the meatballs all over. Drain well on paper towel.

For the sauce, heat the oil in a heavy-based casserole dish and lightly sauté the onions and garlic until they are translucent. Add the tomatoes, cumin, cinnamon, cayenne and salt and pepper to taste and stir well. Then add the water, stir again and bring to the boil. Lower the heat and simmer the sauce, uncovered, for about 30 minutes, or until it has reduced to a very thick gravy.

Add the meatballs to the sauce and continue cooking for a further 8 minutes. Stir in the parsley and coriander. Carefully break the eggs into the sauce, cover the pan with a lid and cook until the eggs are just set, which will take about 5 minutes.

Serve at once, straight from the pot, liberally garnished with the radish leaves and flowers, if using, and with plenty of Arabic flatbread to mop up the runny egg yolks. Alternatively, accompany with a dish of plain buttered couscous and a dollop of thick natural yoghurt.

Those who enjoy a more piquant dish may add one finely chopped bullet chilli while sautéing the onion and garlic.

SERVES **6**

SULTAN'S DELIGHT — LAMB RAGOUT WITH CHEESY EGGPLANT PURÉE

700 g lamb (from the leg or shoulder), trimmed and cut into 3 cm cubes
40 g unsalted butter | 2 purple onions, cut into 1 cm dice | 3 cloves garlic, finely chopped
2 teaspoons chopped oregano | 1 teaspoon honey
2 large vine-ripened tomatoes, skinned, seeded and diced
1 tablespoon hot Turkish red pepper paste | 1 teaspoon sea salt
1/2 teaspoon freshly ground black pepper | 250–300 ml good-quality chicken stock
chopped flat-leaf parsley leaves to garnish

CHEESY EGGPLANT PURÉE 2 eggplants (aubergines) | 80 ml cream (35% fat)
80 g gruyère or gouda, grated | good pinch of ground nutmeg
sea salt and freshly ground black pepper | juice of up to 1 lemon

MELT THE BUTTER IN A LARGE, heavy-based casserole dish over medium heat, then brown the lamb all over and remove from the pan. If necessary, add a little more butter to the pan, then sweat the onion, garlic and oregano over a low heat for about 5 minutes. Add the honey, increase the heat and cook for another couple of minutes. Stir in the tomatoes, pepper paste, salt, pepper and stock, then bring to the boil. Stir well and return the lamb to the pan. Cover the pan, lower the heat and simmer very gently for 1–1 1/2 hours, or until the lamb is tender and the liquid has reduced to a thick sauce.

To make the eggplant purée, prick the eggplants all over with a fork and sit them directly on the naked flame of your stovetop. Cook over a low–medium flame for at least 15 minutes, turning constantly until the eggplants are charred all over and soft. Remove and place on a small wire rack in a sealed container or plastic bag so the juices can drain off. Allow the eggplants to cool for about 10 minutes. (Alternatively, put the eggplants under a hot griller, turning them regularly until charred.)

When the eggplants are cool, gently peel away the skin from the flesh, taking care to remove every little bit or the purée will have a bitter, burnt flavour. Put the eggplant into a bowl of acidulated water for 5 minutes — this soaks away any lingering bits of burnt skin and turns the flesh pale and creamy. Drain the eggplant in a colander, squeeze gently to extract any moisture, then chop finely.

Bring the cream to the boil in a small saucepan and simmer for a couple of minutes to reduce slightly. Stir in the cheese and nutmeg, then season with salt and pepper and a squeeze of lemon juice. Add the chopped eggplant and beat lightly to combine. Taste and adjust the seasonings as required.

To serve, spoon the eggplant purée into the centre of a warmed serving platter. Make a well in the centre of the purée and spoon in the lamb. Garnish with parsley and serve straight away with a green salad.

SERVES 4

This is one of Persia's most famous khoresht dishes — a slow-cooked stew-sauce to serve with rice. When made well, it is a stunner, combining sweet, slow-cooked lamb with tangy dried limes, creamy kidney beans and a veritable mountain of fragrant fresh herbs, including the distinctive fenugreek. Fresh fenugreek can be found in Middle Eastern stores in the summer months. You can substitute crushed fenugreek seeds quite happily all year round, but use them cautiously as they have a tendency to overwhelm if you use too heavy a hand.

FRESH HERB STEW WITH LAMB AND DRIED LIME

3 tablespoons olive oil | 1 onion, finely diced | 1 leek, finely diced
1 teaspoon ground turmeric | 1/2 teaspoon freshly ground black pepper
450 g lamb (from the shoulder), cut into 2 cm cubes | 1 cup coriander leaves
1 cup flat-leaf parsley leaves | 1/2 cup chervil sprigs | 1/3 cup dill sprigs
1/3 cup fresh fenugreek leaves or 1/2 teaspoon fenugreek seeds, lightly crushed
100 g dried kidney beans, soaked overnight and drained
2 large dried limes, lightly cracked | 1 litre good-quality chicken stock
100 g spinach leaves | juice of 1/2 lemon | 1 teaspoon sea salt, or to taste
Persian Chelow (page 217) and thick natural yoghurt, to serve

HEAT THE OIL IN A LARGE, HEAVY-based saucepan or casserole dish over a low heat. Add the onion and leek and fry gently until soft and translucent. Stir in the spices and fry for another couple of minutes.

Add the lamb to the pan and brown over a highish heat for a minute. Add the herbs and fenugreek leaves or seeds and stir well. Stir in the kidney beans, dried limes and stock and bring to the boil. Lower the heat and cook, covered, for 1 1/2 hours, or until the beans and lamb are very tender. As the limes soften, squeeze them against the side of the pan to extract the juice.

Towards the end of the cooking time, bring a saucepan of water to the boil and blanch the spinach briefly. Refresh in cold water, then squeeze very firmly to extract as much liquid as you can. Chop the spinach finely, and stir it into the stew to revive the rich green colour. Allow to bubble vigorously for 5 minutes until the sauce is lovely and thick. Add lemon juice and salt to taste and serve with plain chelow rice and plenty of yoghurt.

SERVES 6

Oxtail is a favourite winter dish — all sticky-sweet and richly tender strips of gelatinous meat which, when cooked long enough and slow enough, fall away from their little knuckle of cartilage. A further bonus of this type of dish is that it requires minimal effort. Once the preparation is done, just put it in the oven and leave it alone.

OXTAIL BRAISED WITH CINNAMON AND PRESERVED LEMON

3 kg oxtail, cut into pieces | 1 generous tablespoon ground ginger | 150 g plain flour | 80 ml olive oil | 2 large onions, roughly diced | 3 cloves garlic, finely chopped | 4 sticks celery, roughly chopped | 1 teaspoon ground cinnamon | 1 preserved lemon (page 394), rind only, diced | 8 cloves | 1 teaspoon sweet paprika | 2 x 400 g cans crushed tomatoes | 100 g pitted green olives | 400 ml gutsy red wine | 2 bay leaves | zest of 1/2 orange | about 500 ml chicken stock or water | 6 baby turnips, peeled and cut into small dice | mashed potatoes to serve

PREHEAT THE OVEN TO 160°C (GAS 3).

Get the butcher to trim any large lumps of fat away from the oxtail for you, and cut it through into nice little sections about 5 cm long.

Mix the ginger with the flour and use it to dust the oxtail pieces.

Heat the oil in a large, heavy-based casserole dish and then brown the meat all over. Once coloured, remove the meat pieces from the pan. Add the onions, garlic and celery with the cinnamon, preserved lemon rind, cloves and paprika. Stir until everything is well mixed. Add the tomatoes, olives and wine. Tuck in the bay leaves and orange peel and return the oxtail to the tomato base. Pour in enough stock or water to just cover the meat, raise the heat and bring to the boil.

Cover the casserole and put it in the middle of the oven. Leave it for an hour, then remove it from the oven and stir everything around gently. Return it to the oven and cook for a further hour, by which time the meat will be a lovely glossy dark brown, and the sauce will have reduced to a sticky glaze.

Steam the turnips for 6 minutes, or until tender. Drain well, sprinkle with a little sea salt and keep warm.

Serve the oxtail in a large serving bowl and scatter on the steamed turnip. Serve straight away with a big bowl of garlicky mashed potatoes.

SERVES 4

SIDE DISHES

Once you've grasped the basic parboil-rinse-steam technique of preparing gorgeously fluffy chelow, you'll be ready to tackle other Persian rice dishes as most follow the same method. A prized part of any Persian rice dish is the crunchy layer that forms under the rice as it cooks — the tah-deeg, which literally means 'base of the pot'. We use oil or ghee to start the tah-deeg, as straight butter burns too easily. There are several popular tah-deeg variations, which are listed on page 218. For a fancy presentation the rice is inverted onto a platter, so the golden crust can be properly admired. But in many households, for everyday eating the rice is spooned onto a platter and the tah-deeg is served on a separate plate.

PERSIAN CHELOW

300 g Iranian or best-quality basmati rice | 2 litres water | 2 tablespoons sea salt | 70 ml vegetable oil | 40 g unsalted butter, melted

WASH THE RICE THOROUGHLY, THEN leave it to soak in a generous amount of lukewarm water for 30 minutes. Swish it around with your fingers every now and then to loosen the starch. Strain the rice, rinsing it again with warm water.

Bring the water to a boil in a large saucepan. Add the salt and stir in the strained rice. Return the water to a rolling boil and cook, uncovered, for 5 minutes. Test the rice by pinching a grain between your fingers or by biting it. It should be soft on the outside, but still hard in the centre. Strain the rice and rinse again with warm water. Toss it several times to drain away as much of the water as you can. Return the saucepan to a medium heat and add the oil and 2 tablespoons water. As soon as the oil begins to sizzle, spoon in enough rice to cover the base of the saucepan in a thin layer, then spoon in the rest of the rice gradually, building it up into a pyramid. Don't tip it all in at once, as this will squash the rice and you won't achieve the proper fluffy lightness. Use the handle of a wooden spoon to poke five or six holes down through the rice to the base of the pan to help it steam.

Mix 2 tablespoons warm water with the melted butter and drizzle this over the rice. Wrap the saucepan lid in a clean tea towel and cover the pan as tightly as you can. Leave the pan on a medium-high heat for 2–3 minutes until the rice is visibly steaming — you will see puffs of steam escaping from the edges of the pan. Turn the heat down to low and leave the pan alone for 40 minutes. Resist the temptation to peek, as this releases the steam and affects the cooking time. The rice can actually sit quite happily over the lowest possible heat for another 20 minutes or so.

When ready to serve, sit the saucepan in a little cold water in the sink; the sudden change in temperature creates a surge of steam that 'shocks' the rice and makes it shrink from the sides, which loosens the crusty bottom.

To serve, invert the pan onto a warm serving platter so that the rice plops out as one glorious, golden-capped mound. Otherwise, spoon the rice into a warm serving dish and when you reach the crisp base, lift it out and drape it over the rice. It doesn't matter in the slightest if the tah-deeg breaks. Alternatively, present it on a separate plate.

SERVES 4–6

Saffron is often used as a garnish to liven up plain white chelow rice. The classic presentation is described below, but another method is to drizzle saffron liquid over the parboiled rice before steaming, to create a pretty marbled effect through the rice as it cooks. In Iran, saffron is nearly always used in powder form and steeped in water to create a saffron liquid. We prefer to buy top-quality saffron threads and grind them as needed. If you like, you can use ¼ teaspoon saffron powder — mix it with the boiling water and proceed as below.

SAFFRON CHELOW

SAFFRON LIQUID **20 saffron threads (or 1/4 teaspoon saffron powder)**
2 tablespoons boiling water

LIGHTLY TOAST THE SAFFRON IN A dry frying pan over a medium heat for about 30 seconds. The threads must be totally dry, but be very careful not to burn them. As they crisp up, they will begin to release a wonderfully pungent aroma. Tip the saffron into a mortar and leave for a moment or two before grinding to a powder.

Mix the ground saffron with the boiling water and set aside to infuse for at least 1 hour before using. The colour will continue to develop for about 12 hours. Prepare the rice as described on page 217. Just before serving, remove 2–3 tablespoons cooked rice and mix with the saffron liquid in a small bowl. Set this saffron rice aside to use as garnish.

Tip the remaining rice onto a serving platter. Sprinkle on the saffron rice and serve the tah-deeg separately.

TAH-DEEG VARIATIONS

SAFFRON TAH-DEEG The simplest tah-deeg can also be jazzed up a bit by sprinkling saffron liquid (above) instead of plain water into the sizzling oil just before you add the parboiled rice to the pan.

YOGHURT TAH-DEEG Beat 2 tablespoons thick natural yoghurt with 1 egg and 1 tablespoon saffron liquid (above). Mix this with a generous scoop of the parboiled rice and spread it over the sizzling oil. Spoon in the rice and steam as described on page 217.

POTATO TAH-DEEG Arrange thin, slightly overlapping slices of waxy potato in the sizzling oil. Spoon in the rice and steam as described on page 217.

BREAD TAH-DEEG Lay a piece of Arabic flatbread split in half in the sizzling oil. Fill any gaps with torn bits of bread. Spoon in the rice and steam as described on page 217.

Broad beans and dill go beautifully together and we tried several versions of this classic dish, Baghali polow, while on our travels. It is particularly good served with lamb, but makes a great vegetarian option, accompanied by a big bowl of creamy yoghurt.

You can make this polow quite happily with frozen broad beans, but don't forget to slip them out of their outer skins. The dried mint and lemon zest are not strictly traditional, but they add an extra dimension of flavour.

BROAD BEAN, BORLOTTI AND DILL RICE

300 g Iranian or best-quality basmati rice | 2 tablespoons sea salt
1 kg broad beans in the pod or 300 g frozen broad beans
600 g borlotti beans in the pod | 70 ml vegetable oil
1/3 cup chopped dill sprigs | 1 heaped teaspoon dried mint
40 g unsalted butter, melted | 1 large clove garlic, lightly crushed
1 long strip lemon zest, all pith removed

WASH, SOAK AND PARBOIL THE RICE as described on page 217.

Bring a saucepan of water to a boil. Pod the broad beans and borlotti beans, then blanch them briefly, separately, in the boiling water. Peel the broad beans. If using frozen broad beans, there's no need to blanch them first; just slip them out of their skins.

Return the rice saucepan to a medium heat and add the oil and 2 tablespoons water. As soon as the oil begins to sizzle, spoon in enough rice to cover the base of the saucepan in a thin layer. Gently toss the remaining rice with the beans, dill and mint and spoon it into the pan, building it up into a pyramid. Use the handle of a wooden spoon to poke five or six holes down through the rice to the base of the pan to help it steam. Mix 2 tablespoons warm water with the melted butter and drizzle over the rice. Sit the garlic clove and lemon zest on top of the rice and continue as described on page 217.

SERVES **4-6**

The Indian influences on Persian Gulf cooking are obvious in this dish, which has more than a hint of heat and many more spices than you find elsewhere in Iran.

PERSIAN GULF-STYLE PRAWN AND HERB RICE

300 g Iranian or best-quality basmati rice | 2 tablespoons sea salt
1 teaspoon fenugreek seeds | 80 ml vegetable oil | 1 small onion, finely diced
1 teaspoon freshly ground black pepper | 1 teaspoon ground turmeric
1/2 teaspoon ground ginger | 1 large tomato, seeded and diced
200 g peeled prawns (tails intact) | 1/3 cup finely snipped chives
1/3 cup finely shredded flat-leaf parsley leaves
1/3 cup finely shredded dill sprigs | 1/3 cup finely shredded coriander leaves
40 g unsalted butter, melted | 2 tablespoons Saffron Liquid (page 218)

WASH, SOAK AND PARBOIL THE RICE as described on page 217.

Meanwhile, soak the fenugreek in cold water for 10 minutes, then drain. Heat 1 tablespoon of the oil in a frying pan over a low heat. Add the onion and spices and fry gently for 5 minutes, or until the onion has softened. Add the tomato and cook for 1 minute. Add the prawns and stir them briefly in the spice mixture until they start to change colour. Remove the pan from the heat and stir in the herbs.

Return the rice saucepan to a medium heat and add the remaining oil and 2 tablespoons water. As soon as the oil begins to sizzle, spoon in enough rice to cover the base of the pan in a thin layer. Scatter a layer of the prawn mixture over the rice. Continue to layer the rice and the prawn mixture, building them up into a pyramid. Use the handle of a wooden spoon to poke five or six holes down through the rice to the base of the pan to help it steam. Mix 2 tablespoons warm water with the melted butter and saffron liquid and drizzle this over the rice. Continue as described on page 217.

SERVES 6

There's no denying that this festive and exquisite Golden Shirin Polow is a bit of a palaver to make — but if you have a sweet tooth, you will find the combination of candied citrus zest, lightly toasted nuts and spices absolutely irresistible. The idea of candying carrot may seem a little strange at first, but, of course, it has an underlying sweetness all of its own and the bright colour adds to the amber glow of the dish.

Serve with grilled or roasted chicken or quail — or with an earthy braised lamb dish.

SWEET RICE WITH SAFFRON, NUTS AND ORANGE ZEST

zest of 2 oranges, cut into julienne strips | 125 g unsalted butter
2 small carrots (about 200 g), peeled and cut into julienne strips
1/2 teaspoon ground cardamom | 1/2 teaspoon ground cinnamon
pinch of ground cumin | 150 g caster sugar | 2 tablespoons Saffron Liquid (page 218)
250 ml water | 50 g flaked almonds, lightly toasted | 50 g slivered pistachios
300 g Iranian or best-quality basmati rice | 2 tablespoons sea salt
70 ml vegetable oil | 2 tablespoons pomegranate seeds (optional)

BRING A SMALL SAUCEPAN OF WATER to the boil. Blanch the orange zest in the boiling water for 20 seconds. Drain and repeat twice more to remove any bitterness.

Melt 75 g of the butter in a medium saucepan over a low heat. Add the carrot and spices and sweat for 5 minutes, stirring constantly. Add the zest, sugar, half the saffron liquid and water to the pan and bring to the boil, then reduce the heat and simmer gently for 10 minutes. Allow to cool, then strain off the syrup and reserve it and the zest and carrot separately.

Set aside a tablespoon each of the almonds and pistachios to use as a garnish and combine the rest with the orange and carrot mixture. Set aside.

Wash, soak and parboil the rice as described on page 217.

Return the rice saucepan to a medium heat and add the oil and 2 tablespoons water. As soon as the oil begins to sizzle, spoon in enough rice to cover the base of the pan in a thin layer. Scatter a layer of the carrot mixture over the rice. Continue to layer the rice and the carrot mixture, building them up into a pyramid. Use the handle of a wooden spoon to poke five or six holes down through the rice to the base of the pan to help it steam.

Melt the remaining butter, mix it with 2 tablespoons warm water, then drizzle this over the rice. Continue as described on page 217. After 20 minutes, quickly drizzle the reserved syrup over the rice, then replace the lid and cook for a further 20 minutes. You will need to keep an eye on the pan to make sure that the sugar syrup doesn't burn on the base.

Garnish with the reserved nuts and pomegranate seeds, if using.

SERVES 6

There are many recipes for morasa polow, the king of Persian dishes, some of which are variations of Sweet Shirin Polow (page 221). This version is less sweet, which to our mind really allows the flavours and textures of the separate 'jewels' to shine through.

Much of the beauty of this dish is in the presentation — and indeed jewelled rice is often served as a centrepiece at lavish wedding celebrations and other feasts. Instead of turning it out with its crunchy tah-deeg crown, we like to spoon the rice into a pyramid shape to really show off the jewels.

JEWELLED RICE

300 g basmati rice | 2 tablespoons sea salt | 70 ml vegetable oil
40 g unsalted butter, melted

JEWELS **zest of 2 mandarins or oranges, cut into julienne strips | 50 g caster sugar**
2 tablespoons dried barberries, stems removed | 30 g unsalted butter
2 tablespoons Saffron Liquid (page 218) | 2 tablespoons currants | 50 g slivered pistachios
50 g flaked almonds, lightly toasted | 50 g roasted hazelnuts, skins rubbed off
various colours of edible rose petals

WASH, SOAK AND PARBOIL THE RICE as described on page 217. Return the saucepan to a medium heat and add the oil and 2 tablespoons water. As soon as the oil begins to sizzle, spoon in enough rice to cover the base of the pan in a thin layer. Spoon in the rest of the rice gradually, building it up into a pyramid. Use the handle of a wooden spoon to poke five or six holes down through the rice to the base of the pan to help it steam. Mix 2 tablespoons warm water with the melted butter and drizzle this over the rice. Continue as described on page 217.

While the rice is cooking, prepare the 'jewels'. Bring a small saucepan of water to a boil and blanch the mandarin zest for 20 seconds. Drain and repeat twice more to remove any bitterness. Add the sugar and 100 ml water to the pan. Bring to the boil, then reduce the heat and simmer gently for 10 minutes. Allow to cool, then strain off the syrup and reserve the zest and syrup separately.

Soak the barberries in cold water for 2 minutes, then drain and dry well. Melt the butter in a small saucepan over a gentle heat. Add the barberries and fry for 4–5 minutes, stirring constantly. Remove from the heat and reserve.

Once the rice is cooked, remove 2–3 tablespoons, mix with the saffron liquid and set aside. Spoon the remaining rice onto a warm serving platter and mound into a pyramid. Sprinkle on the saffron rice followed by the 'jewels'. Drizzle over a little of the reserved syrup, which will make the jewels shine.

For an alternative presentation, gently combine the plain rice with the saffron rice, all the jewels and the rose petals in a large mixing bowl. Tip into a large pudding basin and press in gently but firmly. Turn out carefully onto a serving platter and drizzle with the reserved mandarin syrup.

Serve the crunchy tah-deeg separately.

SERVES 6

In the Middle East, as in other parts of the world, lentils are often combined with rice to add an easy protein boost. This dish is similar to mjaddarah, one of the most popular home-cooked dishes in Lebanon and Syria. In mjaddarah, the rice and lentils are cooked together until they break down to a sludge-coloured porridge. Here, the rice is prepared risotto-style, and the cooked lentils are added towards the end for a pretty speckled effect. Serve with the caramelised onions spooned over the top, and accompany with a mixed leaf salad.

LENTILS AND RICE WITH CARAMELISED ONIONS

LENTILS **150 g brown lentils | 1/2 onion | 1 bay leaf | 1 cinnamon stick**
1 tablespoon extra virgin olive oil

CARAMELISED ONIONS **50 ml olive oil | knob of unsalted butter**
3 medium purple onions, finely sliced

RISOTTO **2 tablespoons olive oil | 1/2 small onion, finely diced**
200 g Vialone Nano rice | 60 ml white wine
up to 1 litre good-quality chicken or vegetable stock, simmering
80 g unsalted butter, chilled and diced | 40 g parmesan, grated
sea salt and freshly ground black pepper

PUT THE LENTILS IN A SAUCEPAN with twice their volume of water, the onion, bay leaf and cinnamon stick. Bring to the boil, then lower the heat and cook for 25–30 minutes, or until the lentils are tender. Remove from the heat, drain, discard the aromatics and stir through the olive oil.

Prepare the caramelised onions while making the risotto. Heat the oil and butter in a heavy-based frying pan and cook the onions over a very low heat for 20–30 minutes until soft and sweet.

To cook the risotto, heat the oil and fry the onion for a few minutes to flavour the oil, then discard. Add the rice and stir for a few minutes to coat each grain of rice with the oil. Pour in the wine and let it bubble away until it evaporates. Next, ladle in enough simmering stock to cover the rice by a finger's width. Cook on medium heat, stirring with a wooden spoon from time to time, until most of the stock has been absorbed.

Add the same quantity of stock. Again, cook on medium heat, stirring from time to time, until most of the stock has been absorbed. Add a third amount of stock (reserve about 100 ml for the final stage) and when half of the liquid has been absorbed, add the lentils. Stir gently until the stock is all absorbed. Add the final 100 ml of stock and the butter and stir until both are completely absorbed. Stir in the parmesan, then taste and adjust the seasoning if needed. Cover the pot and allow to rest away from the heat for a few minutes.

Serve in shallow bowls, topped with a generous spoonful of caramelised onions.

SERVES **4–6**

One of our very favourite rice dishes, this cinnamon-scented Lebanese classic is good enough to eat on its own, with lashings of yoghurt as an accompaniment. It's a little bit of an extravagant dish, given the quantities of nuts used as garnish, but well worth every cent for the crunch and flavour they add. Serve as an accompaniment to all kinds of roasts — and especially with a festive whole baby roast lamb. We always make extra so as to be sure of having leftovers.

LEBANESE NUT RICE

50 ml olive oil | 1 onion, finely diced | 150 g minced lamb
650 g long-grain rice | 1 litre good-quality chicken stock, boiling
1 cinnamon stick | sea salt and freshly ground black pepper

TO SERVE **80 g pine nuts | 80 g unsalted pistachio kernels | 80 g blanched whole almonds**
100 ml olive oil | 1/2 teaspoon ground cinnamon
2 cloves garlic crushed with 1/2 teaspoon salt | juice of 1 lemon | sprigs of fresh coriander

HEAT THE OIL IN A LARGE, HEAVY-based saucepan and sauté the onion and lamb for about 5 minutes, until the onion is soft and the meat has browned. Add the rice and boiling stock. Turn the heat down to a simmer and add the cinnamon stick, salt and pepper. Cover and cook for 16 minutes or until the rice is tender.

Sauté the nuts separately in the olive oil until golden brown. To serve, turn the rice out onto a large serving platter and sprinkle with the cinnamon and nuts. If serving as an accompaniment to a roast, pour the juices from the roasting pan into a small pan and bring quickly to the boil. Stir in the garlic paste and lemon juice and pour over the rice and meat. Garnish with fresh coriander.

SERVES **4–6**

Known as tahcheen-e morgh, this is another attractive layered rice dish from Iran that is great for special occasions. If you have leftover cooked chicken from your Sunday roast, then by all means use it instead of the fresh chicken given here. Try to marinate the meat — whether raw or cooked — for at least 2 hours, as it really does develop the flavours.

BAKED YOGHURT RICE WITH CHICKEN

250 g thick natural yoghurt | 3 egg yolks | 3 tablespoons Saffron Liquid (page 218)
1 teaspoon orange-flower water | finely grated zest of 1 orange
1 teaspoon sea salt | 1/2 teaspoon freshly ground black pepper
500 g boneless free-range chicken breast and thighs, skin removed and cut into 2 cm cubes
400 g best-quality basmati rice | 2 tablespoons sea salt
80 g unsalted butter, plus extra for greasing
thick natural yoghurt and fresh herbs, to serve

BEAT THE YOGHURT WITH THE EGG yolks, saffron liquid, orange-flower water, zest, salt and pepper in a shallow dish. Add the chicken to the yoghurt mixture. Cover and refrigerate for at least 2 hours or up to 12 hours ahead of time.

Wash, soak and parboil the rice as described on page 217.

Preheat the oven to 190°C (Gas 5) and butter a 2 litre ovenproof dish. Remove the chicken from the yoghurt marinade. Mix half the parboiled rice with the marinade and spoon it into the base of the ovenproof dish. Spread the rice over the bottom and up the sides of the dish. Arrange the chicken on top of the rice, then spoon in the rest of the rice to cover, and smooth the surface. Cover tightly with a sheet of lightly buttered foil and bake for 1 1/2 hours. Remove the dish from the oven and dot the surface of the rice with bits of butter. Replace the foil and leave to rest for 10 minutes. Turn the rice out onto a warm serving platter. Serve with a bowl of creamy yoghurt and a selection of fresh herbs such as tarragon, basil, chives and parsley.

SERVES **6**

This Lebanese dish, known as makloube, combines three of our favourite things: nuts, rice and eggplant. We like to serve it with creamy yoghurt cheese.

UPSIDE-DOWN CHICKEN AND EGGPLANT PILAF

POACHED CHICKEN 1 large chicken breast on the bone | 1 small onion, quartered | 1 stick celery | 1 sprig thyme | 2 bay leaves | 1 small cinnamon stick | 1/2 lemon | 1/2 teaspoon white peppercorns | 1/2 teaspoon allspice berries

PILAF 1 medium eggplant (aubergine), peeled and thinly sliced | sea salt | 120 ml olive oil | 50 g pine nuts | 50 g flaked almonds | 1 tablespoon olive oil | 1 small onion, finely diced | 150 g lean minced lamb | 1/2 teaspoon ground cinnamon | 1/2 teaspoon ground allspice | large pinch salt | 250 g long-grain rice, rinsed well | 600 ml chicken stock (reserved from the poached chicken) | extra ground cinnamon | yoghurt or Yoghurt Cheese (page 44) and salad to serve

PUT THE CHICKEN AND ALL THE aromatics into a small saucepan with enough water to cover. Bring to the boil, then lower the heat and simmer gently for 5 minutes. Turn off the heat and leave the chicken for 20 minutes in the hot stock. Reserve the stock for cooking the rice.

To make the pilaf, put the eggplant slices in a colander and sprinkle with salt. After 20 minutes, rinse under cold water and pat dry with paper towel. Heat the olive oil in a large non-stick frying pan and fry the pine nuts until golden brown. Remove them from the pan and drain on paper towel. Repeat the process with the almonds. In the same oil, fry the eggplant slices on both sides until golden brown, adding a little more oil if necessary.

Heat the tablespoon of olive oil in a large saucepan and sauté the onion gently until it softens. Turn up the heat, add the lamb and sauté until all the juices have evaporated. Add the spices and salt, and stir well. Add the rice and stir again before pouring on the reserved chicken stock. Bring to the boil, then lower the heat, cover the pan and simmer gently for 20 minutes.

While the rice is cooking, pull the chicken meat off the bone and shred it roughly into largish pieces. Much of the pleasure of this dish comes from the presentation, so find a deep round bowl and lightly oil the inside. Lay the pieces of chicken inside, going three-quarters of the way up the sides. Arrange the eggplant slices on top of the chicken, then carefully spoon in the cooked rice. Pack it in fairly tightly and smooth the surface flat. Leave to stand for a few moments before inverting onto a serving platter. Garnish with the pine nuts and almonds and dust with cinnamon. Serve with a bowl of cool, creamy yoghurt or yoghurt cheese, and perhaps a green salad.

SERVES 4

This paella is cooked more like a risotto so the rice becomes creamy. It has no cheese, though, in order to maintain the fresh intense flavours of the vegetables.

SPRING VEGETABLE PAELLA

60 ml olive oil | 1 small onion, quartered | 2 cloves garlic
400 g Vialone Nano rice | up to 1 litre good-quality chicken stock, simmering
15 saffron threads, roasted and crushed to a powder
120 g shelled peas, blanched for 2 minutes | 120 g fresh broad beans, blanched and peeled
8 Artichokes Cooked à la Niçoise (page 67), or good-quality purchased artichokes preserved in oil, quartered | 2 medium tomatoes, seeded and diced
2 small red capsicums (peppers), roasted, skinned and diced
sea salt and freshly ground black pepper | 100 g butter, chilled and cut into small cubes
green salad to serve

HEAT THE OIL IN A SAUCEPAN AND fry the onion and whole garlic cloves in the oil for a few minutes to flavour it, then discard the onion (but keep the garlic). Add the rice and stir for 2 minutes to coat each grain with the oil. Ladle in enough simmering stock to cover the rice by a finger's width. Cook on medium heat, stirring with a wooden spoon from time to time, until most of the stock has been absorbed.

Add the same quantity of stock and continue to cook on medium heat, stirring from time to time, until most of the stock has been absorbed.

Add a third amount of stock (reserving some for the next stage) and when half the liquid has been absorbed, add the saffron, blanched peas and beans and the artichokes. Stir gently, then add the tomato, red capsicum and salt and pepper to taste.

Remove from the heat, cover the pan and let sit for 3 minutes. Return the pan to the heat and add the cold diced butter and the last 100 ml of stock and stir gently until the butter has been incorporated.

Adjust the seasoning if necessary and serve with a fresh green salad.

SERVES 4–6

There is nothing hard about making risotto; it simply requires supervision and constant stirring to create the proper creamy texture. Risotto is ready when the individual grains are tender but with some residual bite. The overall consistency of the dish should be a little like that of porridge — creamy and starchy, and definitely not swimming in liquid. One other thing: risotto is not for those watching their cholesterol and calories. The final compulsory touch is a healthy handful of grated parmesan and a big knob of butter — these help to thicken the final dish, enrich it and add a lovely glossy sheen.

Here, the sweet starchiness of pumpkin and mysterious bittersweet pungency of saffron transform the rice into a glorious, golden-hued meal. You could serve this as an accompaniment, or ideally as a vegetarian starter or main course, along with a salad of bitter leaves or peppery watercress.

GOLDEN SAFFRON PUMPKIN RISOTTO

60 ml olive oil | 1 small onion, quartered | 400 g Vialone Nano rice | 60 ml white wine
up to 1 litre good-quality chicken or vegetable stock, simmering
200 g butternut pumpkin, cut into 1 cm dice | 15 saffron threads, lightly toasted and crushed
1 tablespoon chopped flat-leaf parsley leaves | 1 tablespoon chopped celery-heart leaves
100 g unsalted butter, chilled and cut into small cubes
sea salt and freshly ground black pepper | 60 g parmesan, grated | salad to serve

HEAT THE OIL IN A SAUCEPAN AND add the onion. Fry for a few minutes to flavour the oil, then discard the onion. Add the rice and stir for a few minutes to coat each grain of rice with the oil. Add the wine and let it bubble away until it has evaporated. Next, ladle in enough simmering stock to cover the rice by a finger's width. Cook on medium heat, stirring with a wooden spoon from time to time, until most of the stock is absorbed.

Add the same quantity of stock. Again, cook on medium heat, stirring from time to time, until most of the stock has been absorbed. Add a third amount of stock (reserve about 100 ml for the final stage) and when half of the liquid has been absorbed, add the pumpkin, saffron, parsley and celery leaves. Stir gently until the stock is absorbed.

Add the final 100 ml of stock and the butter and stir until both are completely absorbed. Adjust the seasoning, if need be, then stir in the parmesan, cover the pot and allow to rest away from the heat for a few minutes.

Serve straight away, accompanied by a lightly dressed salad.

SERVES **4–6**

This elegant risotto combines fresh, zesty flavours and makes an ideal light lunch with a simple salad.

RISOTTO WITH ZUCCHINI, PRAWN AND PRESERVED LEMON

160 ml olive oil | 1 small onion, quartered | 400 g Vialone Nano rice
up to 1 litre good-quality chicken or vegetable stock, simmering
2 large zucchini (courgette), shredded into small batons | 2 shallots, finely sliced
1 preserved lemon (page 394), rind only, washed and diced finely
1 tablespoon chopped flat-leaf parsley | 100 g butter, chilled and cut into small cubes
sea salt and freshly ground black pepper | 12 king prawns, peeled and deveined
1 teaspoon Ras al Hanout (page 378) | 1 clove garlic, finely sliced
cornflower petals to garnish (optional)

HEAT 60 ML OF THE OIL IN A PAN and add the onion. Fry for a few minutes to flavour the oil, then discard. Add the rice and stir for a few minutes to coat each grain of rice with the oil. Ladle in enough simmering stock to cover the rice by a finger's width. Cook on medium heat, stirring with a wooden spoon from time to time, until most of the stock has been absorbed.

Add the same quantity of stock. Again, cook on medium heat, stirring from time to time, until most of the stock has been absorbed.

Meanwhile, heat a further 50 ml of oil in a frying pan until it is hot. Throw in the zucchini and shallots. Do not stir, but let sit for 30 seconds. Then stir well, remove from the heat and drain in a colander or sieve.

Add a third amount of stock to the rice (reserve about 100 ml for the final stage) and when half of the liquid has been absorbed, add the zucchini, shallots, preserved lemon rind and parsley. Stir gently until all of the stock has been absorbed.

Add the last 100 ml stock and the butter and stir well until both are completely absorbed. Adjust the seasoning, if need be, then cover the pot and allow to rest away from the heat for a few minutes.

Meanwhile, place the frying pan back on the heat, add the remaining 50 ml oil and heat until it is hot. Throw in the prawns and ras al hanout and stir briskly until just cooked through. Add the garlic, season with salt and pepper and stir well.

To serve, divide the risotto among four shallow bowls and top with the prawns. Garnish with cornflower petals, if using, and serve straight away.

SERVES 4-6

ABOVE GOLDEN SAFFRON PUMPKIN RISOTTO (PAGE 230)
OPPOSITE RISOTTO WITH ZUCCHINI, PRAWN AND PRESERVED LEMON (PAGE 231)

When cooked, couscous grains should be fluffy and separate, not gluggy. The traditional method of steaming couscous (below) really does improve the flavour and texture of the couscous. Couscous has an amazing capacity to absorb liquid, and if inadequately cooked will continue to swell in your stomach! For everyday speedy meals, instant pour-on-boiling-water couscous is really quite satisfactory.

QUICK BUTTERED COUSCOUS

POUR BOILING WATER ONTO THE couscous, following the instructions on the box — the rule is to use about the same volume of liquid as of couscous. Add a drizzle of oil and stir in very well. Leave it to stand for at least 10–15 minutes, or until the liquid is completely absorbed. Fork through every couple of minutes. At the end of the standing time, rub a little olive oil on your hands and rub the couscous between your fingers until the grains are loose and you have broken up any little lumps.

Dot with butter or drizzle it with a little more olive oil, cover with plastic wrap and microwave on medium for about 5 minutes. Alternatively, tip it into an oven-proof dish, add butter or oil, cover it with foil and leave it in a low oven for about 20 minutes. This second step allows the couscous to steam gently under cover and greatly improves its texture.

If you want to jazz it up a little, add some aromatics (like a stick of cinnamon, a squeezed-out lemon half, a few sliced dried mushrooms, some raisins or even finely diced apricots) before the second heat-through. When ready to serve, fluff it up with a fork, season and serve. Or sprinkle on finely chopped parsley and mint, or lightly toasted almonds.

STEAMED COUSCOUS

This traditional method takes a bit longer, but achieves a lighter, fluffier result. Sprinkle 250 g couscous in a shallow dish, add 250 ml cold water and let it sit for 10 minutes. Then rake it through with your fingers. Add 1 tablespoon of olive oil, and lightly season with sea salt and freshly ground black pepper. Line a steamer or couscoussier with a damp cloth. Sit it on top of boiling water flavoured with aromatics if desired — such as a cinnamon stick, half an onion, lemon zest and a few sprigs of thyme. Tip the couscous into the top section, steam for 15 minutes, then pour it onto a tray. Fork it through lightly and allow it to cool for about 5 minutes. Sprinkle it with 4 tablespoons cold water and pour 1 tablespoon oil onto your hands. Rub the couscous between the palms of your hands to break down clumps into individual grains. This will take about 5 minutes. Put the couscous back into the cloth and steam it again for about 20 minutes. Pour out and fork 1 teaspoon butter through thoroughly.

SERVES **4**

This is an oven-baked couscous dish with a surprise hidden layer of sweetly spiced pumpkin. It is good served with rich braises or stews or on its own as a vegetarian main course.

PERFUMED PUMPKIN COUSCOUS

120 g couscous | 180 g butternut pumpkin, peeled and cut into 1 cm dice
1 teaspoon melted butter | sea salt and freshly ground black pepper to taste
1/2 teaspoon ground cinnamon | 20 g currants, soaked in water for 10 minutes
1/2 tablespoon butter | orange-flower water for sprinkling

TO PREPARE THE COUSCOUS, FOLLOW the instructions on the box, or use the quick-cook method opposite.

Steam the pumpkin for 5 minutes and then drain well. Brush a 16 cm x 26 cm baking dish with the melted butter and line the bottom with the pumpkin. Season lightly with salt, pepper and cinnamon.

Sprinkle the currants over the pumpkin and then cover them with a layer of couscous. Lightly pack down and smooth the surface. Again, season lightly with salt and pepper. Drizzle a tablespoon of cold water around the edge of the dish and dot a few knobs of butter over the top of the couscous. Cover with foil and bake in preheated 200°C (Gas 6) oven for 15–20 minutes. Remove and sprinkle with orange-flower water to serve.

SERVES **4**

WILD MUSHROOM COUSCOUS

WILD MUSHROOM BRAISE 3 tablespoons extra-virgin olive oil | 2 shallots, sliced finely
2 cloves garlic, finely chopped | 2 tablespoons thyme leaves
6 king mushrooms, cut into quarters | 6 slippery jack mushrooms, cut thickly
2 tablespoons dry sherry | 40 g dried porcini mushrooms, soaked in cold water
200 ml good quality chicken stock | 2 tablespoons verjuice
juice of 1/2 lemon | sea salt and freshly ground black pepper
1/2 teaspoon Turkish chilli flakes | 60 g unsalted butter, cut into pieces
thin slices of yellow baby beetroot to garnish (optional)

2 tablespoons extra-virgin olive oil | 350 ml water | 400 g couscous
2 small tomatoes, skinned, seeded and diced small
3 tablespoons finely snipped chives | butter

HEAT THE OIL IN A LARGE FRYING pan. Add the shallots, garlic and thyme leaves and sauté gently for 2 minutes, or until translucent. Add the king and slippery jack mushrooms and sauté until lightly coloured. Add the sherry and bubble vigorously for a few minutes, stirring gently.

Strain the porcini mushrooms, reserving 2 tablespoons of the soaking liquid. Add both mushrooms and liquid to the pan. Cook for 2 minutes then add the stock. Increase the heat and cook until the liquid has reduced by half. Stir in the verjuice and lemon and season with salt, pepper and chilli flakes. Add the butter, a little at a time, whisking continuously until it is all incorporated and the sauce is thick and shiny.

Meanwhile, prepare the couscous following the method for Quick Buttered Couscous on page 234. Once you have broken up any small lumps, stir in the diced tomatoes and chives. Dot with butter, cover with plastic wrap and microwave on medium for 3 minutes. Stir briefly, then tip into a buttered pudding basin and press in firmly.

To serve, unmould the couscous onto a platter and spoon the wild mushroom braise around. Garnish with baby yellow beetroot slices, if you like.

WILD MUSHROOM COUSCOUS WITH FIORE DI LATTE Combine the prepared couscous and wild mushroom braise then tip into an ovenproof dish. Grate 150 g fiore di latte cheese (or mozzarella) over the top, drizzle with 1 tablespoon extra-virgin olive oil and bake in an oven preheated to 200°C (Gas 6) for 10 minutes, or until the cheese has melted. Sprinkle with sweet paprika.

SERVES 4

This is an absolutely fabulous, over-the-top kind of pilaf, with more 'jewels' than a Lacroix bracelet. You can substitute dried cranberries for the pomegranate seeds, or to be really exotic, use dried Iranian barberries. Serve as a vegetarian main course or to accompany barbecued poultry or lamb.

JEWELLED CRACKED WHEAT PILAF WITH HONEY-GINGER TOMATO SAUCE

175 g coarse burgul, soaked in cold water for 5 minutes
sea salt and freshly ground black pepper | generous knob of butter
30 g currants soaked in 30 ml dry sherry for 30 minutes | 1/2 teaspoon ground allspice
zest of 1/2 orange | 1 sheet brik pastry | clarified butter for brushing | 50 g pine nuts
50 g unsalted pistachio kernels, blanched and peeled | 1/4 cup pomegranate seeds

HONEY-GINGER TOMATO SAUCE 2 tablespoons olive oil | 2 cloves garlic, finely chopped
1 red bullet chilli, seeded, scraped and finely chopped | 400 g can chopped tomatoes
sea salt and freshly ground black pepper | 1 teaspoon ground turmeric
1 thumb fresh ginger, finely grated | 1 tablespoon honey

RINSE THE BURGUL WELL IN COLD water, then put it in a heavy pan with 1 1/2 times its volume of cold water. Season lightly with salt. Bring to the boil and then simmer, covered, on a low heat for 10–15 minutes, or until the liquid has been absorbed. Towards the end of the cooking time, turn up the heat to evaporate any remaining liquid at the bottom of the pan. Take the pan off the heat when you hear the burgul start to crackle and catch, and stir in the butter.

Tip the burgul into a mixing bowl, season with salt and pepper and add the drained currants, allspice and orange zest. Fork it through well, then cover with a snug-fitting lid and leave in a warm place for 10 minutes, or until the burgul has absorbed all the liquid and is tender.

To make the sauce, heat the oil in a pan and sauté the garlic and chilli for a few minutes until they soften. Add the tomatoes, salt and pepper, turmeric, ginger and honey and simmer for 10 minutes.

Preheat the oven to 180°C (Gas 4) .

To make the brik pastry garnish, use a pastry cutter to cut 10 cm circles from the pastry. Then cut smaller circles from the centre of each piece using a 4 cm cutter. Transfer to a baking tray lined with baking paper. Brush with clarified butter, put another sheet of baking paper on top and weight down with another baking tray. Bake for 10 minutes, until crisp.

Toast the pine nuts in a dry frying pan until they colour, then add them to the burgul pilaf with the pistachios. Tip onto a serving plate, pour on the honey-ginger tomato sauce, scatter on the pomegranate seeds and garnish with pastry circles.

SERVES 4

Freekeh has a wonderful smoky flavour that works brilliantly with the sweetness of pumpkin, onions and orange. This makes a good vegetarian main course or a lovely accompaniment. Either way, serve with a big bowl of thick, natural yoghurt.

FREEKEH WITH PUMPKIN, ORANGE ZEST AND PEARL ONIONS

200 g freekeh (smoky green wheat) | 50 ml olive oil | 1/2 onion, finely diced
1 garlic clove, finely diced | 1/2 cup diced celery | 1/2 cup diced pumpkin
3/4 cup cooked chickpeas | 1/2 teaspoon ground cumin
6 pearl onions, peeled and halved | shredded zest of 1 orange
up to 1.25 litres good-quality chicken stock or water
sea salt and freshly ground black pepper | juice of 1 lemon
1/4 cup snipped micro-herbs (optional) | extra-virgin olive oil
natural yoghurt to serve

RINSE THE FREEKEH THEN LEAVE to soak in plenty of cold water for 30 minutes. Drain well.

Heat the oil in a large, heavy-based frying pan. Add the onion, garlic, celery, pumpkin, chickpeas and cumin. Sauté for a few minutes, stirring well to coat everything in the oil. Add the drained freekeh, along with the pearl onions, orange zest and 500 ml of the stock. Season with salt and pepper and bring to the boil. Lower the heat and simmer for 1 hour. Stir well every 10 minutes or so, to make sure it doesn't catch and burn. Add extra stock, if necessary. By the end of the cooking time, most of the liquid should have evaporated.

Just before you serve, stir through the lemon juice and sprinkle on the micro-herbs. Drizzle with a little extra-virgin olive oil and serve straight away.

SERVES **6**

To give this a really good consistency, mix ordinary brushed potatoes, which are light and fluffy but rather tasteless, with flavoursome waxy Desirée potatoes. To get that lovely light texture, you should also push the mashed potatoes through a sieve, which is a bit tedious, but worth it for the result.

GOAT'S CHEESE MASHED POTATOES

3 large brushed potatoes (about 600 g in total) | 1 large desirée potato (about 200 g)
60 ml extra-virgin olive oil | 100 g butter | 100 ml cream (35% fat)
sea salt and freshly ground black pepper | 80 g mild-flavoured goat's cheese

PEEL THE POTATOES AND CUT THEM into large equal-sized dice. Place in a large saucepan and cover with cold salted water. Bring to the boil, then lower the heat and simmer gently for 15–20 minutes, or until the potatoes are cooked, but not mushy.

As they are cooking, place the olive oil, butter and cream in another saucepan. Bring these to the boil and then simmer to reduce by a third. Keep warm.

When the potatoes are cooked, drain, return them to the pan and allow them to dry over the heat for a further 40–50 seconds. Then push them through a sieve and pour over the cream mixture. Beat with a wooden spoon. Adjust the seasoning.

Roughly crumble the goat's cheese into the potato and mix it well with the mash. Serve immediately.

SERVES **4**

This recipe evolved after our visit to a dairy in the Tannail region near Beirut, where they made a type of Gouda cheese flavoured with cumin seeds. It is a variation on a potato purée from the Auvergne in France, known as aligot. It is rich and delicious, and would make a lovely accompaniment to simple grilled or roasted meats.

CHEESY MASHED POTATOES WITH CUMIN

3 large brushed potatoes (about 600 g in total) | 1 large desirée potato (about 200 g)
60 ml extra-virgin olive oil | 100 g butter | 100 ml cream (35% fat)
200 g cumin gouda, grated | sea salt and freshly ground black pepper

PEEL THE POTATOES AND CUT THEM into large equal-sized dice. Put them in a large saucepan and cover with cold salted water. Bring to the boil then lower the heat and simmer gently for 15–20 minutes, or until the potatoes are cooked but not mushy.

Meanwhile pour the oil, butter and cream into a small pan and bring to the boil. Lower the heat and simmer until reduced by a third.

When the potatoes are cooked, drain them well and return them to the pan. Leave them to dry for another minute, then push them through a sieve into the hot cream mixture and beat with a wooden spoon. Leave to cool for a few minutes, then fold in the grated cheese. Return the pan to a gentle heat and leave, without stirring, until the cheese begins to melt. Use the wooden spoon to lift and turn the mixture until all the cheese has been incorporated. Don't let it boil. Just before serving, taste and adjust the seasoning and lift and turn the potato mixture once again to pull the melted cheese into strings.

SERVES 4

We love sautéed potatoes. These Lebanese harkoussa have a chilli buzz and a tang of garlic and coriander to liven them. Use Sebago, King Edward or another type of floury potato, as they will give you the best texture — crisp and crunchy on the outside, and fluffy inside. Serve them with anything — or just eat them on their own, with a dollop of sour cream.

FRIED POTATOES WITH GARLIC, GREEN CHILLI AND CORIANDER

500 g floury potatoes, peeled and cut into 1 cm cubes | 100 ml olive oil
1 small purple onion, finely sliced | 2 cloves garlic, finely chopped
2 long green chillies, seeded, scraped and cut into 5 mm dice
1 teaspoon coriander seeds, roasted and ground | knob of butter | sea salt

BLANCH THE POTATOES IN BOILING water for 2 minutes, then drain and leave to steam dry. Heat the oil in a large heavy-based frying pan. When the oil is sizzling, add the potatoes and fry them for 5–10 minutes, turning them from time to time so they colour evenly. As they begin to brown, add the onion, garlic, chilli and coriander.

Once the potatoes are crisp and the onions a deep golden brown, add the knob of butter. Cook for a few more minutes, then tip into a serving dish and season with salt. Serve piping hot.

SERVES **4**

SPICED ROASTED ROOT VEGETABLES

6 baby turnips, trimmed and peeled
4 baby heirloom (purple) carrots, trimmed and scraped
4 baby orange carrots, trimmed and scraped
2 small parsnips, trimmed, scraped and halved lengthwise
600 g peeled pumpkin, cut into chunks | 4 shallots, peeled and halved
2 long red chillies, split lengthwise and seeded
2 long green chillies, split lengthwise and seeded | 40 g sultanas | splash of verjuice

SPICE PASTE 2 cloves garlic, roughly chopped | 1 shallot, roughly chopped
1 long red chilli, roughly chopped | 1 teaspoon sea salt | 1 teaspoon caraway seeds, ground
1 teaspoon freshly grated nutmeg | 1/2 teaspoon ground cardamom
1/2 teaspoon ground cinnamon | 1/2 teaspoon freshly ground black pepper | 75 ml olive oil

PREHEAT THE OVEN TO 180°C (GAS 4).

To make the spice paste, combine the garlic, shallot, chilli and salt in a mortar and pound to a paste. Add the remaining spices and pound again to incorporate thoroughly. Stir in the oil.

In a large mixing bowl, combine the turnips, carrots and parsnips. Add the spice paste and toss until the vegetables are evenly coated. Tip into a heavy-based roasting pan and roast for 15 minutes.

Scatter in the pumpkin, shallots, chillies, sultanas and verjuice and toss them with the other vegetables until coated with the spicy oil. Return the pan to the oven and cook for a further 20 minutes. Check from time to time and turn the vegetables to ensure they cook evenly. Serve with your favourite roasts.

SERVES 4

Skordalia is a traditional Greek garlic sauce, often made with mashed potatoes, stale white bread, or even almonds. This version uses parsnip for a sweeter, mellower taste. Serve it as an accompaniment to any barbecued or grilled meats.

PARSNIP SKORDALIA

1 kg parsnips | 500 ml milk | 2 cloves garlic crushed with 1/2 teaspoon salt
juice of 1 lemon | 50 g fresh breadcrumbs | 100 ml olive oil
sea salt and freshly ground black pepper

PEEL AND CORE THE PARSNIPS AND cut them into even-sized pieces. Cook them in the milk until they are very soft. Purée them in a food processor with the garlic paste, lemon juice and breadcrumbs. Add the oil, in a very slow dribble, until all of it is incorporated. Adjust the seasoning and allow to cool before serving.

SERVES 4

GREEN BEANS WITH HAZELNUTS

400 g baby French green beans, trimmed neatly | 30 g unsalted butter
20 ml hazelnut oil | sea salt and freshly ground white pepper
100 g hazelnuts, roasted and peeled | 1 small purple salad onion, thinly sliced

BLANCH THE BEANS FOR 2 MINUTES in boiling salted water. Refresh in iced water, then drain. Heat the butter and hazelnut oil in a small saucepan. Add the beans and season lightly. Fry gently for 1 few minutes, tossing to coat with the buttery oil. Lift the beans out of the pan, leaving as much oil in the pan as you can, and keep the beans warm. Add the hazelnuts to the pan and fry for 30 seconds.

To serve, mound the beans onto a warm serving platter and spoon on the hazelnuts. Top with a few rings of onion and serve straight away.

SERVES 4

This braise goes well with the Chermoula-roasted Monkfish (page 155).

BRAISED BABY BEETROOT WITH CHICKPEAS

SAUCE **60 ml olive oil | 1 small onion, finely diced | 1 clove garlic, crushed with1 teaspoon sea salt | 1 tablespoon coriander seeds | 1 heaped tablespoon cumin seeds | 1 heaped tablespoon caraway seeds | 1 teaspoon sweet paprika | 1 teaspoon chili powder | 1 teaspoon ground ginger | 400 g can chopped tomatoes | 1 tablespoon honey | 600 ml chicken or vegetable stock | 2 small bunches baby golden beetroot | 1 bunch baby red beetroot | 8 cloves garlic, peeled | sea salt and freshly ground black pepper | 60 ml olive oil | 150 g cooked chickpeas**

TO MAKE THE SAUCE, HEAT THE OIL in a frying pan and sauté the onion until soft and translucent. Add the garlic paste and fry for a few minutes more.

Use a mortar and pestle to grind the coriander, cumin and caraway seeds to a fine powder. Sieve to remove the husks, and mix them with the remaining dry spices.

Add all the spices to the pan, stir well and continue to sauté for 2 more minutes. Add the tomatoes, honey and stock. Bring to the boil, then lower the heat and simmer uncovered for 45 minutes. Stir the mixture from time to time. It will reduce down to a thick, fragrant sauce.

While the sauce is cooking, preheat the oven to 180°C (Gas 4). Prepare the beetroot by washing them thoroughly to remove any grit, paying special attention to the area close to the stalks. Trim the roots and cut off the stalks. Place in a baking tray and scatter in the garlic cloves. Season lightly with salt, add the oil and toss thoroughly. Cover the tray loosely with a sheet of foil and roast for 30–45 minutes, or until the beetroot are tender.

Remove the tray from the oven and discard the garlic cloves. When the beetroot are just cool enough to handle, peel them and cut them in half horizontally.

Keep the red beetroot warm. Add the golden beetroot only to the sauce, as the red beetroot will discolour the dish, then add the chickpeas to the sauce and stir in well — you might need to add more stock at this stage if the sauce is too thick. Bring the sauce back to the boil and taste for seasoning, adjusting as necessary. Tip into a serving bowl and place the red beetroot on top.

SERVES **4**

This Moroccan classic makes a superb vegetarian main course. Serve with Onion Jam and Green Harissa broth in a separate jug, for each person to help themselves. A bowl of rosewater-flavoured Yoghurt Cheese (page 44) or Basil Tzatziki (page 43) on the side, although distinctly un-Moroccan, is also delicious.

SEVEN-VEGETABLE TAGINE

240 g couscous | 2 medium carrots, scraped and cut into wedges on the angle
1 small butternut pumpkin, peeled and cut into 2 cm dice
2 small turnips, peeled and cut into wedges | 2 small parsnips, scraped and cut into batons
1 small eggplant (aubergine), cut into wedges | 500 ml vegetable stock
1 medium zucchini (courgette), cut into wedges on the angle
100 g chickpeas, soaked overnight and cooked until just tender
4 small waxy potatoes, boiled until tender, peeled and halved | 1 tablespoon sweet paprika
1/2 tablespoon ground ginger | 1/2 tablespoon crushed dried chillies
1/2 tablespoon ground cumin | 1/2 tablespoon ground coriander
1/2 tablespoon freshly ground black pepper | seeds from 4 cardamom pods, crushed
1 clove garlic, crushed with 1/2 teaspoon salt | juice of 1 lemon | 100 ml olive oil
2 teaspoons rosewater | Onion Jam (page 394) and Yoghurt Cheese (page 44) to serve

GREEN HARISSA BROTH 2-3 tablespoons Green Harissa (page 381), or to taste
400 ml vegetable stock or water, simmering | sea salt and freshly ground black pepper

IF YOU HAVE A COUSCOUSSIER, stew the vegetables in the bottom section and steam the couscous on top. Otherwise proceed as follows.

Prepare couscous with aromatics according to the base method (see page 234). During the second steaming, begin to prepare the vegetables. Preheat the oven to 200°C (Gas 6).

In a mixing bowl, combine all the spices with the garlic paste, lemon juice and half the olive oil.

Heat the remaining oil in a large ovenproof casserole and sauté the carrots, pumpkin, turnips, parsnips and eggplant for about 5 minutes, or until all are lightly coloured. Add the spice mixture and stir to coat the vegetables for a further 2 minutes. Add the stock and cook for 5 minutes.

Add the zucchini, chickpeas and potatoes. Mix them in well then place the casserole in the oven and bake for 20–30 minutes or until the vegetables are tender. Remove from the oven, check for seasoning and sprinkle the rosewater over the top.

When ready to serve, mix the green harissa into the simmering stock. Return to the boil, then taste and adjust the seasoning to your liking.

Pile the vegetables into a deep serving dish and stack the couscous on top. Serve immediately with onion jam, the harissa broth and yoghurt cheese.

SERVES 4

One of our favourite side dishes, this is especially good with grilled or roasted red meats.

FETA-CREAMED SPINACH

3 bunches spinach, leaves only | 100 ml cream (35% fat)
1 tablespoon Dijon mustard | 1 tablespoon grated parmesan
1/4 preserved lemon (page 394), rind only, cut into small dice
sea salt and freshly ground black pepper
1/2 teaspoon red Turkish chilli flakes | 80 g feta, crumbled | 30 ml extra-virgin olive oil

BLANCH SMALL BATCHES OF THE spinach leaves in plenty of boiling, salted water for 10 seconds. Refresh in cold water and then squeeze out as much moisture as possible. Loosen the clumps of spinach and chop it finely.

Combine the cream and mustard in a small saucepan and bring to the boil. Lower the heat and simmer until reduced by half, then add the parmesan, preserved lemon and chopped spinach. Season with salt and pepper and stir in the chilli flakes. Add the feta and cook over a high heat until the cheese begins to soften.

Tip into a fine sieve and use the back of a spoon to gently press the creamy liquid back into the saucepan. Heat gently for a few minutes.

Use dessertspoons to form the spinach into golf-balls and arrange on a warm serving dish. Pour the creamy sauce over and drizzle with oil.

SERVES **4**

This simple garden salad is a handy way to use up stale pieces of Arabic bread. It is most delicious when the bread is fried, but you can also toast or grill it.

FATTOUCHE

2 teaspoons ground sumac | 1/4 teaspoon ground allspice
1/4 teaspoon freshly ground black pepper | 1 medium purple onion, sliced
4 cos lettuce leaves, washed and dried | 4 radishes, thickly sliced
2 ripe but firm tomatoes, roughly diced | 2 Lebanese cucumbers, cut into chunky dice
1/3 cup roughly chopped mint leaves or 1 tablespoon dried mint
1/2 cup roughly chopped parsley leaves | 1/2 cup purslane (if available)
1 piece Arabic flatbread | 60 g butter | 60 ml olive oil
1 clove garlic crushed with 1 teaspoon salt | juice of 1 lemon
40 ml extra-virgin olive oil | 1/2 tablespoon balsamic vinegar

SOAK THE SUMAC IN COLD WATER for a few minutes and remove any husks or uncrushed berries that float to the top. Add the sumac, allspice and pepper to the sliced onion, and rub it in well. Cut the cos leaves crosswise into 3 cm strips. Place them in a large salad bowl with the radishes, tomatoes, cucumbers and all the herb leaves.

Split the bread open and cut it into rough 2 cm triangular shapes. Melt the butter and oil in a frying pan until they are foaming and fry the bread in two batches until it is golden brown. Remove it with a slotted spoon and drain it on paper towel. Mix the garlic paste with the lemon juice. Whisk together the extra-virgin olive oil and vinegar.

When you are ready to serve, add the spiced onions to the other salad ingredients, add the lemon-garlic mix and stir well. Finally, pour over the dressing, add the pieces of fried bread, mix everything together gently and serve straight away.

SERVES 6

This is a favourite Turkish salad using raw vegetables, which make it wonderfully crunchy. Sometimes gypsy salads are made with grated hard white cheese, but we prefer to use a tangy yoghurt dressing instead. The dried apricots aren't traditional, but we love their soft, chewy sweetness against the crunch of the vegetables.

GYPSY SALAD

2 vine-ripened tomatoes, skinned and diced
1 Lebanese cucumber, peeled, seeded and diced
1 small purple onion, peeled and diced | 4 dried apricots, diced
3 baby carrots, diced | 1 long yellow banana pepper, diced
1 clove garlic, crushed with 1/2 teaspoon sea salt | 100 g thick natural yoghurt
1 tablespoon extra-virgin olive oil | juice of 1/2 lemon
1 red bullet chilli, seeded and finely shredded
1 teaspoon ground cumin | freshly ground white pepper

PUT THE TOMATOES, CUCUMBER, onion, apricots, carrots and yellow pepper into a large bowl and toss gently.

In another bowl, whisk together the garlic paste, yoghurt and remaining ingredients to make a dressing. Pour on enough to coat the vegetables and toss gently.

SERVES 4

Even though it's called Shiraz salad, this dish is popular all around Iran. The freshness and quality of the ingredients are all-important. The tomatoes, in particular, must be really tasty — vine-ripened, if possible. In some versions, the vegetables are cut into tiny dice and left to stand in the dressing to allow the flavours to develop. Our preference is for a chunkier style, dressed just before serving, for a crisper and fresher result.

Shiraz is the city of roses, so we like to garnish the salad with an exotic sprinkling of edible flowers.

SHIRAZ SALAD

4 vine-ripened tomatoes, roughly chopped
2 Lebanese cucumbers, peeled, seeded and roughly chopped
3 shallots, finely sliced | 6 radishes, cut into thick discs
1 cup flat-leaf parsley leaves | 2 tablespoons chopped dill sprigs
1/4 teaspoon dried mint | 1/2 cup snipped chives in 2 cm lengths
juice of 1 lime | 2 tablespoons extra-virgin olive oil | sea salt | freshly ground black pepper
edible flower petals (rose, nasturtium, chrysanthemum, cornflower) to garnish

COMBINE THE VEGETABLES AND herbs in a large mixing bowl. Whisk the lime juice and oil together and pour over the salad. Season with salt and pepper and toss everything together gently. Scatter with petals, if using.

SERVES 6

A touch of harissa will liven up all sorts of soups and stews, or even a creamy potato salad such as this. If you can't make your own, then a good-quality purchased paste will do.

HARISSA POTATO SALAD

6 medium waxy potatoes | 2 tablespoons Mayonnaise (page 385)
1 tablespoon Red Harissa (page 381) | cream (35% fat), optional
1 tablespoon chopped capers | 4 spring onions, finely chopped
sea salt and freshly ground black pepper

STEAM THE POTATOES UNTIL TENDER. While they are cooking, mix the mayonnaise with the harissa. Thin with a little cream if desired. Peel the potatoes while they are still warm and cut them into 2 cm dice. Mix them with the capers, spring onions and mayonnaise. Season with salt and pepper.

SERVES 4

SHREDDED CARROT SALAD

2 large carrots

DRESSING 1 clove garlic, crushed with 1/2 teaspoon sea salt | 1/4 teaspoon ground cinnamon 1/4 teaspoon ground cumin | 1/4 teaspoon paprika | 1/4 teaspoon chilli powder
juice of 1 large lemon | drizzle of honey | 2 tablespoons extra-virgin olive oil
splash of orange-flower water (optional)

PEEL THE CARROTS THEN USE THE peeler to shred them into long ribbons. Put all the dressing ingredients into a clean jar and shake everything together vigorously until well combined. Tip over the carrots, taste and adjust seasoning if necessary.

SERVES 4

Cucumber and pomegranate is a popular combination in Iran, and in this recipe we've taken the idea and run with it. Creamy white cheese and a toasty crunch of almonds make this a refreshing salad or side dish, and it is especially good with spicier meat dishes.

Sometimes you can find lovely little curled cucumbers, which somehow seem extra tasty. But the Lebanese ones work just as well.

SHAVED CUCUMBER AND POMEGRANATE SALAD

6 Lebanese cucumbers, peeled | 3 tablespoons vegetable oil
60 g flaked almonds | seeds from 1/2 pomegranate
2 tablespoons shredded mint leaves | 2 tablespoons shredded chervil sprigs
2 tablespoons snipped chives in 2 cm lengths | juice of 1/2 lemon
2 tablespoons extra-virgin olive oil | 80 g creamy feta, crumbled
sea salt and freshly ground black pepper

USING A VEGETABLE PEELER, SHAVE the cucumber flesh into long strips, being careful not to include any seeds. Discard the seedy core. Tip the shavings into a colander set on a plate and refrigerate for 10 minutes.

Meanwhile, heat the vegetable oil in a frying pan over a low heat and fry the almonds until golden brown. Drain briefly on paper towel.

Combine the shaved cucumber with the pomegranate seeds and herbs in a large mixing bowl. Whisk the lemon juice and extra-virgin olive oil together and pour over the salad. Scatter on the feta and crisp almonds, then season with salt and pepper and toss everything together gently.

SERVES 6

A bit of fancy presentation turns this perfumed salad into an elegant starter. It is also a lovely light accompaniment to many earthy vegetable dishes and risottos.

HONEY-ROASTED PEAR AND WALNUT SALAD

3 ripe pears | 2 1/2 tablespoons mild-flavoured honey | seeds from 3 cardamom pods
1 tablespoon orange-flower water | 3 teaspoons dry sherry | 25 g butter
120 ml extra-virgin olive oil | 100 g walnuts
2 x 250 g packets Cypriot haloumi, sliced 3 mm thick
100 g plain flour for dusting | 60 ml olive oil | juice of 2 lemons
1 teaspoon chopped fresh thyme leaves | 1 purple onion, finely sliced
1 bunch flowering watercress, leaves picked | 1 cup frisée lettuce
1/2 cup black basil leaves | sea salt | 1/2 teaspoon fresh black pepper

HALVE THE PEARS (OR QUARTER them if they are quite large), and cut out the cores. In a small pot, warm the honey, cardamom seeds, orange-flower water and sherry.

In a heavy frying pan, melt together the butter and 2 tablespoons of the extra-virgin olive oil until bubbling, then sear the pears for 1 minute on each side. Add the honey mixture and sauté for a further 2 minutes until it is a warm caramel colour.

To roast the walnuts, place them in a very hot oven for 5 minutes. Rub away some of the papery brown skin in a tea towel and cut them into quarters.

To grill the haloumi, dust the slices in flour. Heat the 60 ml olive oil in a frying pan over a high heat and cook the cheese slices until they are golden brown. Turn them and cook the other side until coloured. Pour half the lemon juice over the cheese and sprinkle with the thyme leaves.

Rinse the onion slices under cold running water for 5 minutes to reduce their sharpness.

In a large bowl gently mix the pears and haloumi with the watercress leaves, frisée lettuce, basil, onion and two-thirds of the walnuts. In a separate bowl, gently whisk together the remaining olive oil and lemon juice and season with the salt and pepper. Pour the dressing over the salad and gently toss to combine.

To serve as a starter, divide the salad into 6 portions. Set a 5 cm x 5 cm length of PVC tubing on a plate and carefully layer in a portion of salad. Carefully lift away the tubing and repeat with the remaining 5 serves. Garnish with the remaining walnuts and serve straight away.

SERVES **6**

Use really tasty tomatoes for this salad: we like to use a selection of the heirloom tomatoes that are becoming increasingly available from greengrocers and markets, but vine-ripened tomatoes will do well too.

TOMATO SALAD WITH TARRAGON, SHANKLEISH CHEESE AND SUMAC DRESSING

2 shallots, peeled and sliced into wafer-thin rings | 3 tablespoons French tarragon
10–12 small assorted heirloom or vine-ripened tomatoes, thickly sliced
sea salt and freshly ground black pepper | 120 g shankleish cheese, crumbled
fennel pollen, to garnish (optional)

SUMAC DRESSING **1 heaped tablespoon sumac berries | 60 ml warm water**
100 ml extra-virgin olive oil | juice of 1/4 lemon | 1/2 teaspoon caster sugar
drizzle of pomegranate molasses | sea salt and freshly ground black pepper
1/2 sprig thyme | 1/2 clove garlic, crushed

TO MAKE THE SUMAC DRESSING, crush the sumac berries roughly in a mortar. Tip into a small bowl and pour on the warm water. Leave to infuse for 45 minutes, then strain through a fine cloth into a measuring jug and reserve 50 ml.

In a bowl, whisk the sumac water with the oil, lemon juice, sugar and molasses. Season with salt and pepper and add the thyme and garlic. Leave to infuse for 20–30 minutes, then strain into a sealable jar. The dressing will keep, refrigerated, for up to 3 weeks.

To make the salad, soak the shallot rings in iced water for 10 minutes, then pat dry with paper towel. In a small bowl, toss the shallots with the tarragon and enough sumac dressing just to moisten. Stack the sliced tomatoes onto a serving platter and season lightly. Scatter on the shallots and shankleish cheese, then drizzle with a little more dressing, garnish with fennel pollen, if using, and serve.

SERVES **4**

GREEN LEAF SALAD WITH FIGS AND YOGHURT CHEESE

1 head red witlof, leaves trimmed | 1 cup watercress leaves and flowers
1/2 cup chervil leaves | 1/2 cup snow pea tendrils | 1/3 cup black basil leaves
1/3 cup chocolate mint leaves | 6 firm but ripe figs, peeled and quartered
3 French radishes, sliced lengthwise into wafers | 200 g Yoghurt Cheese (page 44)

HAZELNUT DRESSING **50 ml hazelnut oil | few drops sesame oil | 50 ml olive oil**
30 ml Champagne vinegar | 50 ml water | sea salt and freshly ground white pepper

TO MAKE DRESSING, TIP THE OILS into a bowl and whisk in the vinegar, then the water. Season with salt and pepper.

For the salad, tip all the ingredients except the yoghurt cheese into a bowl. Lightly season with salt and pepper and pour in as much dressing as required. Gently mix the salad with your hands and arrange on plates neatly to form a circle. Place blobs of yoghurt cheese around the salad and drizzle on a little more dressing, if needed.

SERVES **6**

BAKERY

These stubby little bread sticks make a nice change from focaccia. This quantity makes 20 sticks, which might seem a lot, but they always disappear quite quickly. Vary the size to make them thicker or thinner, according to preference.

LEBANESE BREAD STICKS WITH ZA'ATAR

BREAD DOUGH **500 g bakers' flour | 20 g salt | 30 g fresh yeast | 20 g white sugar 375 ml warm water**

LEBANESE SPICED OIL **3 tablespoons za'atar | 1 tablespoon sumac | 100 ml olive oil**

olive oil and pomagranate molasses to serve

PLACE THE FLOUR AND SALT IN YOUR electric mixer. In a separate bowl whisk together the yeast, sugar and water to a smooth, creamy liquid and add it to the flour. Mix with the dough hook for 5–10 minutes until the ingredients form a smooth, glossy dough. Cover the dough with a cloth and place in a warm place to prove for about 1 hour.

For the Lebanese spiced oil, mix the za'atar, sumac and olive oil.

Knock the dough back and roll it out on a floured work surface to an 80 cm x 20 cm rectangle, about 1.5 cm thick. Brush it with the Lebanese spiced oil and sprinkle it with a little salt. Then cut it into sticks about 2.5 cm wide. Place them on a baking tray and leave them to prove in a warm place for a further 10 minutes.

Preheat the oven to 180°C (Gas 4) and bake for about 10 minutes until the sticks are golden brown. Serve with a dish of olive oil and pomegranate molasses for dunking.

MAKES **20**

Lavosh — reputedly of Armenian origin — are crisp and delicate with just a hint of dill. They come in many shapes, and may be sprinkled with sesame, caraway or poppy seeds. I like to make them into elongated triangles, which is easy to do by simply cutting a long rectangle in half from corner to corner. Lavosh are a great addition to any cheese board, and we also serve them with dips and spreads.

It's important that the dough is rolled out paper thin, so that you end up with light and crisp crackers. If you happen to have a pasta machine, all the better — just feed the dough through each of the settings until you reach the finest one.

LAVOSH CRACKERS

250 g bakers' flour | 1 teaspoon sea salt | 1 teaspoon caster sugar
1/2 teaspoon dill seeds | 30 g unsalted butter | 150 ml milk | 1 free-range egg
additional 1 tablespoon milk | sesame, caraway or poppy seeds

COMBINE THE FLOUR, SALT, SUGAR and dill seeds in a large bowl and rub in the butter. Use your hands to mix in the milk until the mixture comes together as a ball of dough. Knead for 5 minutes, then cover with plastic wrap and leave to rest for a minimum of 1 hour or overnight.

Preheat the oven to 150°C (Gas 2) and line baking trays with baking paper.

Cut the dough into quarters, and work with one piece at a time (keep the rest wrapped). On a lightly floured surface, roll out the dough until paper thin, or use a pasta machine, working through the settings. Transfer the sheet of dough to a work surface, then cut it into long strips about 6 cm wide, and carefully transfer these to the prepared baking tray. Lightly beat the egg with the extra milk, then brush each strip of dough with this. Sprinkle the dough with seeds of your choice and allow to air-dry for about 5 minutes.

Cut each strip into triangles, rectangles or squares and bake for 10–15 minutes until golden and crisp, then transfer to a wire rack to cool. Repeat with the remaining dough. When all the crackers are cold, store them in an airtight container.

MAKES **20**

These huge oval flaps of golden bread, known as barberi, are enjoyed for breakfast around Iran with clotted cream and honey, fruit conserves, eggs or a warming soup, all equally wonderful. In commercial bakeries, the dough for barberi bread is shaped into large ovals about 60 centimetres long, but for the home baker we suggest making smaller loaves, about half the size. This quantity of dough makes three loaves, sufficient for six people.

BREAKFAST BREAD

2 teaspoons dried yeast | 500 ml warm water | 750 g bakers' flour
1 tablespoon sea salt | 50 ml olive oil | fine polenta for dusting
20 g unsalted butter, melted | sesame or nigella seeds (optional)

DISSOLVE THE YEAST IN 50 ML OF the warm water and set aside in a warm place for 10 minutes.

Combine the flour and salt in the bowl of an electric mixer fitted with a dough hook and make a well in the centre. Mix the oil with the remaining water and stir in the yeast mixture, then gradually work the liquid into the flour. Knead on a slow speed for 10–15 minutes until the dough is smooth, shiny and elastic — add more tepid water if necessary. Transfer to a lightly oiled bowl, then cover with a damp tea towel and leave to prove in a warm place for 2 hours or until doubled in size.

Preheat the oven to 220°C (Gas 7). Knock back the dough, then leave to prove for a further 20 minutes. After 10 minutes, put a large, heavy baking tray into the oven for 10 minutes or until very hot.

Transfer the dough to a lightly floured work surface and knock back again. Divide into six portions and shape into oval balls. Working with one piece of dough, stretch it into a 30 cm long oval with your hands. If it is easier, roll the dough out lightly with a rolling pin. Scatter a little polenta over the base of the hot baking tray and transfer the stretched piece of dough to the tray. Use a sharp knife or pizza cutter to mark narrowly spaced parallel lines along the length of the dough. Brush with melted butter and sprinkle with the seeds of your choice.

Bake for 6–7 minutes, until slightly risen and a rich golden brown. Transfer the cooked loaf to a wooden board and cover with a clean tea towel.

While the bread is baking, prepare the next loaf. Continue with the remaining balls of dough.

Barberi bread is best eaten warm. Alternatively, leave it to cool completely, then wrap in plastic wrap and freeze for up to 1 month. Thaw at room temperature and reheat in a warm oven.

MAKES **3**

These are little versions of the ubiquitous Arabic khobz, also called pita or pocket bread.

JOU JOU BREAD

75 g fresh yeast | up to 1 litre warm water | 1.25 kg bakers' flour | 25 g salt | 75 ml olive oil

DISSOLVE THE YEAST IN 100 ML OF the warm water and set aside in a warm place for 10 minutes.

Combine the flour and salt in the bowl of an electric mixer fitted with a dough hook and make a well in the centre. Mix the oil with 850 ml of the remaining water and stir in the yeast mixture, then gradually work the liquid into the flour. Knead on a slow speed for 10–15 minutes until the dough is smooth, shiny and elastic — add more tepid water if necessary. Transfer to a lightly oiled bowl, then cover with a damp tea towel and leave to prove in a warm place for 2 hours or until doubled in size.

Preheat the oven to 220°C (Gas 7). Knock back the dough, then leave to prove for a further 20 minutes. After 10 minutes, put a large, heavy baking tray into the oven for 10 minutes or until very hot.

Transfer the dough to a lightly floured work surface and knock back again. Divide the dough into 3 equal portions and cover with a cloth.

Work with 1 portion at a time. Knock out the air and roll out to a large, roughly rectangular shape, about 2 mm thick. Use a 10 cm pastry cutter to cut out the jou jou breads. You should get about 8 from each portion.

Lift the jou jou breads onto the hot baking tray and bake in the oven for 1 minute, or until they balloon up and colour very lightly. Remove from the oven and transfer gently to a shallow basket lined with a cloth. Wrap up and leave while you continue with the remaining portions of dough.

MAKES **about 25**

This is our interpretation of a wonderful savoury-sweet bread we tasted in the oasis town of Mahan in south-eastern Iran. Cumin is grown in abundance in the region and flavours many of the local dishes, often in combination with turmeric. The addition of sweet, sticky dates turns this bread into an afternoon treat when served with a cup of fragrant tea.

We use a heart-shaped cutter to make the buns, as this was the way we enjoyed them in Mahan. But, obviously, you can use any shape of cutter with similar dimensions.

DATE BREAD WITH TURMERIC AND CUMIN

2 teaspoons dried yeast | 50 ml warm water | 680 g bakers' flour
60 g sugar | 1 teaspoon ground turmeric | 1 heaped teaspoon sea salt
310 ml tepid water | 30 ml olive oil | 1 egg | 15 fresh dates, pitted and cut into chunks
50 g unsalted butter, softened | 2 egg yolks, lightly beaten
1 tablespoon cumin seeds, lightly crushed | icing sugar to dust

DISSOLVE THE DRIED YEAST IN THE 50 ml warm water and set aside in a warm place for 10 minutes.

Combine the flour, sugar, turmeric and salt in the bowl of an electric mixer fitted with a dough hook and make a well in the centre. In a bowl, whisk together the tepid water, oil and whole egg, then stir in the yeast mixture. Gradually work the liquid into the flour mixture. Knead on a slow speed for 10 minutes until the dough is smooth and shiny. Transfer to a lightly oiled bowl, then cover with a damp tea towel and leave to prove in a warm place for 1 hour or until doubled in size.

Knock back the dough and leave to prove again in a warm place for 1 hour, until doubled in size.

Preheat the oven to 200°C (Gas 6). Knock back the dough again and divide it into eight even portions, then cut each in half. Working with one portion at a time, roll it out to a rectangle about 17 cm x 11 cm (or roll as appropriate for your chosen cutter), and place it crosswise in front of you. Sit a 9 cm x 8 cm heart-shaped cutter on the left side of the dough and place a few pieces of date inside it. Squish on a small piece of butter, then remove the cutter and fold the dough over, from right to left, to cover the filling. Cut out a heart shape and transfer to a baking tray. Repeat with the remaining portions of dough, then re-roll the offcuts. You should get about 20 buns in total. Leave the buns to sit on the baking tray for 15 minutes, then brush lightly with the egg yolk and sprinkle on a good pinch of cumin seeds. Bake for 6–8 minutes until puffed and golden.

Remove from the oven and cool briefly (if you have the willpower) on a wire rack before dusting with icing sugar and eating.

MAKES 20

We came across a number of different versions of hard aniseed breads in bakeries around Syria. This is our interpretation, and although quite different, it is utterly delicious, with a hint of sweetness from the aniseed and figs, a lovely crumbly texture and melting crust. The bread is wonderful served warm from the oven with lashings of cold unsalted butter or a dollop of tart jam, and it works equally well with the savoury flavours of creamy blue cheese, Brie, a strong Cheddar with bite — or, to stay Middle Eastern, a sharp, salty feta.

ANISEED BREAD WITH WILD FIGS

3 teaspoons dry yeast | pinch of sugar | 180 ml warm water
260 g semolina | 225 g bakers' flour
1 tablespoon aniseeds, plus extra to sprinkle
1 tablespoon sesame seeds, plus extra to sprinkle
100 g dried wild figs, stalks removed, diced | 1/2 teaspoon salt
180 ml olive oil | 1 egg, lightly beaten | 1 egg yolk | 1 tablespoon water

DISSOLVE THE YEAST AND SUGAR IN 140 ml of the warm water. Set aside for 10 minutes until it begins to froth.

In a large mixing bowl, combine the semolina, flour, aniseeds, sesame seeds, dried figs and salt, then mix in the oil evenly. Stir in the egg then pour in the frothy yeast. Use your hands to bring the mixture together to form a dough. Add the remaining warm water, plus a little more, if necessary. The dough should be firm, not wet or sticky.

Use your hands or the dough hook on an electric mixer to knead the dough vigorously for 10 minutes, until it is smooth and shiny. Lightly oil the ball of dough and put it into a bowl. Cover and leave in a warm place to rise for 2 hours, by which time it should have doubled in size.

Knock the dough back, then shape it into a round measuring roughly 20 cm x 3 cm thick. Put it on a lightly oiled baking tray. Whisk together the egg yolk and water and brush the top of the loaf. Sprinkle on 1/2 teaspoon aniseeds and 1 teaspoon sesame seeds and leave in a warm place for another 45 minutes.

Preheat the oven to 200°C (Gas 6) and bake the bread for 20–30 minutes, until it is a lovely golden brown. It should sound hollow when you tap the bottom. Transfer to a wire rack and leave until completely cool before eating — if you can resist!

MAKES **1 loaf**

The yoghurt in this dough results in a soft and tender crumb. Use the best-quality olives you can find for the best flavour.

OLIVE BREAD

310 g bakers' flour | 1/2 teaspoon salt | 3/4 teaspoon sugar
1 tablespoon dried yeast | 50 ml warm water | 150 g natural yoghurt
extra-virgin olive oil | 150 g green olives, chopped | 1 teaspoon fresh thyme leaves
1/2 teaspoon chilli flakes (optional)

SIFT THE FLOUR INTO A LARGE mixing bowl and add the salt. Dissolve the sugar and yeast in the warm water. In another small bowl, whisk together the yoghurt and olive oil. Pour the bubbling yeast into the flour with the yoghurt mixture. Knead for about 10 minutes, until the dough is smooth and silky. Lightly oil the ball of dough and put it in a bowl. Cover and leave in a warm place to rise for 2 hours, by which time it should have at least doubled in size.

Knock the air out of the dough then tip it out onto a floured work surface. Knead in the olives, thyme and chilli flakes and shape the dough into a round. Lift onto a lightly greased baking tray and leave in a warm place to rise for a further 45 minutes.

Preheat the oven to 200°C (Gas 6).

Brush the dough with olive oil before baking for 20–30 minutes, until it is golden brown. It should sound hollow when you tap the bottom. Transfer to a wire rack and leave until completely cool before eating.

MAKES **1 loaf**

We use this dough to make the soft, slightly chewy flatbread known throughout Australia as pide or Turkish bread. It's typically shaped into a large rectangle or oval, and the top is marked with parallel rows of indentations and sprinkled with black nigella or sesame seeds. The same dough is used to make the long, open-faced Pide Pies (pages 278–279), with all manner of savoury fillings. Like most Middle Eastern flatbreads, this is greatly improved by baking on a hot stone. Most kitchenware stores stock them — they're often called pizza stones.

TURKISH FLATBREAD

1 tablespoon dried yeast | pinch of caster sugar | 375 ml warm water
480 g bakers' flour plus extra for sprinkling | 1 teaspoon salt | 60 ml extra-virgin olive oil
2 free-range eggs | 50 ml milk | nigella or sesame seeds

DISSOLVE THE YEAST AND SUGAR IN 125 ml of the warm water and set aside in a warm place for about 10 minutes until frothy. Use your fingers to work 90 g of the flour into the yeast mixture to make a sloppy paste. Sprinkle lightly with a little more flour, then cover with a tea towel and set aside in a warm place for 30 minutes to form a 'sponge'. Put the remaining flour and the salt into a large bowl. Make a well in the centre and add the sponge, oil and remaining water. Use your fingers to work it to a soft, sloppy dough. Don't panic: it is meant to be very sticky!

Transfer to an electric mixer fitted with a dough hook and knead on a low speed for 10–15 minutes until very smooth and springy. Transfer to a lightly oiled bowl, then cover with a damp tea towel and leave to rest at room temperature for 1 hour or until doubled in size. (From this point you can proceed to bake the pide bread or filled pide pies. You can also refrigerate the dough until you are ready to use it. It will keep for about 24 hours, but take it out of the refrigerator a good 3 hours before you want to bake it, so it can return to room temperature.)

When ready to bake the bread, preheat the oven to its highest setting with two pizza stones or oiled baking trays in it. Divide the dough in two, then form into rounds and leave, covered, to rest for 30 minutes.

Mix the eggs and milk to make an egg wash. Place the dough on a lightly floured work surface. Use the heels of your hands to press and flatten each piece of dough out to a 20 cm oval. Brush the surface liberally with the egg wash. Dip your fingertips into the egg wash and mark rows of deep indentations across and down the length of the dough, leaving a narrow border.

Now comes the tricky bit. Lightly flour the hot pizza stones or trays. Lift on the pides, stretching them gently and evenly. Sprinkle with nigella or sesame seeds and bake for 8–10 minutes until crisp and golden brown.

MAKES **2**

PIDE PIES

1 quantity Turkish Flatbread dough (page 277) | 1 free-range egg yolk mixed with 50 ml milk your choice of topping (below and opposite)

CUT THE DOUGH INTO SIX EVEN portions and leave, covered, to rest for 30 minutes.

When ready to bake the pide pies, preheat the oven to its highest setting with two pizza stones or oiled baking trays in it.

Roll each portion of dough on a lightly floured work surface to form a long rectangle, about 35 cm x 10 cm. Scatter a sixth of the topping down the pide, leaving a 2 cm border. Quickly fold up the two long sides of the dough, bringing them up and over the topping, but without meeting in the middle. Squeeze the sides together at each end, twisting slightly, so that the pide looks like a long canoe.

Brush the dough with a little egg wash. Bake in batches, two at a time. Carefully transfer the pides to the hot stones or trays and bake for 7 minutes. Eat hot from the oven.

MAKES **6**

SPINACH, RAISIN AND FETA PIDE

Soak 1/3 cup roughly chopped raisins in a little water for 15 minutes, then drain. Meanwhile, bring a large saucepan of salted water to the boil and blanch 250 g washed spinach leaves in batches. Refresh in cold water, then squeeze firmly to extract any liquid. In a large bowl, mix the spinach and raisins with 1 clove garlic crushed with 1 teaspoon sea salt, 1 finely sliced shallot, 1/2 teaspoon freshly grated nutmeg, 1/2 teaspoon freshly ground black pepper, the finely grated zest of 1/2 lemon, 2 tablespoons extra-virgin olive oil and 120 g roughly crumbled feta. Top the pide pies as described above, then crumble 30 g extra feta and dot this over the open surfaces of the pides. Bake as described above.

TOPS **6 pide**

CHEESE, SUJUK AND OLIVE PIDE

Mix 250 g washed and finely sliced haloumi, 150 g finely sliced mozzarella, 18 pitted and halved kalamata olives, 1 seeded and chopped green banana pepper and 2 tablespoons extra-virgin olive oil in a large bowl, then season with sea salt and freshly ground black pepper. Top the pide pies with this mixture, as described opposite, then top the open surface of each pide with 120 g sliced sujuk and bake.

TOPS **6 pide**

CHEESE, EGG AND ONION PIDE

Mix 250 g washed and finely sliced haloumi, 150 g finely sliced mozzarella, 1 heaped teaspoon ground sumac, 1/2 teaspoon freshly ground black pepper, 1/2 teaspoon dried mint, 4 finely sliced shallots and 1 tablespoon extra-virgin olive oil in a large bowl. Top the pide pies with this mixture, as described opposite, making a shallow indentation in the topping down the middle. Carefully transfer two pides to the hot stones or trays and bake for 5 minutes. Crack an egg into a small bowl and break the yolk. When the 5 minutes is up, open the oven door and carefully slip the egg into one of the pides so it runs naturally along the length of the indentation. Repeat with another egg and the other pide. Bake for a further 2 minutes. Bake the remaining pides in two batches, repeating the step with four more eggs. Eat hot from the oven, sprinkled with a little sea salt.

TOPS **6 pide**

Lebanese pizzas — manoushi — are the number one snack food all around Lebanon and Syria. They are very similar to Italian pizzas, although the dough is a little softer and chewier. Use the base for any of the suggested toppings.

LEBANESE PIZZA

355 g bakers' flour | 1 teaspoon dried yeast | 1/2 teaspoon salt
3/4 teaspoon sugar | 175–200 ml warm water | 1 tablespoon extra-virgin olive oil
your choice of topping (below and opposite)

SIFT THE FLOUR INTO A LARGE mixing bowl and add the yeast and salt. Dissolve the sugar in the warm water and dribble it into the dry ingredients until they absorb enough to make a sticky dough. How much water is required will entirely depend upon your flour. Mix in the olive oil and use your hands — or the dough hook on your electric mixer — to knead the dough until it is smooth and silky. It will take about 10 minutes. Lightly oil the ball of dough, put it in a bowl, cover and leave in a warm place to rise for 2 hours, by which time it should have at least doubled in size.

Knock back the dough, then tip it out onto a floured work surface. Cut the dough into 12 portions, then lightly flour each one and put them on a tray, covered, for another 10 minutes. When ready to cook, roll each portion out to the desired size and 3–4 mm thick, then cover with topping and bake on a preheated pizza stone.

MAKES **10–12**

THREE CHEESE MANOUSHI

Mix 180 g chopped Blue Castello (or another mild, creamy blue cheese), 180 g coarsely grated mozzarella, 100 g coarsely grated parmesan cheese, 1 teaspoon Turkish chilli flakes and 1 tablespoon extra-virgin olive oil. Roll the manoushi dough out into rounds 10 cm in diameter and brush with olive oil. Spread the topping thinly over the rounds and bake for 4–5 minutes (a fan-forced oven may take as little as 3–4 minutes).

TOPS **10–12 manoushi**

HALOUMI, CRÈME FRAÎCHE AND SPINACH MANOUSHI

Bring a large saucepan of salted water to the boil and blanch 550 g washed spinach leaves in batches. Refresh in cold water, then squeeze firmly to extract as much liquid as you can. Place the spinach on a large chopping board and on top put 1 finely diced shallot, 1 finely diced small clove garlic, the finely grated zest of 1/2 lemon and 1/2 teaspoon dried mint. Use a very large knife to chop and mix everything together as finely as you can get it until well combined. Tip the spinach mixture into a large bowl and stir in 150 g washed and finely grated haloumi and 60 ml crème fraîche. Season with sea salt and freshly ground white pepper. Roll the manoushi dough out into rounds 10 cm in diameter and brush with olive oil. Spread the topping thinly over the rounds and bake for 6–8 minutes (a fan-forced oven may take as little as 4–5 minutes).

TOPS **10-12 manoushi**

MINCED LAMB MANOUSHI

Don't buy minced lamb from the supermarket for this recipe as it's far too fatty. You don't want the lamb to be too lean, however. Ask the butcher for leg lamb with some fat, but no sinews. Place 250 g minced lamb on a large chopping board and on top put 1 seeded and finely diced tomato, 1 finely diced small purple onion, 1/3 cup finely shredded flat-leaf parsley leaves, 1 teaspoon ground allspice, 1 seeded and finely diced red bullet chilli and 1 teaspoon pomegranate molasses. Use a large knife to chop and mix everything together until well combined. It should be the consistency of a fine paste. Season with sea salt and freshly ground black pepper. Roll the manoushi dough out into rounds 10 cm in diameter and brush with olive oil. Smear the lamb topping thinly over the rounds and bake for 3 minutes.

TOPS **10-12 manoushi**

ZA'ATAR MANOUSHI

Mix 3 tablespoons za'atar and 1 tablespoon ground sumac with enough olive oil to make a thick paste. Roll manoushi dough out into rounds 10 cm in diameter and brush with olive oil. Smear the za'atar topping thinly over the rounds and bake for 3 minutes.

TOPS **10-12 manoushi**

These little pies from Baalbeck, known as sfiha, are renowned across Lebanon.

LITTLE LAMB PIES WITH YOGHURT CHEESE AND POMEGRANATE

DOUGH **310 g bakers' flour | 1/2 teaspoon salt | 3/4 teaspoon sugar**
1 tablespoon dried yeast | 50 ml warm water | 150 g natural yoghurt
3 tablespoons extra-virgin olive oil

1 quantity Minced Lamb Manoushi topping (page 281) | Yoghurt Cheese (page 44) to serve
extra-virgin olive oil and pomegranate molasses to serve

SIFT THE FLOUR INTO A LARGE mixing bowl and add the salt. Dissolve the sugar and yeast in the warm water. In another small bowl, whisk together the yoghurt and olive oil. Pour the bubbling yeast into the flour with the yoghurt mixture. Knead for about 10 minutes, until the dough is smooth and silky. Lightly oil the ball of dough and put it into a bowl. Cover and leave in a warm place to rise for 2 hours, by which time it should have at least doubled in size.

Preheat the oven to 200°C (Gas 6). Knock back the dough then tip it out onto a floured work surface. Dust a rolling pin with flour, then roll the pastry out as thinly as you can. Cut it into 12 rounds, each about 10 cm in diameter. Place a spoonful of minced lamb mixture in the centre of each round. Moisten the edges of the pastry with a little water, then pinch the corners together to form the traditional shape.

Bake the pies for 8–10 minutes. Serve with a big dollop of yoghurt cheese, a drizzle of oil and a splash of pomegranate molasses.

MAKES **12**

In markets and villages throughout Turkey, especially in summer, women sit at low, broad tables rolling out large, thin rounds of yufka dough. These are stuffed with a filling then folded, oiled and cooked on a flat griddle to make gözleme. Hot and oozing with melted cheese, they are irresistible. Yufka pastry requires great skill and patience to make but thankfully it's available ready made from Middle Eastern food stores.

GÖZLEME

2 sheets yufka pastry | melted unsalted butter | your choice of filling (below and page 288)

OPEN OUT A SHEET OF YUFKA PASTRY so you have a large round on your work surface. Use a sharp knife to cut the pastry in half, then cut each half into three equal wedges. Stack them on top of each other and trim the curved edge straight. Repeat with the other sheet of pastry so you have a total of 12 small equilateral triangles. Working with one triangle of pastry at a time, smear a generous tablespoon of filling into the middle of the triangle, leaving a border. Brush a little melted butter on the triangle's points and fold in the points to form a small enclosed triangle. Repeat until all the pastry and filling have been used.

Heat a heavy non-stick frying pan over a medium heat. Brush the gözleme with a little more melted butter and fry for 2–3 minutes, turning once.

MAKES **12**

SPINACH AND GRUYÈRE GÖZLEME

Bring a large saucepan of salted water to the boil and blanch 550 g washed spinach leaves in batches. Refresh in cold water, then squeeze firmly to extract as much liquid as you can. Place the spinach on a large chopping board and on top put 1 finely diced shallot and 1 finely diced small clove garlic. Use a very large knife to chop and mix everything together until well combined. Season with sea salt and freshly ground white pepper and mix in 200 g finely grated gruyère. Prepare and fill the gözleme and fry in melted butter, as described above. Serve hot from the pan with a sprinkle of sea salt and a few pomegranate seeds, if you like.

FILLS **12 gözleme**

FETA AND DILL GÖZLEME

Mix 250 g grated feta, 1 lightly beaten free-range egg, 1 finely diced shallot, 1 finely diced small clove garlic and 1/2 cup chopped dill in a large bowl, then season with sea salt and freshly ground white pepper. Prepare and fill the gözleme and fry in melted butter, as described on page 286. Serve hot from the pan with a sprinkle of sea salt and a few pomegranate seeds, if you like.

FILLS **12 gözleme**

BASTOURMA AND GOAT'S CHEESE GÖZLEME

Take 240 g very thinly sliced bastourma and arrange the slices in the centre of each gözleme triangle, leaving a border. Divide 220 g crumbled soft goat's cheese among the gozleme and sprinkle them with 1 tablespoon dried mint, 1 teaspoon lemon zest and 2 tablespoons extra-virgin olive oil.

Prepare and fill the gözleme and fry in melted butter, as described on page 286. Serve hot from the pan with a sprinkle of sea salt and a few pomegranate seeds, if you like.

FILLS **12 gözleme**

Pecorino is a sharp Italian cheese made from sheep's milk. In these pies it works beautifully with the Middle Eastern combination of spinach and allspice with cubed waxy potatoes. Serve them as a starter or light lunch dish with a salad, or as an accompaniment to roast lamb or other barbecued meats.

SPINACH, PECORINO AND POTATO PIES

60 ml olive oil | 3 shallots, finely sliced | 1 clove garlic, finely chopped
1 small bullet chilli, seeded, scraped and finely shredded
200 g spinach, stalks removed and leaves finely shredded
1 large waxy potato, peeled and cut into 1 cm dice | 1/4 teaspoon ground allspice
sea salt and freshly ground black pepper | 200 ml stock or water
40 g pecorino cheese (or parmesan or grana), grated
4 sheets filo pastry | 20 g melted butter mixed with 20 ml olive oil

HEAT THE OLIVE OIL IN A HEAVY-based pan. Add the shallots, garlic and chilli and stir over a medium heat for 30 seconds. Add the shredded spinach and stir for a further minute until it collapses and softens slightly. Then add the potato dice, allspice, salt and pepper and stock and bring to the boil. Cover the pot, lower the heat and simmer for 4 minutes over a gentle heat. Then raise the heat and cook uncovered for an additional 4 minutes, to let the liquid evaporate. Remove from the heat and tip into a sieve to allow any excess moisture to drain away. Stir in the grated cheese and allow the mixture to cool.

Preheat the oven to 200°C (Gas 6). To make the pies, lay a sheet of filo out widthways and brush one half with the melted butter mixture. Fold this half over the other. Turn this smaller rectangle through 90° so it is again widthwise in front of you, and brush half with the butter mixture. Again fold it in half. You should then have a rectangle of about 14 cm x 20 cm. Trim off 6 cm from one side to make a 14 cm square. Brush with butter. Heap a quarter of the spinach mixture into a high mound in the centre of pastry. Fold the pastry sides up and over the filling and flatten them slightly to form a raised pie. Brush the pastry edges with melted butter to help them stick together and then carefully turn the pie over. Flatten and smooth the top slightly and then use the palms of both hands to shape into a neat round pie. Repeat with the remaining three sheets of pastry. Brush their surfaces with butter and cook for 8 minutes on a tray lined with baking paper.

Remove the tray from the oven and turn the pies over. Return the tray to the oven and cook a further 4 minutes until the pies are golden brown all over. Remove from the oven and serve immediately.

SERVES **4**

Serve as part of a mezze selection with a salad of mixed herbs, pickled turnips, shallots and black olives. They also make brilliant cocktail party nibbles.

LEEK, GOAT'S CHEESE AND CURRANT SPANAKOPITA CIGARS

50 ml olive oil | 2 shallots, finely sliced | 1 clove garlic, finely chopped
1 bunch spinach, stalks removed and leaves shredded | 60 g butter
3 leeks, white parts only, cut into 1 cm dice
1/3 cup currants soaked in dry sherry for 15 minutes
150 g soft goat's cheese, crumbled | 1/4 teaspoon freshly grated nutmeg
1 teaspoon dried mint | sea salt and freshly ground white pepper | 4 sheets filo pastry
vegetable oil for deep-frying

HEAT THE OLIVE OIL IN A LARGE heavy-based pan. Add the shallots and garlic and stir over a medium heat for a few minutes until they soften. Throw in the spinach leaves, turning them as they wilt down. When all the spinach has wilted, tip into a colander and press out the moisture well. Transfer to the fridge to chill.

Melt the butter in a heavy-based pan and fry the leeks very gently until soft but not coloured. Remove from the heat and leave to cool.

Drain the currants. Add to the chilled spinach with the goat's cheese, cooled leeks, currants, nutmeg and mint and season with a little salt and pepper.

Stack the sheets of filo pastry on the work surface and cut crosswise into four strips, each bout 10 cm x 17 cm. Work with one strip of pastry at a time and keep the rest covered with a tea towel. Place a spoonful of filling across one end of the strip. Fold the sides in and roll up like a cigar, sealing the sides and the end with a little water. Repeat with the remaining 15 rectangles.

Heat the oil in a small saucepan or deep-fryer to 180°C. Deep-fry the cigars for 2 minutes or until they are golden brown. Remove with a slotted spoon to drain on paper towel and keep warm while you fry the remaining cigars.

MAKES **16**

This Moroccan specialty is baked for special occasions. However, nearly all Moroccan restaurants serve it, along with the popular tagines and couscous. It is traditionally made as one large pie, from pigeon spiced with saffron and cinnamon and enriched with eggs. An alternative to pigeon is chicken, which is often substituted, but duck legs might be a better choice, with their dark, gamier meat. In Morocco, the whole pie is dusted with cinnamon and icing sugar.

These pies are only small, as the saffron and scrambled eggs make them extremely rich. Serve them on their own as a starter or maybe with some lemon-sautéed spinach as a main course.

LITTLE PIGEON BISTEEYA

3 pigeons (about 300 g each) | sea salt and freshly ground black pepper | 100 ml olive oil
1 large onion, finely chopped | 2 cloves garlic, finely chopped
1/2 teaspoon ground ginger | 8 saffron threads, lightly roasted and crushed
1/2 teaspoon ground cinnamon | 1/2 teaspoon ground cumin
1 bullet chilli, seeded and finely chopped | 60 ml dry sherry
600 ml good-quality chicken stock | 4 egg yolks | 1/2 cup chopped flat-leaf parsley leaves
1/2 cup chopped coriander leaves | 12 sheets filo pastry | 150 g melted butter
100 g flaked almonds, fried in vegetable oil and drained
100 g icing sugar | 20 g ground cinnamon

WASH THE PIGEONS AND PAT THEM dry with paper towel. Remove the necks and cut the pigeons into quarters. Season with salt and pepper.

Heat half the oil in a heavy pan and sauté the pigeon pieces until they are golden brown. Add the onion, garlic, ginger, saffron, cinnamon, cumin and chilli, adding more oil if necessary. Stir so the pigeon is well coated with spices.

Add the sherry and stock, bring to the boil, then lower the heat and simmer for 45–50 minutes, or until the pigeon is tender. When it is cool enough, remove the meat from the pigeon, discarding skin and bones, and shred it finely.

Reduce the poaching liquid by half and then add the eggs and whisk until they are well combined. Pour this mixture into a small saucepan, season and scramble over a gentle heat until it is creamy and nearly set. Stir in the parsley and fresh coriander, and check the seasonings. Allow the mixture to cool completely. Stir the meat into the egg mixture, taste for seasoning and refrigerate until it is ready to use.

To make the pies, lay two sheets of pastry side by side on your work surface and brush them with melted butter. Fold each one in half and then cut into six equal squares. Put these to one side (you will need ten of them). Lay the remaining ten filo sheets on the work surface, one by one, and brush them with melted butter. Fold them in half and brush them with butter. Fold them in half again.

Place a generous tablespoon of the meat–egg mixture in the centre of each filo square. Place one of the small pastry squares on top of the filling and scatter a teaspoon of fried almonds over the square. Brush around the filling with melted butter and then bring the surrounding pastry sides up and over the filling to form a ball. Turn the pie over and, with the palms of your hands, gently shape it into a raised circular pie. Flatten the top slightly and refrigerate the pie until you are ready to bake.

Place the pies on a greased oven tray and bake in preheated 180°C (Gas 4) oven for 10–15 minutes until they are golden brown.

Sift the icing sugar and cinnamon together. Remove the pies from the oven and dust them with cinnamon sugar. Use a paper doily to create a pretty pattern on the surface, if you like. Serve immediately.

MAKES **10 little pies**

OPPOSITE LITTLE PIGEON BISTEEYA (PAGE 292)

CORIANDER AND PRAWN BRIOUATS

240 g raw prawn meat | 1 tablespoon olive oil | 2 shallots, finely sliced
1 tablespoon Chermoula (page 383) | 1/2 cup roughly chopped mint leaves
1/2 cup roughly chopped coriander leaves | 1 egg yolk
sea salt and freshly ground black pepper | 3 sheets filo pastry
1 egg mixed with 1 teaspoon water | 200 ml vegetable oil for shallow-frying
Preserved Lemon Guacamole (page 53), Green Harissa (page 381) or
Chopped Egg, Coriander and Lemon Dressing (page 132) to serve

CHOP THE PRAWN MEAT INTO smallish pieces, about 5 mm.

Heat the olive oil in a frying pan then add the shallots and chermoula and stir for a minute to bring out the flavour of the spices. Remove from the heat and add to the prawn meat. Then add the mint, coriander and egg yolk, season with salt and pepper, and mix together lightly.

Lay a sheet of filo out and cut it into thirds lengthwise. Each strip makes one briouat. Take one strip and brush with egg wash. Place 1 tablespoon of prawn mixture across the corner of one end. Fold this corner up and over on the diagonal, to make a triangle shape. Fold the triangle over, and continue in this fashion all along the pastry strip. Trim any extra little pieces of pastry. You should end up with a nice triangle-shaped pastry parcel. Seal any open edges with egg wash. Repeat to make 7 more pastries.

Shallow-fry the pastries — a wok is ideal — two at a time until they are golden brown. It should take about 2 minutes on each side. If they brown too quickly, lower the temperature, wait a few minutes and try again.

Remove them from the oil and drain on paper towel, then serve hot.

SERVES 4 as a starter

Here, the classic Middle Eastern combination of spinach (you could also use silverbeet) and cheese is lifted with a dash of pomegranate essence. Hazelnuts give crunch, although traditionalists would probably use pine nuts. Serve sambusek as a snack, as party nibbles or as a mezze dish. Sambusek are also good as a starter drizzled with a tangy Parsnip Skordalia (page 248) or the Chopped Egg, Coriander and Lemon Dressing (page 132).

SAMBUSEK

PASTRY **200 g self-raising flour | 30 g butter, chilled | 1/4 teaspoon salt**
pinch of sugar | 50–100 ml warm water

FILLING **30 ml olive oil | 2 shallots, finely chopped**
1 clove garlic crushed with 1/4 teaspoon salt
2 bunches spinach, stems removed, leaves picked and washed twice
100 g toasted hazelnuts, skins rubbed away | 50 g feta cheese
1/4 teaspoon ground allspice | juice and finely chopped zest of 1 lemon
1 tablespoon hazelnut oil (or any other nut oil) | 1 teaspoon pomegranate molasses
1 egg mixed with 1 teaspoon water

TO MAKE THE PASTRY, WHIZ THE flour, chilled butter, salt and sugar in a food processor until the mixture is the consistency of fine breadcrumbs. Gradually add enough lukewarm water for the mixture to just come together in a dough. Allow to rest for half an hour before using.

To make the filling, heat the oil in a pan and sauté the shallots and garlic for 3–4 minutes until they have softened. Throw in the spinach leaves, turning them as they wilt down. When all the spinach has collapsed and softened, tip it into a colander and press out the moisture well.

Lightly crush the hazelnuts in a mortar and pestle. Put the spinach into a mixing bowl and add the hazelnuts, feta, allspice, lemon juice and zest, hazelnut oil and pomegranate molasses and mix together thoroughly.

Preheat the oven to 200°C (Gas 6). To make the sambusek, use an oiled rolling pin (or glass bottle) to roll out the pastry on a floured surface to about 3 mm thick. Cut out pastry circles using an 8 cm pastry cutter and brush half with the egg wash. Place a tablespoon of the mixture into the centre of the circle. Fold the pastry over to make a half-moon shape and pinch or crimp the edges to seal. Brush with more egg wash and place the pastries on a non-stick baking tray. Bake on the middle shelf for 10 minutes or until golden brown.

MAKES **about 15**

This wonderfully useful pastry is perfect for making all kinds of open tarts and savoury pastries, such as Turkish böreks. It's soft, silky, easy to work with and bakes to a lovely short flakiness. The method below is a variation on a classic 'rough puff'; brushing with butter, folding and turning to create meltingly crisp layers.

This makes 600 g pastry, enough for four big böreks, each of which will give about six slices. Serve as part of a mezze selection or as nibbles at a drinks party.

YOGHURT PASTRY FOR BÖREKS

**100 g thick natural yoghurt | 160 g melted unsalted butter (at room temperature)
1 tablespoon extra-virgin olive oil | 1 free-range egg | 220 g self-raising flour, sifted
pinch of sea salt | finely grated zest of 1/2 lemon | your choice of filling (opposite)
1 free-range egg yolk mixed with 50 ml milk**

COMBINE THE YOGHURT, 125 G OF the melted butter and the oil in the bowl of an electric mixer, then beat in the egg. Tip in the flour, salt and zest and beat on a low speed for 5 minutes until silky and soft. Cover the pastry with plastic wrap and refrigerate for 1 hour to rest and firm up a little.

Divide the pastry into two equal pieces. Work with one piece of pastry at a time, keeping the other covered with a damp tea towel. On a lightly floured work surface, roll the pastry out as thinly as you can to make a large round — about 50 cm in diameter or as close to that as you can make it. Brush lightly with some of the remaining melted butter, then fold in two sides of the pastry to meet in the middle. Brush with butter again, then fold one side on top of the other, so you have a rectangle. Brush with butter again, then fold in the short sides of the rectangle to meet in the middle. Brush with butter for a final time and fold one side on top of the other. Set aside, covered with a damp tea towel, to rest for 15 minutes. Repeat with the other piece of dough.

When ready to make the böreks, preheat the oven to 170°C (Gas 3–4) and lightly grease a large baking tray. Cut each piece of pastry in half to give four portions. On a lightly floured work surface, roll out each piece to a large rectangle about 2 mm thick. Sprinkle your choice of filling over the long edge and roll up to form a long log. Pinch the short ends to seal. Repeat with the other pieces of pastry.

Transfer the four logs to the prepared baking trays, seam side down and with the sealed ends tucked underneath. Brush the pastries with egg wash and bake for 20 minutes until golden brown. Allow to cool a little, then cut each log into six slices, using a serrated knife, and serve immediately.

MAKES **4 large böreks**

PUMPKIN AND FETA BÖREK

Steam 700 g peeled and diced butternut pumpkin for about 10 minutes, or until tender, then tip into a large bowl. Meanwhile, melt 20 g butter in a heavy-based frying pan and sauté 1 finely diced small onion and 1 finely diced clove garlic for about 5 minutes, until soft and translucent. Add to the pumpkin with 1/2 teaspoon freshly grated nutmeg, 1/2 teaspoon freshly ground black pepper, 1/2 teaspoon hot paprika, 1/4 cup shredded flat-leaf parsley leaves and 200 g roughly crumbled feta. Mash with a fork until very smooth. Fill the böreks and bake as described opposite.

FILLS **4 large börek**

SPINACH AND CHEESE BÖREK

Bring a large saucepan of salted water to the boil and blanch 550 g washed spinach leaves in batches. Refresh in cold water, then squeeze firmly to extract as much liquid as you can. Place the spinach on a large chopping board and put 1 finely diced shallot and 1 finely diced small clove garlic on top. Use a very large knife to chop and mix everything together until well combined. Season with sea salt and freshly ground white pepper. Transfer to a bowl and mix in 180 g crumbled kashkeval cheese. Fill the böreks and bake as described opposite. (Kashkeval is a stongly flavoured, hard white sheep's milk cheese that is fairly widely available in Middle Eastern stores, but you could substitute feta, mozzarella or even a blue cheese.)

FILLS **4 large börek**

LAMB AND PINE NUT BÖREK

Thoroughly combine 2 tablespoons ground cumin, 2 tablespoons sweet paprika, 1 tablespoon hot paprika, 1 tablespoon freshly grated nutmeg and 1 tablespoon freshly ground black pepper and store in a jar for up to 3 months. Combine 500 g minced lamb, 1 finely chopped small purple onion, 1 finely chopped clove garlic, 1 tablespoon extra-virgin olive oil, 1/4 cup shredded flat-leaf parsley leaves, 3 teaspoons of the spice mix and 1 teaspoon sea salt in a bowl. Use your hands to knead the mixture to a smooth, homogeneous paste. Fill the böreks and bake as described opposite.

FILLS **4 large börek**

The combination of dill and fresh cheese is very popular in the Middle East and Eastern Mediterranean. These airy golden choux balls are terrific with a glass of chilled bubbles as a pre-dinner snack. The quantities will make 30–40 croquettes.

GREEK LEEK CROQUETTES

2 medium leeks, white part only, finely sliced | 1 clove garlic, finely sliced
1 tablespoon butter | 200 ml good-quality chicken stock | 1 bay leaf
sea salt and freshly ground black pepper | vegetable oil, for frying
1–2 teaspoons warmed leatherwood honey or maple syrup to drizzle

PASTRY 500 ml water | 125 g unsalted butter | 250 g plain flour | 1/2 teaspoon sea salt
pinch of nutmeg | 4–5 large eggs | 125 g crumbled goat's cheese
25 g grated parmesan | 1/2 tablespoon finely chopped dill

SAUTÉ THE LEEK AND GARLIC IN THE butter for a few minutes until they soften. Pour in the chicken stock and add the bay leaf, salt and pepper. Cut out a circle of baking paper large enough to cover the leek mixture (this stops a skin forming as it slowly cooks down), lower the heat and cook very gently for 25 minutes, until the mixture has reduced to a lovely soft mass. Remove the pan from the heat and allow the mixture to cool. Peel away the paper and tip the leeks into a food processor. Pulse a few times to make a coarse purée. Set aside.

To make the pastry, put the water and butter in a large saucepan and slowly bring to the boil so that the butter completely dissolves. As the liquid boils, quickly add all the flour and salt at once, and mix well with a wooden spoon to incorporate into the liquid. Continue cooking over a low heat for about 8 minutes, until the mixture is glossy and comes away from the sides of the pan in a smooth ball.

Tip the pastry into an electric mixer and beat for a few minutes on medium speed. Add the leek purée and then the eggs, one at a time, beating constantly. Depending on the flour, you may only need 4 eggs, but if the mixture is too stiff, add another. When all the eggs are incorporated, quickly mix in the cheeses, dill salt and nutmeg. Refrigerate the mixture until completely cold. (You can make the mixture up to a day ahead of time.)

Heat the oil in a deep-fryer or saucepan to 180°C, or until a cube of bread dropped in sizzles to the surface in about 30 seconds. Shape the mixture into mini golfballs and deep-fry until they are golden brown and starting to split. Drain on paper towel and serve immediately, drizzled with a little warmed honey.

MAKES 30–40

These golden puffs of airy choux pastry are rolled in toasted almond flakes before deep-frying and then drizzled with a floral honey syrup. A deep-fryer makes the task easy, but you can manage just as successfully with a small saucepan of oil. If you don't have a thermometer, test whether the oil is hot enough by dropping in a small cube of bread. If it sizzles slowly to the top, turning golden brown in about 30 seconds, you can proceed.

ALMOND FRITTERS

50 g unsalted butter | 3 teaspoons honey | 100 ml milk | 100 ml water
100 g plain flour | 4 free-range eggs | 1 litre vegetable oil for deep-frying
150 g flaked almonds | icing sugar to dust
Saffron-Honey Ice Cream with Candied Ginger (page 338) to serve

BRING THE BUTTER, HONEY, MILK and water to the boil. Add the flour and beat vigorously for 4–5 minutes until the dough comes cleanly away from the side of the pan and forms a ball. Place the dough in an electric mixer and beat in the eggs one at a time. Cover and refrigerate the mixture until ready to fry.

Heat oil to 160°C (or test with a cube of bread). Shape the fritter dough into smallish egg shapes using two dessertspoons. Roll each fritter in almond flakes then deep-fry, four at a time, until the pastry is golden brown and starting to split. Dust with icing sugar and serve immediately with ice cream.

SERVES **4-6**

PROFITEROLES WITH THICK FIG CREAM

THICK FIG CREAM **150 g dried figs, roughly chopped | 50 g caster sugar | 200 ml water | juice of 1/2 lemon | 300 ml cream (35% fat), chilled | 2 tablespoons thick natural yoghurt | 1/4 cup icing sugar | lemon or orange juice (optional)**

CHOUX PASTRY **75 ml water | 75 ml milk | 70 g unsalted butter | 80 g plain flour, sifted | 3 free-range eggs | zest of 1/2 lemon | 1/2 teaspoon ground cinnamon**

3 teaspoons ground cinnamon | 1 1/2 tablespoons caster sugar

TO MAKE THE THICK FIG CREAM, bring the figs, caster sugar, water and lemon juice to a boil in a small, heavy-based saucepan over a medium heat. Lower the heat and simmer gently for about 15 minutes, or until the figs break down to a paste. Cool for a few minutes, then whiz to a smooth purée in a food processor. Set aside until ready to serve, but don't refrigerate.

Whip the cream, yoghurt and icing sugar to medium-stiff peaks, then chill until ready to use.

To make the choux pastry, preheat the oven to 180°C (Gas 4). Line baking trays with baking paper. Combine the water, milk and butter in a heavy-based saucepan over a medium heat until the butter melts, then bring to a boil. Add the flour all at once and beat vigorously with a wooden spoon until the dough comes together as a smooth paste. Lower the heat and continue beating until the paste thickens and dries and comes away from the sides of the pan in a ball.

Tip the choux pastry into the bowl of an electric mixer fitted with a paddle beater and leave to cool for a minute. With the mixer on low speed, add the eggs, one at a time, ensuring that each is thoroughly incorporated before you add the next. Continue beating until you have a smooth, stiff paste. Briefly beat in the lemon zest and cinnamon.

Spoon heaped tablespoons of the choux pastry onto the prepared baking trays, leaving about 5 cm between each one to allow for expansion — you should get 24 profiteroles. Bake for 10 minutes, then decrease the heat to 140°C (Gas 1) and bake for a further 15–20 minutes, or until the profiteroles are puffed and golden. Transfer to a wire rack and pierce the side of each profiterole to release the hot air — this prevents them from becoming soggy.

When ready to serve, take the chilled cream out of the fridge and loosely fold in the fig paste. If the paste is very stiff, loosen it first with a little lemon or orange juice. Use a sharp knife to cut the tops off the profiteroles and fill each with a generous spoonful of the cream, then replace the tops. Mix the cinnamon with the caster sugar and dust on the profiteroles. Serve straight away with a cup of tea or coffee or as a dessert, with fresh berries.

MAKES **24**

Iranian zoolbia — light-as-air, delicate spiral fritters — are known as jalebi in India, and in parts of the Middle East as mushabek. Traditionally they are dropped straight from the hot oil into a sugar syrup, and become sticky and translucent. We prefer to dust them with a spiced sugar, as this way they retain their crispness and are less tooth-achingly sweet.

Some batter recipes call for bicarbonate of soda as a leavening agent but we prefer the texture and flavour yeast provides. This batter holds up really well, and if you leave it to stand overnight, the flavours develop beautifully. Serve the fritters as a sweet treat or with fried bananas and maple syrup for breakfast.

CRUNCHY FRITTERS WITH SPICED SUGAR

120 g icing sugar | 50 g ground pistachios | 1/2 teaspoon ground cardamom
vegetable oil for deep-frying

FRITTER BATTER **175 g plain flour | 1 tablespoon dried yeast | 250 ml warm water**
75 g thick natural yoghurt | 2 tablespoons Saffron Liquid (page 218) | pinch of sea salt

COMBINE THE ICING SUGAR, pistachios and cardamom well and store in an airtight jar until ready to use.

To make the batter, sift the flour into a bowl. Sprinkle on the yeast, then whisk in the warm water and yoghurt to form a batter. Stir in the saffron liquid and salt, then cover and leave to stand for at least 2 hours or up to 12 hours.

Pour vegetable oil into a small, deep, heavy-based saucepan to a depth of 5 cm. Heat the oil to 190°C. If you don't have a candy thermometer, the oil will have reached temperature when it is shimmering, and when a blob of batter sizzles up to the surface in a few seconds.

Pour the batter into a piping bag fitted with a narrow nozzle, or into a plastic squeezy bottle. Pipe the batter into the oil, working from the centre outwards in a spiral. Use the size of the saucepan as the template for your fritter size. Don't worry if you do not make a perfect spiral, as a free-form, lacy effect is just as pretty. Cook for 1–2 minutes, moving the fritter in the hot oil with a slotted spoon so it colours evenly. Once the batter has set, turn it over in the oil to colour. Lift the fritter out of the oil with a slotted spoon and drain on paper towel for a moment. Repeat with the remaining batter. Dust the spiced sugar over the fritters and enjoy with a cup of strong coffee or tea.

MAKES **about 15**

Once the dough has proved and doubled in bulk, you can transfer it to the fridge, where it will keep quite happily for up to four days.

LEBANESE DOUGHNUTS WITH LEMON SYRUP

LEMON SYRUP **300 g caster sugar | 100 ml water | 40 ml lemon juice | 20 g corn syrup | 1 vanilla bean, split and seeds scraped (optional)**

DOUGHNUTS **10 g dried yeast | 600 g plain flour | pinch of salt | 70 g caster sugar | 440 ml milk | 70 g unsalted butter | 3 free-range eggs | 1 egg yolk | candied lemon zest (optional) | ice cream to serve**

COMBINE ALL THE LEMON SYRUP ingredients in a large heavy-based saucepan and heat gently, stirring to dissolve the sugar. Bring to the boil, then remove from the heat and leave to cool.

To make the doughnuts, mix the yeast, flour and salt in a large mixing bowl. Gently heat the sugar and milk in a saucepan to dissolve the sugar. Do not boil. Pour onto the butter and stir to melt. Leave until it cools to lukewarm, then whisk the eggs and egg yolk into the liquid. Pour the liquid into the flour and stir in with a wooden spoon until the batter is smooth. Cover the bowl and leave in a warm, draught-free spot for 1 hour, by which time the dough should have doubled in size.

When ready to cook, heat the oil in a large saucepan or deep-fryer to 180°C, or until a blob of batter sizzles up to the surface in a few seconds. Shape the dough into little quenelles using two teaspoons and drop them into the oil, or spoon the dough into a piping bag fitted with a wide, plain nozzle and hold it above the hot oil. Squeeze gently, snipping the batter with scissors into small, even, round blobs as it falls. The doughnuts should be the size of a small walnut. Fry 8–10 doughnuts at a time for 2–3 minutes until a deep golden brown. Move them around in the oil with a large slotted spoon, so they colour evenly. Scoop the doughnuts out of the oil straight into the pan of syrup and leave for a few minutes to soak.

They are particularly good with a tart ice cream; try the Saffron–Honey Ice Cream with Candied Ginger (page 338) or Syrian Apricot Ice Cream (page 333) or a good-quality purchased vanilla or lemon ice cream. For an extra lemon hit, garnish with candied lemon zest.

MAKES **24 small doughnuts**

Every country in the Middle East and Eastern Mediterranean does its own thing with baklava, small, nutty pastries drenched in a lightly perfumed sugar syrup. Some versions favour ground pistachios as a filling, others prefer ground almonds or walnuts. Sometimes a touch of cinnamon is included with the nuts, or honey is added to the syrup. These cigar baklava are one of our favourite varieties.

GREG'S CIGAR BAKLAVA

100 g walnuts | 100 g whole blanched almonds | 100 g unsalted pistachio kernels
1/2 teaspoon ground cinnamon | 1/4 teaspoon grated nutmeg
1/2 teaspoon ground ginger | 8 sheets filo pastry | clarified butter
2 tablespoons finely ground unsalted pistachio kernels to garnish

ORANGE-FLOWER SYRUP **500 g caster sugar | 350 ml water | 1 cinnamon stick**
1 vanilla pod, split | 2 teaspoons orange-flower water

TIP THE NUTS AND SPICES INTO A food processor and pulse until quite finely ground. Preheat the oven to 160°C (Gas 3) and lightly grease a large baking tray.

Stack four sheets of filo pastry on a work surface, brushing each liberally with clarified butter as you go. Cover the other four sheets with a damp tea towel until needed. Cut each stack crosswise into eight strips and brush with more butter. Sprinkle a line of nut mixture along the length of each strip. Place a metal skewer along the edge and roll the pastry around it tightly. Push the ends together to create a crimped effect. Carefully pull out the skewer and place the cigar on a heavy-based baking tray. Repeat with the remaining filo strips to fill the tray — you should make a total of 16 cigars. Repeat with the other four filo sheets so you have 32 cigars. Brush with more butter and bake for about 30 minutes.

To make the syrup, dissolve the sugar in the water in a small, heavy-based saucepan over a gentle heat, swirling the pan from time to time. Bring to the boil, then reduce to a simmer and add the cinnamon stick and vanilla pod. Simmer for 10 minutes.

Increase the oven temperature to 175°C (Gas 4) and cook the cigars for a further 10 minutes, or until golden brown. Add the orange-flower water to the syrup and increase the heat until it is vigorously bubbling. Remove the tray from the oven and place over a medium flame on the stovetop. Heat for 10 seconds then pour the boiling syrup over the cigars until they are drenched.

Remove from the heat and allow to cool to room temperature (do not refrigerate). When ready to serve, trim the ends with a serrated knife, cut the cigars in half and sprinkle with ground pistachios.

MAKES **32**

Persian baklava is particularly delicious. It's generally made from ground almonds scented with cardamom, and soaked in a light rosewater syrup. Some versions have a base of almonds, topped with a pretty green pistachio layer. Here, a little lime juice added to the syrup helps balance the intense sweetness of the baklava. Serve in small amounts; it is extremely rich.

PERSIAN BAKLAVA WITH ROSE-LIME SYRUP

clarified butter | 300 g ground almonds | 200 g caster sugar | 2 teaspoons ground cardamom
6 sheets filo pastry | 3 tablespoons pistachio slivers (optional) | dried rose petals (optional)

ROSE-LIME SYRUP 300 g caster sugar | 150 ml water | 2 tablespoons rosewater
1 tablespoon lime juice

TO MAKE THE ROSE-LIME SYRUP, dissolve the caster sugar in the water in a small, heavy-based saucepan over a gentle heat, swirling the pan from time to time. Increase the heat and simmer for 10 minutes until the syrup thickens. Remove the pan from the heat and allow to cool for 5 minutes before stirring in the rosewater and lime juice. Set aside.

Preheat the oven to 180°C (Gas 4) and brush a 28 cm x 18 cm baking tin with clarified butter. To make the filling, combine the ground almonds, sugar and cardamom in a bowl.

Work with one sheet of filo at a time and keep the rest covered with a damp tea towel. Lay a sheet of filo on a work surface with the long side facing you. Brush the filo with melted clarified butter and fold it in half from left to right. Line the prepared tin with the pastry (it should be a close fit) and brush with a little more clarified butter. Repeat with two more sheets of filo. Use a sharp knife to trim the layers to fit the base of the tin neatly.

Tip the almond filling into the tin and use your fingers to press it in evenly and firmly. Butter another layer of filo and fold in half, as before, then brush with clarified butter and place it, buttered side down, on top of the filling. Brush with a little more clarified butter and repeat with the remaining two sheets of filo. Finally, brush the top layer of pastry with more butter. Trim the edges neatly.

Cut the baklava on the diagonal into about 30 small diamond shapes with a sharp knife. Make sure you cut right through to the bottom, and try to avoid moving the top pastry layers. Sprinkle the surface with a few drops of water and bake for 15 minutes. Check that the pastry is not browning too quickly; if it is, cover loosely with aluminium foil. Bake for a further 15 minutes, or until golden brown.

Remove from the oven and immediately drizzle the rose-lime syrup over the baklava, allowing it to seep into all the cuts. If you like, garnish with pistachio slivers or rose petals, then set aside to cool. When completely cold, cover tightly with aluminium foil and store in a cool place until ready to serve. The baklava will keep in the refrigerator for up to a week. Return to room temperature before serving with black tea or as an after-dinner treat with strong black coffee.

MAKES 30 pieces

These little raised pies are made from fresh curd cheese, flavoured with honey, orange zest and sherry-soaked currants. Serve them with rose-scented fresh figs, fresh white peaches in caramel, mixed summer berries, or simply a drizzle of maple syrup.

HONEY-CURD PIES WITH ROSE-SCENTED FIGS

225 g fresh curd cheese
2 tablespoons currants, soaked in 2 tablespoons dry sherry for 10 minutes
4 tablespoons flaked almonds | zest of 1 lemon, finely chopped
1 teaspoon ground cinnamon | 1 free-range egg | 4 tablespoons mild honey
6 sheets filo pastry | 30 g butter, melted | 12 fresh ripe figs
6 teaspoons rosewater | 200 g caster sugar | 2 kg ice cubes | icing sugar to dust
cream to serve

PREHEAT THE OVEN TO 200°C (GAS 6).

In a large bowl, mix together the cheese, currants and any excess sherry, almonds, zest, cinnamon, egg and 1 tablespoon of the honey until they are well blended.

Work with one sheet of filo at a time and keep the rest covered with a damp tea towel. Lay a sheet of filo on your work surface with the long side facing you. Brush it with melted butter and fold it in half from left to right. Repeat the folding and brushing twice more. Place a heaped teaspoon of the cheese mixture in the centre of each pastry square. Brush the sides with more butter then gather up the corners and sides over the mixture, and flatten slightly to form a little ball-shaped pie. Repeat with the remaining pastry and filling to make a total of 6 pies. Place the pies on a lightly greased baking tray, brush them all over with butter and cook on the top shelf of the oven for 8–10 minutes until golden brown.

Meanwhile, cut the figs in half and lay them, cut side up, in a flat dish. Sprinkle with the rosewater and sugar. Then pour ice cubes into a deep metal tray and lay the dish of figs on top of them (this ensures the figs don't cook through). Place the tray under a very hot preheated griller for 1–2 minutes until the figs caramelise.

To serve, remove the pastries from the oven and dust them with a little icing sugar. Serve immediately with the rose-flavoured figs and cream.

SERVES 6

There are endless different ways to make cheesecake, but this has to be a winner. It is baked in a water bath, which keeps the cooking gentle, and results in a smooth, creamy filling. The topping adds a pretty line of colour, and helps tone down the honey sweetness.

HONEY AND CINNAMON CHEESECAKE

BASE **150 g ginger biscuits | 75 g unsalted butter, melted**

FILLING **625 g cream cheese, softened | 125 g honey | 3 large free-range eggs 3 large egg yolks | 2 teaspoons vanilla extract | 1 tablespoon lemon juice**

TOPPING **200 ml sour cream | 1 tablespoon caster sugar | 1/2 tablespoon ground cinnamon**

BUTTER THE BASE OF A 23 CM springform tin, then line with a circle of baking paper.

To make the base, put the biscuits in a food processor and whiz to fine crumbs. Add the butter and pulse until combined. Tip into the springform tin and press firmly and evenly into the base only. Put into the freezer for 10 minutes to set.

Preheat the oven to 160°C (Gas 3).

To make the filling, beat the cream cheese until soft and smooth, then gradually pour in the honey. Beat in the eggs and egg yolks one by one, mixing well after each addition. Finally, add the vanilla and lemon juice.

Wrap the outside of the springform tin with two large sheets of strong foil. This is important as it prevents water from seeping into the cheesecake through the base of the tin during the cooking. Place the tin in a deep baking dish. Pour the filling into the springform tin.

Pour enough hot water into the baking dish to reach halfway up the sides of the cake tin. Put the dish in the centre of the oven and cook for 50 minutes, by which time it should be slightly firm on top, but still a little wobbly beneath the surface.

To make the topping, whisk together the sour cream, sugar and cinnamon and pour carefully over the cheesecake. Return it to the oven and cook for a further 10 minutes.

Remove the tin from the oven and carefully remove the foil case. Place the tin on a wire rack and allow to cool completely. Then refrigerate until ready to eat. It is best at room temperature, so remove from the fridge about 20 minutes ahead of time and unmould it from the tin only at the very last moment. Serve on its own, or with chilled fresh black figs.

SERVES **10-12**

This cake uses both fresh grated ginger and ground ginger. It is deliciously moist, and mouth tinglingly hot and gingery. Serve at tea-time with lemon icing or as a dessert with whipped cream, a dollop of crème fraîche or Toasted Almond-orange Praline Ice Cream (page 333).

STICKY GINGER CAKE

220 g golden syrup | 170 g sour cream | 110 g soft brown sugar | 2 eggs
4 teaspoons grated fresh ginger | 1 teaspoon grated lemon zest | 280 g unsalted butter
130 g plain flour | 130 g self-raising flour | 1 teaspoon baking powder | 1/2 teaspoon salt
1 teaspoon ground ginger | 4 tablespoons ground pistachios

PREHEAT THE OVEN TO 180°C (GAS 4). Thoroughly grease a 20 cm springform tin.

Whisk together the golden syrup, sour cream, brown sugar, eggs, grated ginger and lemon zest. Melt the butter and whisk it into the mixture. Sift the flours, baking powder, salt and ground ginger together twice. Fold into the warm batter, whisking gently if necessary to break down any residual lumps of flour. The batter will be fairly runny.

Tip the batter into the prepared tin and bake in the centre of the oven for 35–45 minutes, or until a skewer comes out clean.

Remove the cake from the oven and cool for a few minutes before removing from the tin. When completely cold, smother the cake with lemon icing or whipped cream. Sprinkle with ground pistachios and serve.

SERVES **8**

A sophisticated and exotic variation on the more familiar flourless chocolate almond cake. Pistachios are pricier than almonds (especially if you use top-notch Iranian ones), but they are worth it for the subtle yet distinctive flavour they add. Like its almond-based cousin, this cake cracks and sinks after baking. Don't panic! Feel free to serve it with a heavy dredging of icing sugar to cover the cracks, and perhaps some fresh raspberries. For a special occasion, and an impressive presentation, top with a mounded dome of cream and cover with a glossy coating of ganache icing.

CHOCOLATE PISTACHIO CAKE

CAKE **150 g best-quality dark chocolate | 150 g caster sugar | 150 g unsalted pistachio kernels | 150 g unsalted butter, softened | 6 large eggs, separated | pinch of salt | 2–4 tablespoons pistachio slivers to garnish**

ICING **200 g best-quality dark chocolate | 2 tablespoons honey | 80 g unsalted butter**

CREAM DOME **300 ml cream (45% fat) | 1 tablespoon honey | splash of orange-flower water**

PREHEAT THE OVEN TO 190°C (GAS 5). Grease and line a 23 cm springform tin.

To make the cake, melt the chocolate. In a food processor whiz 50 g of the sugar with the pistachios until they turn into a fine dust. Add the butter and an additional 50 g of the sugar, and process until smooth. Add the egg yolks, one at a time, mixing well after each addition. When all the eggs have been added, and with the motor running, slowly pour in the melted chocolate.

In a spotlessly clean bowl of an electric mixer, whisk the egg whites with the salt. As peaks start to form, slowly add the remaining 50 g sugar until you have a glossy and firm mound. Add a large spoonful to the batter in the food processor and pulse a few times to slacken the mixture. Then carefully fold the remaining batter into the egg whites.

Pour the batter into the prepared tin and bake for 20 minutes, then turn the oven down to 180°C (Gas 4) and cook for a further 20–30 minutes, or until cooked. The cake will be ready when it starts to come away from the sides of the tin. Allow to cool in the tin before carefully turning it out. The cake should be completely cold before icing.

To make the icing, break the chocolate into pieces and place in a heavy pan with the honey and butter. Heat gently, whisking from time to time, until the chocolate has completely melted. Remove from the heat and leave to cool. The icing should be at the same temperature as the cream or it will melt it.

While the icing is cooling, whip the cream with the honey and orange-flower water to form stiff peaks. Dollop the cream on top of the cake and smooth it into a generous dome shape. Pour on the icing very slowly so it covers the surface and sides of the cake evenly. Don't be tempted to rush, or to use a spatula, or you will not achieve a smooth, glossy finish. Decorate with the pistachios and serve.

SERVES **10–12**

We love the intense orangeness of this delicious moist cake, accentuated by the warm syrup that is spooned over the cake as it cools. The crumb is delectably soft, and the touch of cardamom in the batter adds an exotic note.

ORANGE CARDAMOM SOUR CREAM CAKE

CAKE **130 g unsalted butter, softened | 200 g caster sugar | grated zest of 1 orange and 1 lemon | 1/2 teaspoon vanilla extract | 2 large free-range eggs | 225 g plain flour | 1 teaspoon cardamom seeds, finely ground and sieved | 1 1/2 teaspoons baking powder | 1/2 teaspoon salt | 200 ml sour cream**

SYRUP **juice of 1 orange | juice of 1/2 lemon | 3 tablespoons Cointreau | 3 tablespoons caster sugar | 6 cardamom pods, cracked | 1 cinnamon stick**

PREHEAT THE OVEN TO 170°C (GAS 3–4). Grease and line a 23 cm springform cake tin.

To make the cake, cream the butter and sugar together until pale, then add the citrus zests and vanilla extract. Beat in the eggs, one at a time. Sift the flour with the cardamom, baking powder and salt. Add the flour mixture to the batter, alternating with the sour cream, mixing well on low speed after each addition. Tip the mixture into the prepared tin and bake for 50–60 minutes, or until the cake is springy to the touch and a skewer inserted in the middle comes out clean.

While the cake is cooking, combine all the syrup ingredients in a small saucepan and heat gently to dissolve the sugar, then simmer for 2–3 minutes. Strain and discard the cardamom and cinnamon.

As soon as the cake is out of the oven, pierce the top all over with a skewer and pour over the syrup. Try to ensure it is soaked up evenly. Place the tin on a wire rack and leave it to cool completely before releasing from the tin.

SERVES **10–12**

These moist, tangy cakes are delicious on their own with a cup of coffee, or served with a big blob of thick cream and some fresh berries.

LITTLE LEMON-YOGHURT CAKES

250 g unsalted butter, softened | 200 g caster sugar | 4 teaspoons lemon zest | 4 eggs | 50 g plain flour | 2 teaspoons baking powder | 250 g fine semolina | 200 g ground almonds | 6 tablespoons lemon juice | 120 g natural yoghurt

SYRUP **250 ml lemon juice | 175 g caster sugar | 1/2 tablespoon brandy**

PREHEAT THE OVEN TO 180°C (GAS 4). Thoroughly grease two large six-hole muffin tins or twelve 10 cm rectangular mini-loaf tins.

Cream together the butter, sugar and lemon zest until the mixture is pale and smooth. Beat in the eggs, one by one, ensuring each one is completely incorporated before adding the next. Sift the flour and baking powder over the top, add the semolina and ground almonds and gently fold in. Then mix in the lemon juice and yoghurt.

Pour the mixture into the prepared tins so they are two-thirds full. Bake for 20–30 minutes, or until the cakes are firm to the touch and golden brown.

While the cakes are cooking, combine the lemon juice, sugar and brandy in a small pan and bring to the boil. Reduce the heat and simmer for 5 minutes. Remove the cakes from the oven and pierce them all over with a skewer. Pour the syrup over the hot cakes and allow it to soak in. Leave to cool in the tins before turning out. The cakes will keep well in an airtight container for 2–3 days.

MAKES **12 small cakes**

CARDAMOM-ORANGE WAFERS

60 g caster sugar | 60 g plain flour | finely grated zest of 1 orange
1/4 teaspoon cardamom seeds, finely crushed | 2 egg whites
75 g unsalted butter, melted and cooled | 1/2 teaspoon orange-flower water | milk

PREHEAT THE OVEN TO 160°C (GAS 3). Line baking trays with baking paper.

Mix together the sugar, flour, orange zest and cardamom. Add the egg whites and mix to a smooth paste. Add the butter and orange-flower water to the mixture and stir to incorporate. The batter will be quite loose and sloppy. Place well-spaced teaspoons of batter on the prepared baking trays. Wet your finger in some milk and carefully flatten then smear the batter out to circles 8–10 cm round and 1 mm thick. Refrigerate for 10 minutes before baking in the centre of the oven for 5–7 minutes, or until golden brown. Remove the tray from the oven and lift the wafers onto a wire rack with a spatula. When cool, store them in an airtight container for up to 3 days.

MAKES **30–35**

HONEY WAFERS

125 g unsalted butter, softened | 200 g caster sugar | 4 teaspoons honey | 100 g plain flour
1/2 teaspoon ground ginger | 2 egg whites | milk | 100 g sesame seeds

PREHEAT THE OVEN TO 160°C (GAS 3). Line two baking trays with baking paper.

In an electric mixer, cream the butter and sugar at high speed. Add the honey, flour and ground ginger. When they are fully blended, add the egg whites and mix well. Place well-spaced teaspoons of batter on the prepared baking trays. Wet your finger in some milk and carefully flatten then smear the batter out to circles 8–10 cm round and 1 mm thick. Bake the wafers on the middle shelf of the oven for 7–10 minutes, or until they are golden brown. Carefully transfer to a wire rack to cool, then store in an airtight container for up to 3 days.

SESAME-HONEY WAFERS Sprinkle the battter circles liberally with sesame seeds, pouring off any excess, then bake as described above.

MAKES **about 30**

Rice flour gives these biscuits a slightly sandy, shortbready texture. You could use cornflour instead for a softer, more melting biscuit.

GINGER SHORTBREAD

150 g unsalted butter, softened | 75 g icing sugar | 1 free-range egg yolk | 150 g plain flour | 75 g rice flour | 2 generous tablespoons finely chopped crystallised ginger

PREHEAT THE OVEN TO 150°C (GAS 2). Line two baking trays with baking paper.

Chill the bowl and blade of your food processor for 10 minutes in the freezer. Then cream the butter and icing sugar in the food processor. Add the egg yolk and mix in well. Sift in the two flours and then add the chopped ginger. Pulse carefully until the mixture just comes together. Refrigerate for about 10 minutes to firm the dough.

Tip the dough onto a clean work surface lightly dusted with plain flour. Roll it out evenly and gently to a thickness of 3–4 mm. Use a sharp knife to cut out three rounds 12 cm in diameter. With the back of a knife, mark each round into eight wedges.

Lift the rounds onto the prepared baking trays and bake for 15–20 minutes, or until the biscuits are just starting to colour and feel a bit firm to the touch. Cool on the tray for a few minutes, then carefully lift onto a wire rack and leave until completely cold. They will keep in an airtight container for a week.

MAKES **24**

Tiny melt-in-your-mouth biscuits are popular throughout the Middle East. Some are made with rice or chickpea flour, some with wheat flour, while others incorporate finely ground nuts, but all use a high ratio of butter or ghee to give that crisp, melting 'shortness'. Iranian versions are usually flavoured with cardamom, but for a change we think hazelnut and orange work beautifully together. Perfect with a cup of tea at any time.

HAZELNUT-ORANGE SHORTBREAD

80 g icing sugar | 110 g clarified butter or ghee
100 g plain flour, sifted, plus extra for dusting
45 g self-raising flour, sifted | 50 g roasted hazelnuts, finely ground
grated zest of 1 orange | 2 teaspoons grated orange zest, dried in a cool oven

PREHEAT THE OVEN TO 150°C (GAS 2). Line two baking trays with baking paper.

Mix the icing sugar with the clarified butter thoroughly. Fold in all the remaining ingredients, except for the dried orange zest. Take care not to overwork the mixture. The dough will be very soft, but if it feels too wet add a little more flour. Refrigerate for 10 minutes or so to firm the dough.

Tip the dough onto a clean work surface lightly dusted with plain flour. Roll it out evenly and gently to a thickness of 3–4 mm. Use a sharp knife to cut out three rounds 12 cm in diameter. With the back of a knife, mark each round into eight wedges. Sprinkle the edges of each round with the dried orange peel, pressing it in gently and evenly.

Lift the rounds onto the prepared baking tray and bake for 15–20 minutes, or until the biscuits are just starting to colour and feel a bit firm to the touch. Cool on the tray for a few minutes, then carefully lift onto a wire rack and leave until completely cold. They will keep in an airtight container for a week.

MAKES **24**

RAYBEH BISCUITS

225 g icing sugar | 250 g clarified butter or ghee | 225 g plain flour, sifted
75 g self-raising flour, sifted | 60 g blanched almond halves

PREHEAT THE OVEN TO 145°C (GAS 2). Line two baking trays with baking paper.

Add the icing sugar to the liquid clarified butter, stirring well with a wooden spoon. Add the flours and mix well. Now use your hands to knead the mixture until you have a smooth, pliable paste, adding more flour if it feels too wet.

To shape the biscuits, roll a small section of dough into a fat little snake about the size of your middle finger, then join the ends to form a round. Press an almond half over the join. Lay them on the baking tray and cook for about 20 minutes. The biscuits should remain snowy white, but the almonds should turn a light golden brown. When cool, remove from the tray and store in an airtight tin.

MAKES **about 40**

BAZARAK BISCUITS

40 g soft brown sugar | 45 g icing sugar | 150 g unsalted butter, softened
1 teaspoon vanilla extract | 1 egg | 200 g self-raising flour
50 g pistachio kernels, cut into slivers | 60 g sesame seeds, lightly toasted

PUT THE SUGARS AND BUTTER IN A large bowl and cream together well. Mix in the vanilla extract and egg, followed by the flour. The dough softens easily, so transfer it to the fridge for 30 minutes before baking.

Preheat the oven to 180°C (Gas 4). Grease and line two baking trays. Take little pieces of dough and roll them between the palms of your hands into small marble-sized balls. Flatten gently to form little discs about 1 cm thick. Line up two dishes, one with the pistachio slivers and one with the sesame seeds. Press one side of the dough into the pistachios, then turn over and press the other side into the sesame seeds. Carefully brush off any excess and place on the prepared baking trays, allowing about 5 cm between them for spreading.

Bake for 10–12 minutes, or until golden brown. Transfer the biscuits to a wire rack and leave to cool.

MAKES **25–30**

TURKISH DELIGHT FLORENTINES

50 g unsalted butter | 125 ml cream (45% fat) | 125 g caster sugar
440 g flaked almonds | 60 g plain flour | 300 g best-quality dark chocolate
8 pieces rosewater Turkish delight, finely chopped

PREHEAT THE OVEN TO 160°C (GAS 3). Grease baking trays and line with baking paper.

In a small, heavy-based saucepan, bring the butter, cream and sugar to the boil.

Remove from the heat. Allow to cool slightly then stir in the almonds and flour. Drop teaspoonfuls onto the baking trays, leaving plenty of room between each one for spreading. Flatten slightly with a wet fingertip. Bake for 8–10 minutes, until the biscuits are a light golden brown. If you like, at this stage you can cut the biscuits into neat circles with a pastry cutter, before returning them to the oven to finish cooking. Bake biscuits for a further 8 minutes until they are a deep golden brown.

Remove from the oven and, while they are still warm, scatter with the pieces of Turkish delight. (Alternatively, scatter the Turkish delight onto the melted chocolate before it sets.) Once the biscuits are cool and firm, transfer them to a wire rack. Melt the chocolate and brush a thick coat onto the flat sides of the biscuits. Use a fork to create the traditional wavy pattern.

MAKES **about 15**

SWEET

Pretty as a picture, this light, cleansing sorbet combines sweet-sour blood orange and pomegranate juices with the delicate perfume of orange-flower water. There is absolutely no need to mess around squeezing fresh fruit for this sorbet. We use good-quality commercial fresh or bottled juices from the supermarket.

POMEGRANATE AND BLOOD-ORANGE SORBET WITH ORANGE-FLOWER WATER

250 g caster sugar | 250 ml water | 250 ml blood-orange juice | 150 ml pomegranate juice juice of 1/2 lime | 1 tablespoon orange-flower water | 50 g liquid glucose

IN A HEAVY-BASED SAUCEPAN, gently heat the caster sugar and water over a low heat until the sugar has dissolved. Increase the heat, then bring to a boil and simmer for 1 minute. Remove from the heat and leave to cool slightly.

Mix the fruit juices with the orange-flower water. Stir in the warm syrup and the liquid glucose, then transfer to the fridge to cool completely. Tip the cold mixture into an ice-cream machine and churn according to the manufacturer's instructions. Transfer to the freezer until ready to serve.

MAKES **1 litre**

CHOCOLATE AND CINNAMON SORBET

500 ml water | 250 ml milk | 100 g caster sugar | 50 g liquid glucose | 2 cinnamon sticks | 200 g best-quality dark chocolate | 20 g cocoa powder

PUT THE WATER, MILK, SUGAR, glucose and cinnamon sticks in a large saucepan and slowly bring to the boil. Break the chocolate into pieces and put it in a mixing bowl with the cocoa powder. Pour on the boiling milk mixture, stirring until the chocolate and cocoa have melted and dissolved. Cool, stirring from time to time. Strain the mixture to remove the cinnamon sticks, then pour into an ice-cream machine and churn according to the manufacturer's instructions. Transfer to the freezer until ready to serve.

MAKES **1 litre**

This is a silky, smooth sorbet with a light tang and subtle sweetness. It makes a wonderfully refreshing end to a rich meal. Serve it drizzled with a little more honey, or with a salad of fresh berries or stone fruits.

YOGHURT AND HONEY SORBET

350 ml water | 225 g caster sugar | 1 tablespoon liquid glucose | 250 g thick natural yoghurt | 80 ml crème fraîche | 60 ml cream (45% fat) | 2 tablespoons honey | 2 tablespoons lime juice

IN A SMALL SAUCEPAN, GENTLY HEAT the water, sugar and liquid glucose until the sugar has dissolved. Increase the heat and bring to a gentle boil. Simmer for 3 minutes, then remove from the heat and leave to cool. When cool, refrigerate until chilled.

Whisk together the yoghurt, crème fraîche and cream, then chill. Stir the honey and lime juice into the cold syrup, then stir this into the chilled yoghurt mixture. Tip into an ice-cream machine and churn according to the manufacturer's instructions. Transfer to the freezer until ready to serve.

MAKES **500 ml**

WATERMELON AND ROSEWATER SORBET

800 g watermelon flesh | 200 g caster sugar | 70 g liquid glucose | 200 ml water
juice of 2 limes | splash of rosewater

CHOP THE WATERMELON INTO largish chunks and discard the seeds. Whiz to a purée in a food processor then push through a fine sieve to remove any fibrous bits.

Combine the sugar, glucose and water in a saucepan and bring to the boil over a medium heat, then lower the heat and simmer for 5 minutes. Mix the fruit purée with this syrup and allow to cool. Add the lime juice and rosewater. Pour into an ice-cream machine and churn according to the manufacturer's instructions. Transfer to the freezer until ready to serve.

MAKES 1 litre

APPLE-LIME SORBET

200 ml water | 100 g caster sugar | 60 g liquid glucose
180 g chopped Granny Smith apples (cored but not peeled) | lime juice to taste

GENTLY HEAT THE WATER, SUGAR and glucose in a heavy-based saucepan until the sugar has completely dissolved. Increase the heat and bring to the boil, then simmer for 2 minutes. Remove from the heat and set aside to cool.

Whiz the chopped apples in batches in a blender or food processor, gradually adding the cold syrup to make a fine, smooth purée. Add lime juice to taste then push the purée through a fine sieve. Use a rubber spatula or the back of a ladle to push and extract as much juice as possible.

Tip into an ice-cream machine and churn according to the manufacturer's instructions. Transfer to the freezer until ready to serve.

MAKES 500 ml

This very useful Italian-style vanilla ice-cream mixture can be used as the base for all sorts of flavourings. We find it simpler to make than a French custard-based method; it is quick and virtually foolproof and results in a luscious, creamy ice cream.

VANILLA ICE CREAM BASE

250 g caster sugar | 1 vanilla bean, split and seeds scraped | 250 ml water
10 free-range egg yolks | 1 litre cream (35% fat)

PUT THE SUGAR, VANILLA SEEDS AND water in a small saucepan and dissolve over a gentle heat, stirring occasionally. (Use the scraped pod to perfume your sugar canister.) When the syrup is clear, increase the heat and bring to a rolling boil.

Meanwhile, put the egg yolks into an electric mixer and whisk until thick, pale and creamy. With the motor running, slowly pour the sugar syrup onto the egg yolks. Continue whisking for about 5 minutes, or until the mixture cools. You will see it dramatically bulk up into a soft, puffy mass. Fold in the cream and chill in the refrigerator.

Pour the chilled mixture into an ice-cream machine and churn according to the manufacturer's instructions. Transfer to the freezer until ready to serve.

MAKES **about 1.5 litres**

LIQUORICE ICE CREAM

200 g liquorice | 300 ml water | Vanilla Ice Cream Base (above)

CUT THE LIQUORICE INTO SMALL pieces and put into a saucepan with the water. Heat slowly, stirring from time to time, until the liquorice dissolves to a smooth paste.

Stir about a third of the vanilla ice cream base into the melted liquorice, a bit at a time, so that it is incorporated gradually and remains smooth. Tip back into the remaining base mixture, stir and chill in the refrigerator. Pour the chilled mixture into an ice-cream machine and churn according to the manufacturer's instructions. Transfer to the freezer until ready to serve.

MAKES **about 1.5 litres**

TOASTED ALMOND-ORANGE PRALINE ICE CREAM

zest of 2 oranges | 1 quantity Almond Praline (page 399)
Vanilla Ice-cream Base (opposite)

PREHEAT THE OVEN TO 100°C (GAS 1/4). Dry the orange zest in the oven for 3 hours, then grind to a fine powder.

Make the almond praline as described on page 399. After you pour the hot mixture into a lined tray, sprinkle on the ground orange zest. When the brittle is cold, pound to crumbs.

Make the vanilla ice cream base as described opposite and chill in the refrigerator. Pour the chilled mixture into an ice-cream machine and churn, according to the manufacturer's instructions, until nearly set. Add half the almond and orange praline towards the end of the churning time (freeze the rest in an airtight container for another recipe). Transfer to the freezer until ready to serve.

MAKES **about 1.5 litres**

SYRIAN APRICOT ICE CREAM

200 ml water | 250 ml dry sherry | 4 cardamom pods | 500 g best-quality dried apricots
Vanilla Ice Cream Base (opposite) | 100 g Walnut Praline (page 399), optional

COMBINE THE WATER, SHERRY AND the seeds from the cardamom pods in a heavy-based saucepan. Bring to the boil, then lower the heat. Add the apricots and simmer gently, stirring occasionally, until they dissolve into a thickish, smooth consistency. Allow to cool, then blitz to a smooth purée.

Make the vanilla ice cream base as described opposite and chill in the refrigerator. Fold in the apricot purée then pour into an ice-cream machine and churn according to the manufacturer's instructions. Add the walnut praline, if using, towards the end of the churning time. Transfer to the freezer until ready to serve.

MAKES **1.5 litres**

A luscious toffee-ish ice cream, with bits of chewy date folded through for textural interest.

CONFIT DATE ICE CREAM

DATE CONFIT **125 ml water | 125 g caster sugar | 250 g fresh dates, pitted | 100 ml Kahlúa**

ICE CREAM **8 free-range egg yolks | 100 ml water | 100 g liquid glucose | 50 g caster sugar 1 litre cream (35% fat)**

TO MAKE THE DATE CONFIT, BRING the water and sugar to a boil in a saucepan until the sugar dissolves. Add the dates and Kahlúa and stir well. Cover the surface with a circle of baking paper to keep the dates submerged and to prevent a skin from forming during cooking. Bring the mixture back to the boil, lower the heat and simmer gently for 10 minutes until the dates are meltingly soft but not mushy.

Remove the pan from the heat and allow to cool. When cold, remove the dates from the syrup, reserving both dates and syrup. Remove the skins, chop the dates roughly and sit them in a sieve to drain off excess liquid.

To make the ice cream, whisk the egg yolks in an electric mixer until they are light and fluffy. Put the water, glucose and sugar into a saucepan and bring to the boil, then pour onto the egg yolks, whisking slowly as you go. Add the cream and turn off the beaters. Allow the mixture to cool completely, then pour into an ice-cream machine and churn according to the manufacturer's instructions. At the end of the freezing process, just before it gets too stiff to churn any further, tip in the date confit and allow the paddle to swirl it briefly through the ice cream. Transfer to the freezer until ready to serve.

Just before serving, pour over the reserved syrup.

MAKES **about 1.5 litres**

MUSCAT ICE CREAM

600 ml muscat | 55 g sultanas or seedless raisins | 100 ml water | 100 g liquid glucose | 50 g caster sugar | 6 free-range egg yolks | 500 ml cream (45% fat)

IN A HEAVY-BASED SAUCEPAN, BRING the muscat and sultanas to the boil. Lower the heat and simmer until reduced to 100 ml. Strain through a fine sieve and reserve both the sultanas and the intense, syrupy muscat.

Put the water, glucose and sugar in a heavy-based saucepan and bring to the boil.

Meanwhile, whisk the egg yolks in an electric mixer until thick, pale and creamy. With the motor running, slowly pour the sugar syrup onto the egg yolks. Next, pour on the muscat and continue whisking for about 5 minutes, or until the mixture cools. You will see it dramatically bulk up into a soft, puffy mass. Fold in the cream and chill in the refrigerator.

Pour the chilled mixture into an ice-cream machine and churn according to the manufacturer's instructions. Towards the end of the churning time, add the sultanas and let the machine stir them in thoroughly. Transfer to the freezer until ready to serve.

MAKES **about 850 ml**

TURKISH COFFEE ICE CREAM

200 g caster sugar | 1/2 cup water | 100 g liquid glucose | 3 cardamom pods, cracked | 100 g dark-roasted, plain Turkish coffee, finely ground | 60 g best-quality dark chocolate | 12 free-range egg yolks | 60 ml Tia Maria | 1 litre cream (35% fat)

IN A SAUCEPAN, SLOWLY BRING THE sugar, water, glucose, cardamom and coffee to the boil so the sugar dissolves completely. Simmer for 5 minutes. Pour the syrup over the chocolate and stir until it melts. Whisk the egg yolks at high speed until light and fluffy. Strain the coffee-chocolate mixture though a coffee filter into the egg yolks and beat for 1 minute. Add the Tia Maria and cream and refrigerate for 1 hour. Pour the mixture into an ice-cream machine and churn according to the manufacturer's instructions. Transfer to the freezer until ready to serve.

MAKES **about 1.5 litres**

As well as being the sand-coloured, sesame-based confectionery with which westerners are familiar, halva is also a type of Turkish dessert made from semolina or flour. Turkish confectioners often have displays of huge blocks of halva — many studded with nuggets of emerald-green pistachios. Because it is not too sweet, it works brilliantly in ice cream.

PISTACHIO-HALVA ICE CREAM

250 ml full-cream milk | 250 ml cream (35% fat)
1 vanilla bean, split and seeds scraped | long piece of zest from 1 lemon
100 g caster sugar | 5 egg yolks | 70 g pistachio halva | 25 g unsalted pistachio kernels

PUT THE MILK, CREAM, VANILLA BEAN, seeds and zest into a large, heavy-based pan and heat gently. Meanwhile, whisk the sugar and egg yolks by hand in a large bowl until thick and pale. Pour on the hot cream mixture and whisk in quickly. Pour the mixture back into the rinsed-out pan and cook gently until it thickens to the consistency of custard. You should be able to draw a distinct line through the custard on the back of a spoon. Remove from the heat immediately and cool in a sink of iced water. Stir from time to time to help the custard cool down quickly. Remove the vanilla bean and zest. Refrigerate the custard until chilled.

Pour the chilled custard into an ice-cream machine and churn according to the manufacturer's instructions.

While the ice cream is churning, crush the halva in a mortar to even crumbs. Whiz the pistachios in a food processor to form coarse crumbs. At the end of the churning, add the halva and pistachio crumbs and churn in briefly. Transfer to the freezer until ready to serve.

MAKES **600 ml**

We are particularly fond of traditional Persian ice cream, which is often tinted yellow with saffron. It's hard to re-create at home because you need sahlab, the ground root of an orchid, to create the distinctive stretchy consistency. Instead, here is an alternative saffron ice cream that uses a duo of molten gold — saffron liquid and honey — and chunks of sparkling candied ginger. It is rich, luscious and intensely flavoured.

Serve with wafers, other crisp biscuits, or Stone Fruits with Sugar and Spice (page 344).

SAFFRON-HONEY ICE CREAM WITH CANDIED GINGER

100 ml honey | 350 ml water | 200 g caster sugar | 25 g liquid glucose
3 tablespoons Saffron Liquid (page 218) | 1 teaspoon ground ginger
juice of 1/2 lime | 250 g thick natural yoghurt | 3 tablespoons cream (45% fat)
80 ml sour cream | 1/3 cup finely diced crystallised ginger

BRING THE HONEY TO THE BOIL IN A small saucepan over a medium heat and simmer to form a dark caramel — 145°C if you have a candy thermometer. As the caramel darkens, swirl the pan constantly and move it on and off the heat to ensure you don't burn the honey.

Remove from the heat straight away and stir in the water (be careful, the caramel will spit and splutter). Stir gently to combine, then return to the heat. Stir in the sugar, liquid glucose, saffron liquid and ground ginger. Return to the boil, stirring gently to dissolve the sugar and glucose, then simmer for 3 minutes. Remove the pan from the heat and leave to cool.

Refrigerate until chilled, then stir in the lime juice. Whisk the yoghurt, cream and sour cream together, then gently fold in the chilled honey-saffron syrup. Tip into an ice-cream machine and churn according to the manufacturer's instructions. At the end of the churning, add the crystallised ginger to the ice cream and churn briefly to distribute it evenly. Transfer to the freezer until ready to serve.

For an attractive presentation, sandwich a scoop of the ice cream between wafers or other crisp biscuits. Alternatively, serve the ice cream in bowls with wafers on the side.

MAKES **1 litre**

A lovely dinner party dessert to make at the start of summer when cherries are in season. Parfaits are good ices to make for those who don't have an ice-cream machine, as they don't require churning. You will need a 30 cm x 9 cm terrine mould, loaf tin or plastic container, lined with plastic wrap, for the parfait.

CHERRY-VANILLA PARFAIT WITH ROSEWATER SYRUP

CHERRY PURÉE **250 g cherries (stoned weight) | 75 g caster sugar | juice of 1 lemon**

PARFAIT **10 eggs | 200 g caster sugar | 200 ml water | 1 vanilla bean, split and seeds scraped | 600 ml cream (35% fat), whipped to soft peaks**

SYRUP **100 g caster sugar | 100 ml water | zest of 1 lemon | 1 cinnamon stick | 1-2 tablespoons rosewater | 1 tablespoon cherry purée (above)**

100 g pitted and halved cherries | 100 g unsalted pistachio kernels, roughly chopped

TO MAKE THE CHERRY PURÉE, combine all the ingredients in a heavy saucepan. Bring slowly to the boil, stirring gently from time to time to ensure that the sugar dissolves completely. Lower the heat and simmer for about 5 minutes. Remove from the heat and purée in a blender, then strain through a sieve to remove the skins. Allow to cool completely. Reserve 1 tablespoon of the purée for the syrup.

To make the parfait, whisk the eggs in an electric mixer until they are light and fluffy. Bring the sugar, water and vanilla bean to the boil in a saucepan. Carefully remove the vanilla bean and then pour the boiling syrup onto the eggs, whisking slowly as you go. Continue whisking until cool, then fold in the cream. Pour the custard into the terrine mould, swirl the cherry purée through and freeze.

To make the syrup, put all the ingredients and the reserved tablespoon of cherry purée into a saucepan. Bring to the boil and then simmer gently for about 3 minutes. Remove from the heat and set aside until ready to use. Remove the lemon zest and cinnamon stick just before serving.

To serve, turn the parfait out of the mould and slice into eight thick tiles. Drizzle with the syrup and sprinkle with a few cherry halves and pistachios.

SERVES **8**

Fresh fruit curds and purées swirled into softly whipped cream with a little caramel make some of the simplest and most delectable desserts. Serve with wafer biscuits (page 318) with fresh or poached fruit salads (pages 341–344) or your favourite cakes. Fruit curds and purées can also be folded into Vanilla Ice-Cream Base (page 332) for a stunning ice cream.

FRUIT FOOL

500 ml cream (45% fat) | 60 ml Caramel Orange Syrup (page 400) | fruit curd or purée

WHIP THE CREAM TO SOFT PEAKS and swirl in the caramel and fruit curd or purée of your choice. Serve in a glass bowl, or individual glass dishes for the prettiest presentation.

SERVES **6**

FRUIT CURDS AND PURÉES

LEMON CURD Combine the juice and finely chopped zest of 2 lemons, 175 g caster sugar and 90 g unsalted butter in the top of a double boiler. Heat and stir until the sugar is completely dissolved, then pour in 3 beaten eggs. Continue to heat gently, stirring all the time, until the mixture thickens to the consistency of pouring cream. Do not allow it to boil. Strain and chill.

PASSIONFRUIT CURD Combine 110 g caster sugar and 60 g unsalted butter in the top of a double boiler. Heat and stir until the sugar is completely dissolved, then pour in 2 beaten eggs. Continue to heat gently, stirring all the time, until the mixture thickens to the consistency of pouring cream. Do not allow it to boil. Strain, allow to cool completely then fold in the pulp of 6 passionfruit. Chill.

FRESH RASPBERRY PURÉE Whiz 250 g raspberries to a purée then push through a sieve. Stir in 3 teaspoons sifted icing sugar and chill.

RHUBARB AND ROSEWATER PURÉE Combine 300 g chopped rhubarb and 100 g caster sugar in a heavy-based saucepan with a few spoonfuls of water. Heat until the water begins to boil, then cover with a lid and cook over a medium heat for 5 minutes. Remove the lid and stir well. Cook for a few minutes until it softens and collapses completely. Whiz to a very smooth purée then stir in a generous splash of rosewater.

MAKES **about 600 ml (serves 6)**

Dried fruit compotes are widely enjoyed, especially in Persia and Turkey. In Turkey they are called hoşaf, and are sometimes served after the main part of a meal spooned over plain pilav rice. Hoşaf range from simple raisin compotes to brightly coloured combinations of apricots, figs, prunes and currants, sometimes with the addition of nuts. You'll find the barberries and tiny dried wild figs in Middle Eastern food stores, and some gourmet shops.

DRIED FRUIT COMPOTE

250 g caster sugar | 250 ml water | 1/2 cinnamon stick | 2 cloves | 4 cardamom pods
long piece of zest from 1 orange | long piece of zest from 1/2 lemon | 75 g dried wild figs
100 g dried apricots | 1/3 cup currants | 1/4 cup barberries

COMBINE THE SUGAR AND WATER IN a heavy-based saucepan and heat gently, stirring occasionally until the sugar dissolves. When the syrup is clear, add the spices and citrus zests, then increase the heat and bring to the boil. Add the dried fruit and simmer for 5 minutes. Remove from the heat and leave the fruit to cool in the syrup.

Transfer to an airtight container and refrigerate until ready to use. The compote will keep for up to a week.

SERVES **4-6**

A lovely summer dessert using perfectly ripe berries and sweet refreshing watermelon in a light vanilla syrup. Add little nuggets of sweet-bland halva for textural contrast. Serve with wafers and vanilla ice cream or your favourite sorbet — we like Watermelon and Rosewater (page 331) or Yoghurt and Honey (page 329) — for a more elaborate dessert.

WATERMELON, BERRY AND HALVA SALAD

VANILLA SUGAR SYRUP **100 g caster sugar | 100 ml water**
1 vanilla bean, split and seeds scraped | zest of 1 lemon

1 small seedless watermelon (about 500 g) | 250 g blackberries | 250 g raspberries
250 g strawberries | 1/3 cup finely shredded baby mint leaves
sprigs of elderflower (optional) | 100 g pistachio halva, crumbled

TO MAKE THE VANILLA SUGAR SYRUP, put the sugar, water, vanilla bean and lemon zest in a small saucepan. Bring to the boil, then simmer gently for about 5 minutes. Remove from the heat. When cool, remove the vanilla bean; this can be washed and reused to flavour your canister of sugar. Chill the syrup until ready to use.

Use a melon baller to scoop out balls of watermelon. Put into a mixing bowl with the berries, mint and elderflower sprigs, if using, and pour on half the vanilla sugar syrup (use the rest in another dessert). Toss gently, then divide among four serving bowls. Sprinkle on the halva and serve at once.

SERVES **4**

STONE FRUITS WITH SUGAR AND SPICE AND BRIK WAFERS

150 g caster sugar | 200 ml water | 4 cardamom pods, cracked | 1 cinnamon stick | 4 strips lemon zest | 2 ripe but firm white peaches | 2 ripe but firm yellow peaches | 2 ripe but firm white nectarines | 2 ripe but firm apricots | clotted or pure cream to serve

BRIK WAFERS **2 sheets brik pastry | 60 g clarified butter or ghee | icing sugar to dust**

COMBINE THE SUGAR AND WATER IN a saucepan and heat gently, swirling occasionally. When the sugar is completely dissolved, bring to the boil, then add the cardamom pods, cinnamon stick and lemon zest. Simmer until reduced by a third, then remove from the heat and leave to cool.

Bring a large saucepan of water to a boil. Blanch the stone fruits separately, in batches, for 1 minute, then refresh in a bowl of iced water. Use a small paring knife to peel away the skins and cut thick 'cheeks' from each piece of fruit. Transfer to a bowl and cover with the strained syrup. Refrigerate until ready to serve.

Preheat the oven to 180°C (Gas 4) and line a baking tray with baking paper. Lay a sheet of brik pastry out on a clean work surface. Cut in half and brush generously with clarified butter. Brush a 1 cm diameter metal rod with clarified butter and neatly wrap the pastry around it to form a tube. Place on the prepared baking tray and bake for 10 minutes, or until crisp and golden. While hot, carefully slide the pastry tube off the rod. Repeat to make three more tubes. When cool, dust with icing sugar.

Divide the fruits among four shallow bowls and add plenty of syrup. Garnish with a brik wafer and serve with a dollop of clotted or pure cream.

SERVES **4**

RICH CHOCOLATE AND CARDAMOM TART WITH TURKISH DELIGHT JEWELS

SWEET CHOCOLATE PASTRY **20 g cocoa powder | 480 g plain flour**
360 g unsalted butter, diced | 150 g icing sugar | 4 free-range egg yolks
25 ml hot water mixed with 25 g instant espresso-style coffee

CHOCOLATE FILLING **150 ml cream (35% fat)**
150 ml milk | 3 free-range egg yolks (70 g) | 60 g sugar
180 g best-quality dark chocolate (minimum 64% cocoa solids)
1 tablespoon rosewater | 1 teaspoon ground cardamom

TURKISH DELIGHT 'JEWELS' **1 tablespoon icing sugar | 1 tablespoon cornflour**
120 g rosewater Turkish delight

TO MAKE THE CHOCOLATE PASTRY, sift the cocoa powder and flour together. In an electric mixer fitted with a paddle, beat the butter and icing sugar until well mixed. Then add the yolks and espresso coffee. Once evenly blended, pulse in the flour until the dough just comes together. Tip it out of the bowl and shape into a ball. Wrap in plastic wrap and refrigerate for an hour.

Roll the chilled pastry out on a floured work surface until 2–3 mm thick. Lift it carefully onto a buttered 33 cm x 10 cm rectangular tart tin, pressing it in gently to the edges. Trim the edges, leaving some overhang, then return to the refrigerator for another hour.

When ready to blind bake the tart, preheat the oven to 180°C (Gas 4). Line the tart with foil, fill with baking beans, place on a baking tray and cook for 10 minutes. Remove the foil and beans and cook the shell for a further 10 minutes, or until firm.

To make the chocolate filling, combine the milk and cream in a small saucepan and bring to the boil. In a large mixing bowl, whisk the egg yolks with the sugar until well incorporated. Pour on a third of the hot cream mixture and whisk thoroughly. Pour back into the pan with the rest of the hot cream and heat over a medium heat until the custard thickens enough to coat the back of a wooden spoon. Remove from the heat and cool. Pour through a fine sieve into a small bowl and set aside.

Roughly chop the chocolate and place in a small bowl set over a saucepan of simmering water. Once the chocolate has melted, stir the cardamom through gently and remove the bowl from the heat. Sit the custard mixture over the simmering water and warm through gently. Pour into the melted chocolate and stir to blend evenly. Pour into the prepared tart shell and refrigerate for 2 hours to set.

To make the Turkish delight 'jewels', mix the icing sugar with the cornflour in a small mixing bowl. Cut each piece of Turkish delight into quarters and use your hands to roll into little worm shapes. Cut these into tiny discs and dust in the icing sugar mixture. Scatter on the tart just before serving.

SERVES **10**

The various components of this dessert can be prepared ahead, then the tart assembled just before serving. You only need half the given amount of pastry for this tart, but it can be tricky working with smaller quantities of nuts and seeds. Freeze the rest for another use.

SESAME TART WITH BERRY-ROSE MOUSSE

ALMOND AND SESAME PASTRY **150 g blanched almonds, roasted | 65 g sesame seeds, lightly roasted | 130 g caster sugar | 450 g plain flour | 1 teaspoon ground cinnamon | 1/3 teaspoon salt | zest of 1/2 lemon | 335 g unsalted butter | 2 free-range eggs | splash of vanilla extract**

BERRY-ROSE MOUSSE **350 g mixed berries (reserve a few for a garnish) | 130 g caster sugar | 2 x 1.6 g sheets of gold-strength gelatine, softened in water | splash of vanilla extract | splash of rosewater | 375 ml cream (35% fat)**

BERRY SAUCE **250 g mixed berries | 100 ml Vanilla Sugar Syrup (page 342)**

PUT THE ALMONDS, SESAME SEEDS and sugar into a food processor and pulse to fine crumbs. Be careful not to overwork, as the oils will start to come out of the nuts and make the pastry oily. Add the flour, cinnamon, salt and lemon zest to the mixture and pulse quickly to combine. Add the butter and pulse to form crumbs. Add the eggs and vanilla and pulse until the pastry just comes together into a ball. Push it together with your hands and remove from the food processor. Shape into a round, wrap in plastic wrap and chill for at least 1 hour. After chilling, roll the pastry out thinly onto a well-floured work surface. Lift into a 28 cm tart tin and gently press into shape. Trim the edges and return to the refrigerator for another hour.

When ready to blind bake the tart, preheat the oven to 180°C (Gas 4). Line the tart shell with foil, fill with baking beans and bake for 15 minutes. Remove the foil and beans and bake for another 15 minutes, or until the pastry is golden. Remove from the oven and cool on a wire rack.

To make the berry mousse, blend or process the berries to a purée. Push through a fine sieve to remove the seeds. Put half the purée into a small saucepan with the sugar and warm gently until the sugar dissolves. Add the gelatine sheets, stir to dissolve and leave to cool. Add to the rest of the berry purée and stir in the vanilla and rosewater. Whip the cream to stiffish peaks. Fold into the berry purée, then chill.

To make the sauce, blend or process the berries and vanilla syrup to a smooth purée. Pour into a saucepan and bring to the boil, then remove from the heat and leave to cool.

When ready to serve, spoon the berry mousse into the tart and scatter on the reserved berries. Serve each slice with a generous drizzle of berry sauce.

SERVES **6–8**

Known as muhallabeya, this is the classic Middle Eastern milk pudding recipe, which we've tweaked by adding strained yoghurt to give it a lovely tang.

Mastic is the resinous gum from the Mediterranean acacia tree. It is sold as small crystals and has a subtle pine flavour. Mastic is used to flavour milk puddings, ice creams, sweets and even coffee. It is available from Greek or Middle Eastern delicatessens and good specialty food stores.

LEBANESE MILK PUDDING WITH LABNEH, PASSIONFRUIT AND FAIRY FLOSS

4 grains mastic | 120 g caster sugar | 50 g cornflour | 1 litre full-cream milk
long strip of zest from 1/2 lemon | long strip of zest from 1/2 orange
30 ml orange-flower water | 200 g Strained Yoghurt (page 42)
orange-flavoured Turkish or Persian fairy floss to garnish

PASSIONFRUIT SAUCE **500 g passionfruit pulp [about 10 passionfruit]**
100 g caster sugar | 60 g liquid glucose

IN A MORTAR, GRIND THE MASTIC with 1/2 teaspoon of the sugar, then mix with the remaining sugar and the cornflour in a bowl. Stir in 100 ml of the milk to make a paste.

Put the rest of the milk into a large, heavy-based saucepan, then whisk in the paste until smooth. Add the citrus zests and bring to the boil, whisking continuously, then lower the heat and simmer for 4–5 minutes, whisking continuously to make sure it doesn't catch and burn.

Remove from the heat, strain into a bowl and cool in a sink of iced water, whisking continuously so that the mixture becomes light and fluffy. When the mixture cools to blood temperature, stir in the orange-flower water, then fold in the strained yoghurt. Spoon into serving glasses and refrigerate until chilled.

To make the passionfruit sauce, whiz the passionfruit pulp in a food processor for a minute to break it down. Strain through a fine sieve, reserving the juice. Add the juice to the sugar and glucose in a small pan. Bring to the boil, lower the heat and simmer for 10 minutes to make a thick sauce.

Spoon a little of the sauce onto the milk puddings and keep them chilled until ready to eat. Serve garnished with a topknot of fairy floss.

SERVES **8**

The buttermilk in these little milk puddings gives them a delicate tang. They are firm enough to turn out, but are just as pretty served in small ornate dishes or pretty glasses.

Turkish or Persian fairy floss is available in a range of different flavours in Middle Eastern food stores and some delis. As well as looking spectacular, its delicate texture and melting sweetness are irresistible to young and old alike.

BUTTERMILK CREAMS WITH GOLDEN FRUITS AND LIME SYRUP

BUTTERMILK CREAMS **500 ml cream (35% fat) | 1 vanilla bean, split and seeds scraped (or use a splash of extract) | 75 g caster sugar | 3 x 4 g leaves titanium-strength gelatine | 500 ml buttermilk | 1/4 teaspoon rosewater | 150 ml cream (35% fat), lightly whipped**

LIME SYRUP **200 g caster sugar | 1 cup water | strips of zest from 1–2 limes | few slices fresh ginger (optional) | 1 vanilla bean, split and seeds scraped**

TO SERVE **peaches, apricots, nectarines, blood plums and cherries, peeled and cubed | edible flowers (optional) | vanilla-flavoured Turkish or Persian fairy floss**

TO MAKE THE BUTTERMILK CREAMS, put the cream, vanilla and sugar in a heavy-based pan and heat gently, stirring to dissolve the sugar. Once the sugar has completely dissolved, bring to the boil then remove from the heat and leave to cool a little. Remove the vanilla bean.

Soak the gelatine in cold water for 4 minutes then squeeze it dry. Add the gelatine to the hot cream mixture and stir until completely dissolved. To remove any residual lumps, pour through a fine sieve into a bowl set over ice.

When cold, add the buttermilk and rosewater and fold in the lightly whipped cream. Pour into ten lightly oiled small dariole moulds and leave to set in the refrigerator.

To make the lime syrup, combine the sugar and water in a saucepan and heat gently, swirling occasionally, to dissolve the sugar. When completely dissolved, bring to the boil, then add the lime zest, ginger, if using, and vanilla bean. Simmer for 5 minutes, then remove from the heat and leave to cool. When cold, remove the aromatics. The vanilla bean can be washed and reused to flavour your canister of sugar.

To serve, turn the set creams out of their moulds onto dessert plates. Mound the cubed fruit next to the creams and drizzle on a generous amount of lime syrup. Garnish with a few petals, if using, and top with a swirl of fairy floss.

MAKES 10

Sweet mandarins add a delicious perfumed dimension to this satiny smooth, thickly luscious crème caramel. We like to serve them with tangy mandarin segments, wafers for crunch, and perhaps some softly whipped cream.

MANDARIN CRÈME CARAMEL

MANDARIN CARAMEL **100 g caster sugar | 120 ml mandarin or orange juice**

CUSTARD **50 g sugar | 100 ml water | zest of 2 mandarins**
300 ml cream (45% fat) | 200 ml mandarin juice | 50 ml brandy | 50 ml Cointreau
6 free-range egg yolks | 2 whole free-range eggs | 100 g caster sugar

TO MAKE THE CARAMEL, HEAT THE the sugar with half the fruit juice until it dissolves. Bring to the boil, lower the heat and simmer until it thickens and darkens to form a caramel. Remove from the heat and add the remaining cold juice. Stir well and allow to cool.

To make the custard, dissolve the sugar in the water over low heat to make a syrup. Blanch the mandarin zest in boiling water twice, then place it in a saucepan with the sugar syrup, bring to the boil and simmer for 5 minutes. Strain off and discard the syrup and tip the zest into a small saucepan. Add the cream and bring it to the boil, then remove from the heat and allow to cool and infuse with the zest for about 20 minutes.

Meanwhile, put the mandarin juice, brandy and Cointreau in a saucepan, bring to the boil then simmer until reduced by two-thirds to about 100 ml.

Preheat the oven to 150°C (Gas 2).

Return the cream to the heat and bring to the boil. Put the egg yolks, eggs and sugar in a large bowl and whisk well to combine. Pour on the boiling cream and whisk briefly. Pour on the reduced mandarin juice and mix in well.

Pour a little caramel into eight 100 ml capacity ramekins. You just need enough to coat the bottom and reach about 5 mm up the sides. Carefully strain the custard through a sieve into the moulds and place in a baking tray. Pour hot (but not boiling) water into the tray to come about halfway up the sides of the moulds. Cover the baking tray loosely with a sheet of foil and place in the centre of the oven to bake for 45–60 minutes. The caramels should be soft, glossy and a little wobbly looking when ready. Leave to cool before refrigerating. Invert onto serving plates and serve with your choice of accompaniments.

SERVES **8**

Chilled rice puddings are popular all around the eastern Mediterranean. Some are exotically flavoured with mastic, others with orange-flower water or rosewater. Some have currants, pine nuts or pistachios lurking in their creamy depths, and some are served with the top browned under the griller to form a dark, burnt layer. This saffron-scented version from Persia is ethereal, delicate and creamy — the antithesis of gluggy Anglo-style rice puddings. Ruby-hued blood oranges make a lovely colour contrast, but you can, of course, use normal oranges — or any sweet citrus — instead.

SAFFRON RICE PUDDING WITH CARAMEL BLOOD ORANGES

1.2 litres full-cream milk | 120 g caster sugar | 1 tablespoon finely grated orange zest | 1 small cinnamon stick | 1/2 vanilla bean, split and seeds scraped | 1 tablespoon Saffron Liquid (page 218) | 160 g short-grain rice | 1 free-range egg yolk | 200 ml cream (35% fat)

CARAMEL BLOOD ORANGES **4 small blood oranges, peeled and pith removed | 100 g caster sugar | 100 ml orange juice | 1 tablespoon orange-flower water**

TO MAKE THE CARAMEL BLOOD oranges, use a very sharp knife to slice the orange segments out of their skin casings (make sure there's not a trace of pith or membrane).

Combine the sugar and orange juice in a small saucepan over a low heat until the sugar dissolves, swirling the pan occasionally. Bring to a boil, then simmer for 8–10 minutes or until a deep golden brown. Remove from the heat straight away and stir in the orange-flower water and orange segments (be careful, the caramel will spit). Stir gently and refrigerate until ready to serve.

To make the rice pudding, combine the milk, sugar, zest, cinnamon stick, vanilla bean and seeds and saffron liquid in a large, heavy-based saucepan over a medium heat. Bring to the boil, then stir in the rice and boil briskly for a minute, stirring. Lower the heat and simmer very gently for 50 minutes, or until the rice is creamy and the milk has been absorbed. If you have a heat-diffuser, this is the time to use it. You don't need to stir constantly, especially during the first 20 minutes or so, but you do need to keep an eye on it to make sure the rice doesn't stick to the bottom of the pan.

Remove the pan from the heat and allow to cool for a few minutes. Meanwhile, whisk the egg yolk with a few tablespoons of the cream, then whisk this into the rice. Leave to cool completely — you can speed this up by scraping the mixture into a bowl set in cold water. Remove the vanilla bean and cinnamon stick.

Whip the rest of the cream to stiff peaks. Fold it into the cold rice, then cover with plastic wrap and refrigerate until chilled.

Serve the rice in pretty bowls, accompanied by caramelised oranges and a drizzle of caramel.

SERVES **6**

DATE BRÛLÉE WITH KAHLÚA

CUSTARD **1.25 litres cream (45% fat) | 10 free-range egg yolks | 60 g caster sugar | 1 vanilla bean, split and seeds scraped | 1 cinnamon stick**

DATE CONFIT **125 g caster sugar | 125 ml water | 250 g fresh whole dates | 125 ml Kahlúa | 100 g caster sugar for dusting | Honey Wafers (page 318) to serve**

TO MAKE THE CUSTARD, BRING THE cream to a rolling boil then pour it onto the egg yolks, sugar, split vanilla bean and cinnamon stick, whisking well.

Pour the mixture back into the pan and cook gently for 15–20 minutes, stirring constantly with a wooden spoon, until the custard thickens. It should be as thick as honey and just beginning to catch on the bottom of the pot.

Strain the mixture into a stainless steel or glass bowl and sit it on ice or in a sink of very cold water for 5–10 minutes. This is important, as it stops the custard from cooking further. Remove from the ice and allow to continue cooling naturally.

To make the confit, heat the sugar with the water until it is completely dissolved. Add the whole dates and Kahlúa and cover the surface with a circle of baking paper to keep the dates submerged and prevent a skin from forming during cooking. Gently cook for 15–20 minutes. Remove from the heat and allow to cool. When cold, remove the seeds and skins from the dates and chop them finely.

Put a heaped teaspoon of the confit at the bottom of ten small glasses or ramekins. Spoon in enough custard to fill to just below the rim and chill until ready to serve.

Remove the custards from the fridge and lightly dust with sugar. Use a domestic blowtorch to caramelise the sugar, then return to the fridge for another 5 minutes. Dust with a little more sugar and repeat. This ensures a good, even layer of crunchy toffee. If you are using heatproof glasses, you could alternatively grill the brûlées under a very hot griller until the sugar is brown and bubbling. Serve with honey wafers if desired.

MAKES **10 small brûlées**

TOFFEED FIG PAVLOVAS

PAVLOVAS **150 g egg whites (about 4) | 220 g caster sugar | 2 tablespoons cornflour | 2 teaspoons white vinegar | 1 tablespoon orange-flower water**

TOFFEED FIGS **60 g caster sugar | 50 g honey | 100 ml strained orange juice | 3 strips lemon zest | 1 tablespoon orange-flower water | 4 figs, peeled and cut into wedges**

LEMON MASCARPONE **100 g mascarpone | 50 m cream (45% fat) | 30 g icing sugar | 1 teaspoon finely grated lemon zest | elderflowers to garnish (optional)**

TO MAKE THE PAVLOVAS, PREHEAT the oven to 150°C (Gas 2). Line two baking trays with baking paper and draw on 10 cm circles to act as templates.

Put the egg whites into the scrupulously clean bowl of a electric mixer. Start whisking at low speed, until the mixture begins to foam. Increase the speed to high and whisk until the foam thickens to smooth, soft peaks. Sift on the sugar, a little at a time, and continue whisking until the meringue stands in stiff, glossy peaks. Finally, sift on the cornflour, sprinkle on the vinegar and orange-flower water and whisk briefly until they are incorporated.

Spoon the meringue into a piping bag and pipe in concentric circles to fill the drawn circle, or dollop on spoonfuls and smooth into shape by hand. Reduce the oven temperature to 120°C (Gas 1/2) and bake the meringues for 1 hour 20 minutes. Turn the oven off and leave the pavlovas to cool completely, then remove from the oven and transfer to a wire rack to decorate.

To make the toffeed figs, heat the sugar and honey with half the orange juice until the sugar dissolves. Bring to the boil, then lower the heat, add the lemon zest strips and simmer until it thickens and darkens to form a caramel. Remove from the heat and add the remaining cold juice and the orange-flower water. Stir well and allow to cool.

Whisk the mascarpone with the cream then add the icing sugar and lemon zest.

To assemble, arrange the pavlovas on individual dessert plates or a large serving platter. Spread on a spoonful of lemony mascarpone and top with a few segments of fig. Drizzle on the caramel and garnish with elderflowers, if using.

MAKES **6**

GREEN APPLE SOUFFLÉ WITH PISTACHIO-HALVA ICE CREAM

GREEN APPLE SOUFFLÉ BASE **3 Granny Smith apples, cored but not peeled**
1 litre milk | 250 g caster sugar | 4 free-range eggs | 100 g cornflour

80 g unsalted butter, melted | caster sugar for dusting, plus 80 g extra
1 teaspoon cornflour | 150 g free-range egg whites (5–6 eggs)
icing sugar for dusting | cornflower petals to garnish (optional)
Pistachio-Halva Ice Cream (page 336)

CHOP THE APPLES ROUGHLY, THEN whiz in a food processor to a very smooth purée. Push through a sieve to remove any fibrous bits.

Combine the milk and half the sugar in a saucepan and bring to a boil. In a separate bowl, beat the eggs with the rest of the sugar and the cornflour. Pour on half the boiling milk and whisk well, then tip back into the saucepan with the remaining milk. Cook over a medium heat, whisking constantly, for about 2 minutes, or until the custard thickens. Stir in the apple purée and bring back to the boil. Remove from the heat, tip into a bowl and cover with plastic wrap.

When ready to bake the soufflés, preheat the oven to 160°C (Gas 3). Use a pastry brush to grease the insides of eight 150 ml soufflé dishes with melted butter. Brush in an upward direction only. Dust evenly with caster sugar, discarding any excess.

Mix the 80 g caster sugar with the cornflour. Put the egg whites in the clean bowl of an electric mixer and whisk at moderate speed to form soft peaks. Lower the speed of the mixer and sprinkle in the sugar-cornflour mixture. Increase the speed to high and whisk until evenly mixed and the whites are beginning to become stiff and shiny, about 3 minutes.

Put 250 g of the apple soufflé base into a large mixing bowl. Spoon on half of the whipped egg whites and use a spatula to fold them in gently but evenly. Add the rest of the whites and fold in evenly.

Fill the prepared soufflé dishes to the rim and use a spatula to level the surface evenly. Arrange the soufflé dishes on a baking tray and bake for 8–12 minutes, by which time they should be well risen and lightly browned. Dust with icing sugar and scatter on the cornflower petals, if using. Serve immediately with pistachio-halva ice cream.

SERVES **8**

A stunningly rich and delicious hot pudding, ideal for cold winter nights. This is definitely a deluxe bread and butter pudding — perfect for dinner parties and you can make it up to two days ahead of time. The key is to use stale bread that is unsliced and of good quality. Ready-sliced varieties are too moist, which prevents good absorption of the custard.

CHOCOLATE BREAD AND BUTTER PUDDING WITH TURKISH DELIGHT

150 g best-quality dark chocolate | 210 ml cream (35% fat) | 210 ml milk
4 tablespoons rum or brandy | 110 g caster sugar | 75 g unsalted butter, cubed
pinch of ground cinnamon | 3 large free-range eggs
1/2 loaf of stale white bread, about 400 g, cut into 2 cm cubes
100 g rose or orange-flower flavoured Turkish delight, quartered
whipped cream to serve | orange-flower water to serve (optional)

BREAK THE CHOCOLATE INTO PIECES and put in a bowl with the cream, milk, rum or brandy, sugar, butter and cinnamon. Sit the bowl over a pan of simmering water (it is best not to let the bowl touch the water) and allow the chocolate and butter to melt completely and the sugar to dissolve. Don't stir, and be patient — this can take a few minutes. Chocolate can be temperamental, so don't be tempted to do this directly over the heat. When the chocolate and butter have melted and the sugar has dissolved, stir well.

In a separate bowl, whisk the eggs and then pour the chocolate mixture on. Whisk thoroughly.

Lightly butter an 18 cm x 23 cm ovenproof baking dish. Cover the bottom of the dish with a layer of the chocolate mixture, then tip in the cubed bread. Pour the remaining custard over evenly, and squish gently to ensure that all the pieces of bread are well coated. Cover the dish with plastic wrap and allow to sit for a few hours at room temperature, then refrigerate for at least 24 hours, or 48 if you can.

Preheat the oven to 180°C (Gas 4).

Remove the plastic wrap and carefully dot in the pieces of Turkish delight. Bake on the top shelf of the oven for 30–35 minutes. The top should be crunchy, the centre soft and squishy. Allow it to stand for 5 minutes before serving with lightly whipped cream, flavoured, if you like, with a few drops of orange-flower water.

SERVES **8**

This fabulous recipe was invented by talented chef Kurt Sampson, who worked with me for a number of years before heading off to open his own restaurant. It's a little lighter than your average steamed pudding, and the combination of tangy sour cherries and white chocolate is inspired.

KURT SAMPSON'S WHITE CHOCOLATE-SOUR CHERRY PUDDING

250 g unsalted butter, softened | 200 g caster sugar | 2 free-range eggs
400 g self-raising flour | pinch of salt | 1 teaspoon vanilla extract
250 ml milk | 100 g dried sour cherries, chopped into small pieces
60 g white chocolate, chopped into small pieces

PREHEAT THE OVEN TO 180°C (GAS 4). Cream the butter and sugar until smooth, then add the eggs, one at a time.

Sift the flour and salt together and stir the vanilla extract into the milk. Gently fold the flour into the creamed mixture, alternating with the milk. Finally, gently fold in the chopped cherries and chocolate pieces, taking care not to overwork.

Lightly grease a pudding basin or small dariole moulds and pour in the pudding mixture. Cover the basin or each mould with baking paper and seal tightly with a layer of foil. Put into a deep baking tray and pour in enough boiling water to come halfway up the sides of the moulds or pudding basin. Bake for 30–40 minutes if using moulds, 40–50 minutes if you're using a pudding basin. Test by inserting a skewer, which should come out clean when the puddings are cooked.

SERVES **8–10**

This classic is given a decidedly exotic twist with the addition of orange-flower water.

MIDDLE EASTERN TIRAMISU

MASCARPONE MIXTURE **3 free-range eggs | 1 tablespoon brandy | 1 tablespoon Marsala | 100 g caster sugar | 600 g mascarpone, at room temperature**

350 ml very strong espresso coffee | 140 ml water | 1 tablespoon dry sherry | 1 tablespoon brandy | 60 ml Marsala | 1 tablespoon orange-flower water | 20 sponge fingers | 200 g cocoa nibs or best-quality dark chocolate, coarsely grated | fresh berries and Turkish coffee to serve

TO MAKE THE MASCARPONE MIX, whisk the eggs, brandy, Marsala and sugar in a bowl over simmering water until thick and pale (about 6 minutes). While still warm, gently fold in the mascarpone. Allow to cool.

Line a 15 cm x 20 cm deep dish with baking paper and spread over a third of the mascarpone mixture.

Combine the coffee, water, sherry, brandy, Marsala and orange-flower water in a shallow dish. Dip the sponge fingers in the mixture one at a time, quickly, and turn them over once in the liquid. Lay them on the mascarpone. Spread over another layer of mascarpone; add a second layer of biscuits; then finish with a final layer of mascarpone. Refrigerate overnight.

When ready to serve, invert the tiramisu onto a serving plate and peel away the baking paper. Sprinkle on the cocoa nibs or grated chocolate in an even layer. Cut into portions with a very sharp knife and serve with fresh berries or a cup of strong Turkish coffee.

SERVES **4**

Deep amber and ivory in tone, these popular Turkish sweet treats are exquisitely pretty. Make sure you use good-quality, large dried apricots. It can be difficult sometimes to find whole dried apricots, in which case you'll have to use apricot halves and sandwich them together. The cream used in Turkey is kaymak, a thick clotted cream made from buffalo milk. Lightly sweetened mascarpone, crème fraîche and strained yoghurt are the best alternatives if you can't find kaymak.

STICKY APRICOTS STUFFED WITH CLOTTED CREAM

350 ml water | 2 tablespoons caster sugar | 1/2 cinnamon stick
6 cardamom pods, lightly crushed | 2 tablespoons pekmez
1 tablespoon lemon juice | 250 g dried apricots (preferably whole)
250 g clotted cream, mascarpone or Strained Yoghurt (page 42)
additional caster sugar | 2 tablespoons finely ground or slivered unsalted pistachio kernels

IN A HEAVY-BASED SAUCEPAN, gently heat the water and sugar, stirring occasionally, until the sugar dissolves. When the syrup is clear, add the cinnamon, cardamom, pekmez and lemon juice, then increase the heat and bring to the boil. Add the apricots, then lower the heat a little and simmer for 20 minutes. Remove the pan from the heat and leave the apricots to cool in the syrup.

Remove the apricots from the syrup and let them drain for a moment in a sieve. Reserve the syrup. Sweeten the cream with a little sugar to taste. If you are using whole apricots, slit them carefully along one side and fill them generously with cream. If using apricot halves, sandwich them together with a spoonful of cream. Arrange the stuffed apricots on a serving plate and chill. When ready to serve, sprinkle each apricot with pistachios and drizzle with a little reserved syrup.

SERVES 4-6

A kind of Middle Eastern panforte, this ancient Arabic sweetmeat known as alaju comes from Spain courtesy of the Moors. It's a bit fiddly skinning the blanched pistachios, and not essential if you can't be bothered, BUT the resulting nuggets of brilliant jade green are a joy to behold. Toast them for a few minutes brushed with a little oil in a really hot oven to make them nice and crunchy. Similarly, it is worth shallow-frying the almonds to a golden brown, for a toastier flavour and a superior crunchy texture. Once the nuts are out of the way, the rest of the recipe is simple.

ARABIC HONEY SLICE

50 ml vegetable oil | 125 g whole blanched almonds
30 g blanched and peeled unsalted pistachio kernels | 250 g honey
coarsely grated zest of 1/2 lemon and 1 orange
150 g stale white bread, crusts removed | 1 teaspoon orange-flower water
1 teaspoon aniseeds, roasted and lightly crushed
2 sheets rice paper, each 24 cm square

HEAT THE OIL IN A FRYING PAN AND sauté the almonds over a gentle heat until golden brown. Remove and drain on paper towel. Repeat with the pistachios.

Put the honey in a saucepan with the citrus zests and slowly bring to a simmer.

Meanwhile, whiz the bread in a food processor to make coarse crumbs. Add the nuts to the hot honey, then the breadcrumbs. Stir continuously for about 5 minutes. It will look very unpromising to start with, and after a few minutes it will begin to come together in a solid mass and thicken to a stiff, almost glutinous paste. Keep stirring and turning, which will become increasingly hard work, until the 5 minutes is up. Then remove the pan from the heat and add the orange-flower water and aniseeds, stirring again to incorporate them into the mass.

Turn the mixture out onto on sheet of rice paper and pat it into a round disc about 20 cm in diameter. Cover with the second piece of rice paper and press down gently to about a finger's width in height. You may find it easier to use a small jar or a rolling pin to roll the paste out to a smooth, even height. Neaten the edges with a sharp knife and allow to cool. Store in an airtight tin and slice off pieces to serve with coffee as a petit four.

MAKES **18–24 pieces**

I created these crazy-shaped meringues as a reminder of the rocky, wild Cappadocian landscape, with its twisted pillars, cones and knobbed turrets that are nicknamed 'fairy chimneys'. You'll need a piping bag to make these meringues, but only basic piping skills. You're not aiming for perfection here; in a way, the wilder they look, the better!

The addition of cornflour makes the meringues slightly soft and marshmallowy inside. The idea is to make a tall base pillar and to top it with a broader, domed meringue. If you make it large enough, the base pillar can be filled with cream. Otherwise, serve a big bowl of cream on the side so that everyone can help themselves. These meringues make a wonderful dessert, served with fresh summer fruits in a lime syrup (page 351).

FAIRY CHIMNEYS

5 free-range egg whites | 200 g caster sugar | 200 g icing sugar | 1 tablespoon cornflour
400 ml cream (35% fat) | additional caster sugar (optional) | vanilla extract (optional)
2 tablespoons pure icing sugar sieved with 3 tablespoons finely ground pistachio slivers

PREHEAT THE OVEN TO 120°C (GAS 1/2). Line two baking trays with baking paper. Put the egg whites and a few tablespoons of the caster sugar into the scrupulously clean bowl of an electric mixer. Whisk on a low speed until the mixture begins to foam, then increase the speed to high and whisk until the foam thickens to form smooth, soft glossy peaks. Sift on the remaining caster sugar a little at a time, whisking to firm peaks as you go. Finally, sift on the icing sugar and cornflour and whisk in briefly until incorporated.

Spoon the meringue into a piping bag fitted with a smallish nozzle and pipe ten pillars, each about 4 cm in diameter and 5 cm high. Refill the bag and pipe the ten tops: make them a bit shorter, and slightly broader in diameter than the bases and coming to a peak at the top.

Bake for 1 1/2 hours until the meringues are ivory-coloured and crisp. Leave to cool on the baking trays for 10 minutes before carefully lifting them onto a wire rack to cool completely.

When ready to serve, whip the cream, sweetening it with a little sugar and flavouring it with a drop or two of vanilla extract if you like — or add your own flavourings. Fill the pillars with the cream and sit the peaked domes on top, using a little of the cream to secure them, if necessary. Otherwise, serve the cream alongside. Either way, spinkle with the ground pistachio mixture and serve straight away as a tea-time treat, or with fruit salad as a dessert.

MAKES **10**

This is gaz, the famous nougat from Isfahan in Iran. It can be tricky to make at home, but the result is so pretty and delicious that we felt it was worth including. We recommend you read the method through carefully first to be sure of the timing. It's important to have all ingredients and implements ready at the start, and imperative that you warm the fruit and nuts before adding them to the nougat mixture. Be organised and you'll be rewarded!

PISTACHIO-SOUR CHERRY NOUGAT

140 g unsalted pistachio kernels, roughly chopped
250 g dried sour cherries, roughly chopped | 50 g (2-3) egg whites, at room temperature
380 g caster sugar | 120 g liquid glucose | 100 ml water | 230 g honey

PREHEAT THE OVEN TO 110°C (GAS 1/4). Scatter the pistachios and dried cherries onto a baking tray and warm them in the oven while you make the nougat. It's important that the nuts and dried fruit are warm when added to the nougat mixture, or it will seize up and be unworkable.

Prepare all the ingredients: put the egg whites into the bowl of an electric mixer fitted with a whisk; put the sugar, liquid glucose and water into a saucepan; put the honey into another small saucepan. Line a 30 cm x 15 cm baking tray with edible rice paper or baking paper.

Begin cooking the honey over a medium heat and measure the temperature with a candy thermometer. When the temperature reaches 108°C, begin whisking the egg whites on medium-high speed. Continue cooking the honey until it reaches 120°C, by which time the egg whites should have reached the stiff-peak stage. Turn off the mixer and take the honey off the heat.

Now begin gently heating the sugar, glucose and water until the sugar has dissolved, then increase the heat and bring to a boil.

Meanwhile, turn the electric mixer back on to a low speed and mix the hot honey into the egg whites. When incorporated, increase the speed to high.

Continue whisking until the boiling sugar syrup reaches 155°C. Slow the speed of the mixer down again and pour in the boiling sugar syrup slowly and carefully until incorporated. Increase the speed of the mixer again and whisk for 3 minutes.

Turn off the mixer and, working quickly, take the warm fruit and nuts out of the oven and tip them into the nougat. Fold in with a wooden spoon as quickly as you can, then scrape into the prepared baking tray. Smooth out the nougat with a large, strong spatula to a rough rectangle, about 3 cm deep — don't try to make it fit the shape of the tray. The nougat will be very stiff to work with, but try to make the surface as even as possible; use a rolling pin if you like. Cover with a second sheet of rice paper or baking paper. Rest the nougat overnight, then cut into portions using a wet knife and store in an airtight container.

MAKES **750 g**

This wickedly buttery, cardamom-scented sweet is from the religious city of Qom, about an hour south of Tehran, and is famous all around Iran. The texture is hard to define — it is perhaps closer to fudge than brittle or toffee — but it is absolutely addictive.

Make it in one large slab, then cut or break it into random pieces, or drop spoonfuls of the mixture onto the prepared tray to make individual round portions. The high butter content means it can 'sweat' a little bit, so store it in a cool place in an airtight tin, rather than a plastic container. It will keep well for up to two weeks.

CARDAMOM-PISTACHIO BUTTER FUDGE

500 g caster sugar | 80 ml corn syrup | 80 ml water | 300 g unsalted butter, roughly diced
2 teaspoons ground cardamom | 2 tablespoons Saffron Liquid (page 218)
50 g unsalted pistachio kernels | 50 g slivered pistachios

LINE A BAKING TRAY WITH BAKING paper. Combine the sugar, corn syrup and water in a heavy-based saucepan over a low heat until the sugar dissolves. Increase the heat and cook until the mixture begins to become golden in colour, then whisk in the butter, cardamom and saffron liquid and cook for a few minutes more, until it is an even butterscotch colour.

Pour the mixture onto the prepared baking tray and use a spatula to smooth it out as thinly as you can. Sprinkle on the pistachios, pressing them gently into the surface of the toffee. Leave to cool completely before cutting into pieces with a sharp knife.

MAKES **650 g**

We saw several different kinds of toffee and nut brittles on our journeys around Iran, some flavoured with cardamom, others with honey, others with saffron. This is our version of a thin, crunchy pistachio brittle, with a sprinkling of rose petals added.

This recipe produces a fairly large quantity, but it's a little tricky to make in small amounts. Brittles are very versatile — you can serve them as is, or crush them to make a crunchy praline topping for desserts or ice creams (keep a bag of it in the freezer for instant gratification).

PISTACHIO-ROSE BRITTLE

200 g unsalted pistachio kernels | 330 g caster sugar | 80 ml corn syrup
50 g unsalted butter | 125 ml water | $\frac{1}{2}$ teaspoon bicarbonate of soda
pinch of sea salt | grated zest of 1 orange | $1\frac{1}{2}$ teaspoons ground cardamom
10 edible dried rosebuds, petals separated (optional)

PREHEAT THE OVEN TO 160°C (GAS 3). Roast the pistachios on a baking tray for 10–12 minutes, shaking the tray frequently. You don't want them to colour, just to dry out a little. Tip into a bowl and cool.

Line a baking tray with baking paper. Combine the caster sugar, corn syrup, butter and water in a heavy-based saucepan over a low heat until the sugar dissolves. Increase the heat, bring to a boil and cook over a medium heat for 15–20 minutes until the mixture is a light golden caramel — if using a candy thermometer, at 160°C it will be approaching the hard-crack stage. Remove from the heat and immediately stir in the bicarbonate of soda, salt, zest, cardamom and pistachios.

Scrape the mixture into the prepared baking tray and use a spatula to smooth it out as thinly as you can. Sprinkle with rose petals, if using, pressing them gently into the surface of the brittle. Leave to cool completely before breaking into pieces with a rolling pin.

MAKES **500 g**

STRAWBERRY-ROSE MARSHMALLOWS

STRAWBERRY PURÉE **280g strawberries, hulled and roughly chopped | 1 teaspoon rosewater**

300 g caster sugar | 255 g trimoline (invert sugar)
12 x 1.6 g leaves gold-strength gelatine, soaked in 60 ml cold water for 10 minutes
240 g cornflour sifted with 70 g icing sugar

TO MAKE THE STRAWBERRY PURÉE, whiz the strawberries and rosewater in a blender until finely puréed, then pass through a sieve.

Oil a 36 cm x 26 cm baking tray.

To make the marshmallows, combine the sugar with 105 g of the trimoline and 70 g of the strawberry purée in a saucepan and bring to a boil.

In the bowl of an electric mixer, combine the remaining 150 g trimoline with another 70 g strawberry purée and the soaked gelatine then whisk on medium speed to combine. With the motor running, slowly pour on the boiling syrup. Continue whisking for about 5 minutes, or until the mixture cools to room temperature — the same way you would make an Italian meringue.

Pour the mixture into the prepared baking tray, cover with oiled baking paper, then leave for about 2 hours in the fridge until it sets firm. Use a hot knife to cut the marshmallow into 6 cm x 3 cm rectangles, or the shapes of your choice. Roll in the cornflour-icing sugar mixture until coated and store in an airtight container until required. The marshmallows will keep for up to 2 weeks in the fridge.

MAKES **about 800 g**

LARDER

Baharat means, literally, 'spices', and Arab households purchase this all-purpose mix by the sack from specialist spice shops. As with many spice blends, there are variations on the basic theme, and recipes vary according to region and family. The overall flavour of baharat is similar to that of allspice, and baharat is used extensively in marinades, braises and stews.

BAHARAT

Working with each ingredient separately, finely grind 4 tablespoons black pepper, 3 tablespoons cumin seeds, 2 tablespoons coriander seeds, 2 tablespoons cloves and 1 tablespoon cardamom seeds. Mix together with 5 tablespoons sweet paprika, 2 tablespoons ground cinnamon, 1 tablespoon ground star anise and 1 teaspoon grated nutmeg. Transfer to a jar with a tight-fitting lid. It will keep for up to 3 months.

MAKES about 200 g

Za'atar is the Arabic word for wild thyme, and for the spice mix made with the herb, roasted sesame seeds and the ground sour red berries of the sumac tree. It is dearly beloved in the Middle East, where it is eaten virtually daily, sprinkled on dishes as a garnish, or mixed with olive oil to make a paste for pizzas and breads. I always have a little jar of it in the fridge, which I eat on toast for breakfast. Za'atar is also delicious spread on meat or on robustly flavoured fish before grilling or roasting.

To make za'atar, you need to buy a bag of ground sumac and a bag of za'atar (which will actually be a mixture of wild thyme and sesame seeds) from a Middle Eastern food store.

ZA'ATAR

Combine 1/3 cup ground sumac with 1 cup za'atar and store in an airtight jar. To make larger quantities, combine the ingredients in a ratio of three parts za'atar to one part sumac.

To make a paste, stir in enough olive oil to make a loose paste and store in a sealed jar in the fridge.

Za'atar and za'atar paste will keep happily for a couple of months.

MAKES 130 g

Dukkah is a coarsely ground mixture of sesame seeds, hazelnuts and fragrant coriander and cumin. Originating in Egypt, its popularity has spread and these days you can find it in trendy restaurants and cafés around the world, offered with oil and bread before a meal. Don't feel constrained to use it only as a dip — it is terrific added to crumbing mixtures and sprinkled on all kinds of salads, and works particularly well with the unctuous richness of soft-boiled eggs (see page 76).

DUKKAH

Working with each ingredient separately, roast 50 g hazelnuts, 8 tablespoons sesame seeds, 4 tablespoons coriander seeds and 3 tablespoons cumin seeds in a hot, dry frying pan. Keep an eye on the heat — it should not be so hot that they burn or colour too quickly. Shake the pan gently from time to time so that they brown evenly, then tip straight away onto paper towel. After roasting the hazelnuts, tip them into a tea towel and rub them briskly between your fingers to loosen and flake away the dark papery skin.

Grind the ingredients using a mortar and pestle, food processor or spice grinder. You can grind the coriander and cumin seeds together, but do the sesame seeds and hazelnuts separately — be careful not to overgrind or you may end up with an oily paste, rather than the desired coarsely ground crumb.

Mix the nuts and seeds with 1 teaspoon sea salt and ½ teaspoon freshly ground black pepper and store the dukkah in an airtight jar in the refrigerator, where it will keep for several weeks, or in an airtight container in the freezer for several months.

MAKES **200 g**

There are myriad spice blends used to flavour köfte — ground lamb patties and kebabs. This Turkish blend is one of our favourites.

KÖFTE SPICE MIX

Combine ⅓ cup ground cumin, ⅓ cup dried mint, ⅓ cup dried oregano, 2 tablespoons sweet paprika, 2 tablespoons freshly ground black pepper and 2 teaspoons hot paprika. Mix thoroughly and store in a jar for up to 3 months.

MAKES **160 g**

Every moroccan spice vendor has his own ras al hanout blends, which vary in price according to the scarcity of the ingredients. The most prized and exotic blends can include thirty or more spices, plant roots and other unusual aromatics. For daily use, MOST cooks tend to use a humbler blend similar to the one below. Use ras al hanout in soups and tagines, with rice and couscous, or mix it with a little oil and rub onto meat or poultry as a marinade. Add ras al hanout to dusting flour or crumbing mixes before frying.

RAS AL HANOUT

Working with each ingredient separately, lightly roast and finely grind 1 teaspoon cumin seeds, 1 teaspoon coriander seeds, the seeds from 6 cardamom pods, 1/2 teaspoon fennel seeds and 1/2 teaspoon black peppercorns. Sieve to remove the husks. Mix with 2 teaspoons sweet paprika, 1 teaspoon ground cinnamon, 1 teaspoon ground turmeric, 1 teaspoon cayenne pepper, 1 teaspoon sea salt, 1/2 teaspoon sugar and 1/2 teaspoon ground allspice and store in an airtight jar. The mixture keeps well for up to 3 months.

MAKES 50 g

A variation of ras al hanout that is particularly good with seafood — especially shellfish. Add to dusting flour or crumbing mixes before frying.

GOLDEN SPICE MIX

Sieve together 1 tablespoon ground coriander, 1 tablespoon ground cumin, 1/2 tablespoon ground turmeric, 1/2 tablespoon ground ginger and 1/4 tablespoon chilli powder and store in an airtight jar for up to 3 months.

MAKES about 40 g

A popular mix from the Persian Gulf region of Iran, where the extensive use of spices — and even the odd touch of chilli heat — reflects this region's long trading history with the nearby Arab countries and Africa and India. This blend is widely used in the many fish and seafood dishes found there.

BANDARI SPICE MIX

Combine 1½ teaspoons ground cumin, 1 teaspoon ground coriander, 1 teaspoon ground turmeric, ½ teaspoon finely ground caraway seeds, ½ teaspoon finely ground cardamom seeds, ½ teaspoon freshly ground black pepper and ½ teaspoon freshly grated nutmeg. Transfer to an airtight jar. Store for up to 3 months.

MAKES 40 g

Little bowls of spiced salts are wonderful to have on the table for dipping, or sprinkling on food as it is eaten. Fragrant salts can be rubbed onto meat and the skin of poultry before grilling or frying. We also use them in curing and pickling solutions.

The recipe below is for coriander salt, which we serve with Crisp Egyptian Pigeon (page 173). Reverse the quantities of coriander and cumin to make cumin salt, which is equally delicious — especially North African-style, with hard-boiled eggs.

FRAGRANT SALT

Lightly roast, grind and sieve 4 tablespoons coriander seeds and 2 teaspoons cumin seeds. Grind 3 tablespoons sea salt to a fine powder. Heat a non-stick frying pan and warm the salt, coriander and cumin powders together so they merge into one fragrant powder. Allow to cool, then store in an airtight jar for up to 3 months.

MAKES 60 g

Harissa adds depth and character to sauces, soups and stews. Add it to marinades for a blast of heat or use it as a condiment. In Morocco it's drizzled on just about everything.

RED HARISSA

Preheat the oven to 200°C (Gas 6). Place 1 red capsicum (pepper) on a baking tray and roast until the skin starts to blister and blacken, turning from time to time. Transfer to a bowl, cover with plastic wrap and leave to steam for a further 10 minutes. Carefully peel away the skin and discard the stalk and seeds.

Pour enough boiling water to cover over 10–15 dried long red chillies and leave to rehydrate for 10 minutes. Seed 10 red bullet chillies, but leave the white inner fibres intact. Crush 2 cloves garlic with 1/2 teaspoon sea salt. In a blender, combine the skinned capsicum, drained rehydrated chillies, seeded chillies, garlic paste, 1 teaspoon roasted and crushed cumin seeds, 3/4 teaspoon roasted and crushed caraway seeds and 60 ml olive oil. Blend to a paste, then taste carefully for seasoning — it is extremely hot — adding more salt if needed. Tip into a jar and pour on a thin layer of olive oil. It will keep for 3–4 weeks in the fridge.

MAKES about 200 ml

An adaptation of the more commonly found red harissa, green harissa is more fragrant than fiery, with a milder and sweeter taste. Use in soups and stews or to accompany grills, roasts and tagines. Add to mayonnaise and creamy dressings or to vinaigrettes, or spread on sandwiches.

GREEN HARISSA

In a food processor, combine 125 g seeded, scraped and shredded large green chillies, 1 clove garlic, 100 g fresh spinach leaves (stalks removed), 2 cups fresh coriander leaves, 1 teaspoon roasted and crushed caraway seeds, 1 teaspoon roasted and crushed coriander seeds, 1 teaspoon dried mint and 1/2 teaspoon chilli powder. Whiz for a minute, and then, with the machine still running, slowly add 60 ml olive oil until the mixture is the consistency of pouring cream. Season with sea salt and freshly ground black pepper. Pour into a jar, top with a thin layer of olive oil and refrigerate. It will keep for about a week.

MAKES 250 ml

This intensely flavoured, versatile paste is especially popular in the north of Syria. It is often spread onto savoury breads and pastries, added to dips, soups and stews or used to flavour marinades. All varieties of red capsicum can be used — hot and sweet.

RED PEPPER PASTE

In a food processor, put 4 seeded, scraped and roughly chopped large red capsicums (peppers) and 2 seeded, scraped and roughly chopped red bullet chillies, and purée to a smooth paste. Tip the paste into a large heavy-based frying pan and add 1 teaspoon salt and 1 teaspoon sugar. Bring to the boil, then lower the heat and simmer for 40–45 minutes, stirring from time to time to make sure it doesn't catch and burn.

Preheat the oven to its lowest temperature. Scrape the paste into a large, shallow baking tray and spread out evenly. Place in the oven for 5–6 hours, or overnight, until it dries to a very thick consistency. Remove from the oven and leave to cool. Spoon into sterilised jars and pour on a film of olive oil. Seal and store in the fridge or freezer.

MAKES **250 ml**

Chermoula is one of the signature spices of North Africa. It is most often used as a fragrant marinade for seafood dishes, but also works well with poultry and meat. The dominant flavours are garlic, cumin, paprika, coriander and lemon, with a chilli content that can be varied according to your taste.

CHERMOULA

Roast and grind separately 45 g cumin seeds and 15 g coriander seeds. Put into a food processor with 25 g sweet paprika, 15 g ground ginger, 2 roughly chopped cloves garlic, 2–4 seeded, scraped and roughly chopped bullet chillies, the juice of 2 lemons, 100 ml olive oil, 1/2 teaspoon freshly ground black pepper and 1/2 teaspoon sea salt. Whiz until the garlic and chillies have been ground to a paste. Tip into a jar and seal with 1 tablespoon olive oil. It will keep for about three months in the fridge.

TOMATO CHERMOULA For tomato chermoula, add 250 g crushed tomatoes. Refrigerate for up to 1 week.

MAKES **200 g**

Taklia is a very simple, all-purpose savoury spice paste found in Lebanon and Syria. It is usually added at the end of cooking for its aromatic flavouring. It can also be thinned with a little olive oil and used as a condiment, or enlivened with a touch of chilli.

TAKLIA

Place 6 sliced cloves garlic and 1 tablespoon olive oil in a heavy-based pan and sauté for 1 minute, taking care not to let the garlic colour. Put the garlic into a mortar with 2 teaspoons ground coriander and 1 teaspoon sea salt and grind to a very thick paste. Spoon into a jar. It will keep for up to 2 months in the refrigerator.

MAKES **40 g**

Zhoug is a fiery-hot chilli relish that comes originally from Yemen but has now become a firm favourite in Israel. It is eaten with bread as an accompaniment to just about everything, and works particularly well with fish, meats and chicken dishes. For a touch of heat, we also swirl it into stews and soups and even mayonnaises or flavoured butters. Its ferocious chilli heat makes it addictive!

ZHOUG

In a mortar and pestle, crush 1 teaspoon black peppercorns and 1 teaspoon caraway seeds with the seeds from 4 cardamom pods. Sift to remove any husks and dust.

Wash and thoroughly dry 2 cups fresh coriander (roots removed). Put into a blender with 4–6 seeded and scraped red bullet chillies, 6 cloves garlic, 1/4 teaspoon sea salt and a splash of water. Add the spices and whiz to a smooth paste. Tip into a jar and seal with 1 tablespoon olive oil. It will keep for about a week in the fridge.

MAKES **100 ml**

This good all-purpose mayonnaise recipe can be used on its own, or livened up with the addition of red harissa, preserved lemon or green olives.

MAYONNAISE

Crush 1 clove garlic with 1/2 teaspoon salt and whisk with 2 egg yolks. Combine 100 ml extra-virgin olive oil with 100 ml vegetable oil. Very gradually whisk the oils into the egg, drop by drop, making sure each amount is thoroughly incorporated before adding the next drop. Once the mixture has thickened to a stiff paste, thin it with the juice of 1/2 lemon. Continue to add the oil slowly, until all has been incorporated. Taste and add salt and white pepper, and the juice of another 1/2 lemon.

RED HARISSA MAYONNAISE Add 1 tablespoon Red Harissa (page 381) to the base recipe.
PRESERVED LEMON MAYONNAISE Finely chop the rind of 1 preserved lemon (page 394) and add to the base recipe.
GREEN OLIVE MAYONNAISE Add 1 tablespoon finely chopped green olives and 1 tablespoon baby capers to the base recipe.

MAKES **200 ml**

This rich, garlicky mayonnaise is much loved in the south of France. We like to temper the pungency of the raw garlic with a touch of mild honey.

HONEY-GARLIC AÏOLI

Preheat the oven to 180°C (Gas 4). Cut 3 whole heads of garlic in half crosswise and drizzle them with 1 tablespoon honey. Wrap them in foil and roast them for about 20 minutes, or until they are very soft. Squeeze out the garlic into a blender and whiz with 2 egg yolks, 1 teaspoon Dijon mustard and 30 ml Champagne vinegar. Combine 150 olive oil with 100 ml vegetable oil then add the oils, drop by drop, until the mixture emulsifies. Loosen with 30 ml extra Champagne vinegar and the juice of 1 lemon, then add the remaining oil and season with salt and pepper.

MAKES **350 ml**

Strictly for garlic lovers, Toum is the Middle Eastern version of aïoli and there is no compromise with this intense sauce. Uncooked garlic has a uniquely hot pungency, but when combined with an emulsion of oil and lemon juice, it softens to become smooth and almost fluffy. There is simply nothing like it for serving with grilled chicken.

TOUM

Peel and roughly chop the cloves from 1 whole head garlic, then put them into a blender or liquidiser with 1 teaspoon sea salt and the juice of 1 lemon. Blend until very smooth, which will take about 2 minutes. Scrape down the sides from time to time to make sure no chunks of garlic get left out of the paste.

Next, very slowly start to add 200 ml sunflower oil, as though you are making a mayonnaise — be sure to emulsify each addition well before adding more oil. Continue to dribble in the oil until it is fully absorbed. Finally, add 2 tablespoons water. The whole process should take no longer than about 5 minutes.

If the sauce splits as you're making it, you can save it as follows. Clean out the blender. Put in 2 egg yolks and blend, then very slowly pour in half the split mixture. When it begins to emulsify and thicken, add a teaspoon of cold water to loosen it. Then gradually add the rest of the mix. You end up with a straight mayonnaise rather than a sauce, but it is equally delicious! The sauce keeps, covered and refrigerated, for about a week.

MAKES **300 ml**

Hugely popular in Provençal cuisine, rouille is sometimes thickened with breadcrumbs or potatoes. Variations abound — with saffron, orange zest, roasted capsicums or chilli. Here, we add a touch of warm cumin and serve it with Grilled Seafood Bouillabaise (page 158).

CUMIN ROUILLE

Place 250 g peeled potatoes into a saucepan with 300 ml water or Crab Stock (page 13). Add 5 cloves garlic, 10 lightly roasted and ground saffron threads and 2 seeded and roughly chopped bullet chillies.
Cook until the potatoes are soft and the water has nearly evaporated. Roast, skin and dice 2 red capsicums (peppers). Roast, grind and sieve 1 tablespoon cumin seeds. Combine everything in a blender and add a big squeeze of lemon juice. Whiz to a purée. While the motor is running, slowly drizzle in 250 ml olive oil until all is incorporated. Add another big squeeze of lemon juice and season with salt and white pepper. Add more lemon juice to taste. The consistency should be that of a thin honey, not a stiff mayonnaise.

MAKES **350 ml**

LEMON-GARLIC DRESSING

Crush 2 cloves garlic with 1/2 teaspoon salt. Transfer to a mixing bowl and whisk with the juice of 2 lemons, 100 ml water and 1 teaspoon honey, then stir in 250 ml extra-virgin olive oil. Drop in 3 halved shallots and 4 sprigs of thyme and season with a generous grind of pepper. Cover and leave for 6 hours or, even better, overnight so that the flavours mingle and intensify. Taste and add extra salt if necessary. Strain through a fine sieve into a jar. It will keep, sealed and refrigerated, for up to 2 weeks.

MAKES **about 400 ml**

LEMON-CORIANDER DRESSING

Trim and clean the roots of 1 cup fresh coriander then put it — leaves, stalks, roots and all — into a food processor. Crush 2 cloves garlic with 1/2 teaspoon salt. Add to the coriander along with 2 tablespoons water and whiz to a purée. Put 200 ml extra-virgin olive oil into a large mixing bowl and whisk in the coriander purée. Add 1 teaspoon roasted and finely ground caraway seeds, 4 lightly bruised whole cardamom pods, 1/2 teaspoon crushed black peppercorns, 1 seeded, scraped and diced red bullet chilli, the juice of 1 lemon and the segments of 1 lemon and stir together well. Taste and adjust the seasoning, if necessary. Pour into a sealable jar and store in the fridge. It will keep for 3–4 days. Strain before using.

MAKES **about 350 ml**

À LA GRECQUE DRESSING

In a saucepan, mix 10 roasted and finely crushed saffron threads, 80 ml white wine vinegar, 40 ml white wine and 1 teaspoon honey. Warm the pan gently to dissolve the honey, then add 5 evenly and finely diced shallots, 2 finely chopped cloves garlic, 1 finely chopped bullet chilli and the leaves from 2 sprigs fresh thyme. Pour into a large mixing bowl and allow to cool. Add 1 teaspoon roasted and crushed coriander seeds, 1/2 teaspoon roasted and crushed white peppercorns, 1/2 teaspoon roasted and crushed fennel seeds, then whisk in the juice of 1 lemon and 250 ml extra-virgin olive oil. Taste for seasoning and add salt and freshly ground black pepper as required. Pour into a sealable jar and store in the fridge. It will keep for 5 days.

MAKES **about 360 ml**

TOMATO-POMEGRANATE DRESSING

In a bowl, combine 4 finely diced shallots, 1 finely chopped clove garlic, 2 ripe tomatoes, seeded and cut into 5 mm dice, 3 tablespoons pomegranate seeds, the juice of 1 lemon, 1 teaspoon pomegranate molasses, 180 ml extra-virgin olive oil, sea salt and freshly ground black pepper. Whisk well. Taste and adjust the seasoning to your liking. Pour into a sealable jar and store in the fridge. It will keep for 5 days.

MAKES **about 400 ml**

SPICY TOMATO DRESSING

In a food processor, combine 3 peeled, seeded and diced medium tomatoes, 2 seeded, scraped and finely diced red bullet chillies, 1 finely diced clove garlic, 3 tablespoons grated ginger, 2 tablespoons sugar and the juice of 2 lemons. Whiz to a fine, smooth purée. With the motor running, gradually add 150 ml olive oil and 100 ml walnut oil until the oils are fully absorbed. Check the seasoning and add salt and white pepper, to taste. Pour into a sealable jar and store in the fridge. It will keep for 5 days.

MAKES **about 450 ml**

These lightly pickled onion rings are delicious with cold and smoked meats and make a great addition to any salad — especially tomato salads. This is not a pickle to set aside and store; it needs to be eaten soon after it's made. The main benefit of using long purple onions, or 'Tuscan onions', is that when cut the rings are fairly even in size, and not too large.

PICKLED ONION RINGS IN ROSE VINEGAR

In a bowl, stir together 100 ml red-wine vinegar, 1/4 teaspoon sea salt and 1 teaspoon mild honey until the salt and honey have dissolved. Cut 2 long purple (Tuscan) onions into thickish rings, add them to the vinegar mixture and toss thoroughly, then leave to macerate for an hour. Just before serving, add a splash of rosewater and, if you like, a scattering of slivered pistachios.

SERVES **4**

Marinating olives in herbs and other aromatics is a great way to spice them up a bit. Serve the olives with chunks of sweet melon or spiced nuts with pre-dinner drinks. They also make a great addition to the dinner table to enjoy with fresh white cheese and warm bread.

PERSIAN GULF SPICY OLIVES

In a large bowl, mix 1 kg plump green olives, 3 finely chopped cloves garlic, 3 chopped long green chillies, 2 tablespoons chopped dill sprigs, 2 tablespoons chopped coriander leaves, 1 teaspoon fennel seeds, 1 teaspoon dried chilli flakes, 1 lemon, quartered and thinly sliced, 1 bay leaf and the grated zest of 1 orange. Cover and refrigerate for 24 hours so the flavours develop, then transfer to sterilised jars. Keep, refrigerated, for up to 2 weeks.

MAKES **1 kg**

PICKLED CUCUMBERS WITH FENNEL

Wash 700 pickling cucumbers, then prick them all over with a thin skewer or toothpick. Evenly trim the stalks of 6 baby fennel bulbs and cut the bulbs into quarters lengthwise. Prick 4 bullet chillies all over with the point of a small knife. Sterilise two 500 ml jars. Working in layers, pack each jar with half the cucumbers, half the fennel, 2 chillies, 4 cloves garlic, 1/2 tablespoon fennel seeds, 1/2 tablespoon coriander seeds and 1/2 cinnamon stick.

Bring 1 litre water, 150 ml white-wine vinegar, 60 g salt and 2 tablespoons sugar to the boil in a large, non-reactive saucepan. Pour the boiling liquid into the jars, ensuring there are no air pockets and that the vegetables are submerged. Seal the jars and turn them upside down a few times to distribute the ingredients evenly. Leave in a cool, dry place for a week before using. The pickles will keep in the refrigerator for up to a month after opening.

MAKES **1 kg**

This recipe for one of our all-time favourite pickled vegetables comes from my sister-in-law, Amal Malouf.

PICKLED EGGPLANTS WITH WALNUTS AND CHILLIES

Wash and dry 1 kg baby Lebanese eggplants (aubergines), no more than 5 cm long, and cook them in boiling water for 5 minutes. Refresh them under cold water and drain. Split each eggplant in half lengthwise to within 1 cm of the stem. Open them up and, using a total of 100 g salt, rub salt into each side, then lay them in a colander, weight down and allow to drain for 24–48 hours.

Chop 150 g walnut halves into quarters. Pick 2 tablespoons leaves from oregano sprigs. Thinly slice 4 cloves of garlic. Into each eggplant stuff a few oregano leaves, garlic slivers and walnuts. Pack the eggplants tightly in a large sterilised jar and turn it upside down for an hour in a colander — this will allow more liquid to drain away.

Invert the jar, fill it with 1 litre olive oil and drop in 2–3 split red bullet chillies. Seal and leave for at least 3 weeks. Unopened, the pickles will keep up to a year. Once opened, keep refrigerated and eat within 6 weeks.

MAKES **600 g**

This chutney is delicious with all kinds of grills, especially poultry or rich, creamy offal. Alternatively, mix it with a little olive oil and brush the mixture over meat or chicken as a last-minute glaze when barbecuing. A spoonful of chutney added to a vinaigrette adds a lovely citrus-sweet dimension to a dressing for bitter-leaf salads.

DATE-LEMON CHUTNEY

Finely chop the zest and flesh of 6 medium lemons, mix with 2 teaspoons salt and leave overnight. The next day place the lemon mixture in a heavy non-reactive pan with 4 finely minced cloves garlic, 100 ml lemon juice, 100 ml cider vinegar, 1 tablespoon finely grated fresh ginger, 1 teaspoon finely ground cardamom seeds, 1 teaspoon finely ground coriander seeds and 1/4 teaspoon chilli flakes. Bring slowly to the boil and simmer for 5 minutes. Then add 225 g brown sugar and 200 g pitted and finely chopped fresh dates, and simmer gently for 45 minutes to 1 hour, until thick and well reduced. Stir from time to time so it doesn't stick and burn. Pour into sterilised jars and store for at least 6 weeks before eating.

MAKES **600 g**

One of our favourite relishes, this is wonderful with any charcuterie and cold meats or with leftovers from the Sunday roast.

SPICY EGGPLANT RELISH

Peel 2 eggplants (aubergines) and cut them into 2 cm cubes. Put them in a colander and sprinkle with salt. After 20 minutes, rinse them under cold water and pat them dry with paper towel.

Heat 100 ml olive oil in a frying pan and sauté the eggplant, turning from time to time, until it is a light golden brown. Use a slotted spoon to transfer the eggplant to a colander to drain off excess oil. Add 2 purple onions cut into 1 cm dice, 1 finely sliced clove garlic, 1 teaspoon ground cumin, 1/2 teaspoon turmeric, 1/2 teaspoon sweet paprika and a pinch of cayenne pepper to the pan. Fry in the remaining oil on a gentle heat for 5 minutes, stirring from time to time. Return the eggplant to the pan with 2 seeded and diced tomatoes, 1/2 teaspoon salt, 1 teaspoon sugar, juice of 1 lemon and 175 ml water, and simmer gently for a further 8 minutes. Remove from the heat and stir in 1/4 cup finely chopped flat-leaf parsley leaves, 1/4 cup finely chopped coriander leaves and 1/4 cup finely chopped mint leaves. The relish will keep, refrigerated, for up to 5 days. Serve at room temperature.

MAKES **450 g**

There is just no substitute for the distinctive flavour that preserved lemons add to Moroccan-influenced dishes. They are very easy to make, but need a minimum of a month to mature, so it is well worth making a big batch.

PRESERVED LEMONS AND LIMES

Wash and dry 1.5 kg thin-skinned lemons (or limes). Cut them lengthwise into quarters, from the point of the lemon to three-quarters of the way down, but leave them joined together at the base. Place them in a plastic bag in the freezer for 24 hours. This dramatically speeds up the maturing process.

Thaw the lemons. Measure 350 g sea salt and 1 tablespoon lightly crushed coriander seeds. Stuff the centre of each lemon with a heaped teaspoon of salt. Arrange them neatly in a 2 litre jar, sprinkling each layer with more salt and some coriander as you go. Stuff 2 cinnamon sticks into the jar with 2 lemon leaves or bay leaves.

Mix 2 tablespoons honey, 250 ml lemon juice and 750 ml warm water until the honey dissolves. Pour into the jar to completely cover the lemons. Screw on the lid and put the jar into a large pot on top of a piece of cardboard (this stops the jar vibrating). Pour in enough warm water to come halfway up the sides of the jar and slowly bring it to the boil. Boil for 6 minutes, then remove from the heat. Lift the jar out of the water and store in a cool, dry place for at least a month before opening. Once opened, keep refrigerated.

MAKES **1.5 kg**

Sticky, sweet onion jam is an indispensable accompaniment to cold meats or cheese platters. We add currants, for a Moorish touch, and serve it with Seven-Vegetable Tagine (page 250).

ONION JAM

Soak 50 g currants in 50 ml dry sherry. Melt 50 g unsalted butter in a heavy-based pan, and slowly sweat 5 finely sliced medium purple onions until they're soft and translucent (about 5 minutes). Add 250 ml dry sherry and 250 ml tawny port and continue to cook for a further 45 minutes over a very low heat, stirring from time to time to ensure the jam doesn't stick to the bottom of the pan. Add the currants and the soaking liquor and cook for a further 10 minutes, or until the onions have become very sticky and almost caramelised. Season with salt and pepper.

The relish will keep, refrigerated, for up to 4 weeks.

MAKES **300 g**

PERSIAN-STYLE ROSE-SCENTED PLUM JELLY

Place 2.5 kg plums in a large heavy-based pan and boil for about 10 minutes until they are soft and pulpy and have released a lot of juice.

Strain them overnight through a jelly cloth (a piece of muslin or cheesecloth, or even an ordinary kitchen cloth like a clean Chux will do just as well). Do not force them through, as this will make the jelly cloudy, but allow them to drip through naturally. The amount of juice yielded will vary, depending on the fruit, but you should have about 2 litres. Pour the juice into the pan and for every 600 ml, add 500 g sugar. Stir well over a low heat until the sugar has completely dissolved, then bring to the boil.

Boil for 20–25 minutes, until the jelly reaches the setting point. To test, spoon a small amount onto a cold plate and place it in the refrigerator to cool. The jelly is at setting point if it forms a skin which wrinkles when you push your finger through. When it reaches the setting point, remove the pan from the heat and skim the froth from the surface. Stir in 50 ml rosewater and then carefully ladle the jelly into sterilised jars. Seal while hot and store in a cool place. Keeps for up to 12 months.

MAKES **about 3 kg**

ORGANIC ROSE PETAL AND VANILLA JAM

Remove the central stamens from 1.5 kg organic roses. Wash the flowers very gently to ensure they don't bruise. Drain on a tea towel to absorb some of the moisture, then weigh out 1 kg of petals.

Tip into a large stainless steel bowl (this prevents the petals from discolouring) and pour on 1.2 kg caster sugar. Add the scraped seeds from 1 vanilla pod and gently massage the petals, using your fingers, until you have soft pulp. Cover and leave to macerate overnight in a cool place. Do not refrigerate.

The next day, tip the petals into a large stainless steel saucepan and add 200 ml water. Bring to the boil, then lower the heat and simmer, uncovered, for 45–60 minutes, until the pulp turns syrupy. Remove from the heat and stir in the juice of 3 limes. Carefully ladle the jam into sterilised jars. Seal while hot and store in a cool place. This jam will keep, unopened, for up to 3 months. Once opened, refrigerate and use within 4 weeks.

MAKES **about 2 kg**

BITTER ORANGE MARMALADE WITH ROSEWATER AND ALMONDS

Very thinly slice 6 Seville oranges (about 1.5 kg whole weight) and 2 lemons, reserving the pips. Put the slices of fruit in a large bowl and cover with 3 litres water. Put the pips into a small bowl and cover with 500 ml water. Leave both to soak for 24 hours.

Put the fruit and its soaking water into a large pan. Scoop the pips into a small square of muslin and tie it loosely to form a little bag. Tuck it into the fruit in the pan. The soaking water from the pips should also go into the pan with the fruit.

Bring the pan to the boil, then lower the heat and simmer gently for 2 hours. Remove the bag of pips and add 2.2 kg sugar. Stir over a low heat until the sugar has dissolved. Increase the heat and squeeze the bag of pips over the pan to extract as much pectin as you can. Stir well. Bring to a fast boil and cook for 20–30 minutes, or until the marmalade reaches setting point. While it is boiling away, put a couple of saucers in the freezer to chill them.

Test to see if the marmalade has reached setting point by placing a spoonful on one of the chilled saucers and returning it to the fridge to cool. It is at setting point if it forms a wrinkly skin when you push your finger across the surface. When it reaches setting point, remove the pan from the heat and skim the froth from the surface. Stir in 60 ml rosewater and 50 g flaked almonds that have been toasted in a dry pan, and leave to settle for 10 minutes. Skim off any more froth, then carefully ladle the marmalade into hot, sterilised jars. Seal while hot and store in a cool place. Keeps for up to 12 months.

MAKES **about 4.5 kg**

QUINCE AND CARDAMOM PRESERVE

Wash and dry 3 quinces and cut into sixths. Remove the cores and cut the wedges into thickish chunks — there is no need to peel them.

Put the quinces into a large, heavy-based saucepan, then cover with cold water and bring to a boil over a medium heat. Lower the heat and simmer gently for 30 minutes, or until the quinces are just tender.

Lift the fruit out of the pan and weigh it. Weigh out the same amount of sugar and add it to the water in the pan. Stir over a gentle heat until the sugar has dissolved, then put the fruit back into the pan. Cook at a fairly brisk boil for 1 hour, or until the quince is a deep, almost translucent amber and the syrup is very thick and sticky. Skim from time to time to remove any scum that rises to the surface. Add 8 lightly bruised cardamom pods to the pan and simmer for a few more minutes, then remove from the heat.

Leave to cool for a few minutes before ladling into sterilised jars. Seal while hot and store in a cool place. Keeps for up to 12 months.

MAKES **about 1.2 kg**

SOUR-CHERRY PRESERVE WITH LIME

Rub the finely grated zest of 1 lime into 180 g sugar to release its oils. Spoon the sugar onto 200 g dried sour cherries and leave to macerate for 2 hours.

Tip the sugar and cherries into a heavy-based saucepan, add 500 ml water and heat slowly, stirring until the sugar has dissolved, then increase the heat and bring to a boil. Lower the heat and simmer for 45 minutes or until the syrup coats the back of a spoon thickly. Stir regularly and skim from time to time to remove any scum that rises to the surface.

Add the juice of 2 limes, then ladle the cherries into a sterilised jar and pour on enough syrup to cover completely. Seal while still hot and store in a cool place. Keeps for up to 12 months.

MAKES **300 g**

Praline has endless uses in desserts and cakes. It works with all flavours from chocolate to fruits, and is particularly useful for adding a bit of textural crunch to creamy smooth desserts and ice creams. Alternatively, fold it into whipped cream to accompany rich chocolate cakes, or mix it into ice creams, custards and mousses to add sweet crunch.

PINE NUT PRALINE

Place 150 g caster sugar and 2 tablespoons water in a saucepan and heat slowly to dissolve the sugar. Bring to the boil and cook for about 5 minutes until the syrup reaches the thread stage (when a drop of the syrup falls from a wooden spoon in a long thread) at about 110°C.

Stir in 200 g pine nuts, which will make the sugar mixture crystallise. Don't panic! Turn the heat down a little and stir gently until the crystallised sugar redissolves to a caramel. This will take 10–15 minutes. Carefully (as it's hot) pour the mixture into a baking tin lined with baking paper or greased foil. Smooth with the back of a fork and allow to cool and harden. When completely cold, bash it with a rolling pin to break it into chunks and then pound to crumbs in a mortar and pestle, or pulse in a food processor. The praline should be the consistency of coarse breadcrumbs. Store in an airtight container in the freezer for up to 2 months.

ALMOND OR WALNUT PRALINE Replace the pine nuts with 200 g lightly roasted whole almonds or 200 g shelled walnuts.

MAKES **150 g**

SUGAR-DRIED OLIVES

Begin first thing in the morning, on a day when you don't plan to use the oven for anything else. Preheat the oven to its lowest temperature. Line an oven rack with baking paper and set it in a baking tray. Wash 500 g pitted large organic kalamata olives thoroughly and place in a large mixing bowl. While they are still wet, add 200 g caster sugar and toss the olives around so they are all well coated. Scatter the olives evenly on the rack and transfer to the oven. Check after an hour. If the sugar is beginning to colour, the oven temperature is too hot and you may need to prop the oven door slightly ajar.

Leave the olives in the oven for the rest of the day, checking from time to time. Before you go to bed, turn the oven off (with the door closed) and leave the olives inside overnight.

Check the olives the next morning. If they still feel very moist, reduce the oven to its lowest temperature and cook for a further 6 hours, or until completely dried out (they can remain slightly moist in the centre).

MAKES **250 g**

Citrus fruit breathe their warm perfume into all kinds of sweet and savoury Persian dishes. The zest is mainly used dried, but this recipe for candied citrus peel makes a gorgeous sticky garnish for all sorts of creamy desserts and ice creams — or add a few strands to cake batters or biscuit doughs for a sweet citrus scent. The saffron intensifies the golden-amber hue and adds its own subtle layer of flavour. Seville oranges are best, but you can use any oranges or citrus fruit you like.

CANDIED SAFFRON ORANGE PEEL

Peel 4 oranges, removing as much white pith as you can from the peelings. Cut the zest into julienne strips, then put these into a small, non-reactive saucepan and cover with boiling water. Return to a boil and blanch for 20 seconds, then drain and repeat twice more to remove any bitterness.

Combine 250 ml water and 150 g sugar in a heavy-based saucepan over a low heat, stirring until the sugar has dissolved, then increase the heat and bring to a boil. Add the blanched orange zest and 2 tablespoons Saffron Liquid (page 218) and cook at a gentle simmer for 30 minutes, until the zest is soft and translucent.

Spoon into a sterilised jar, then seal while still hot and store in a cool place. Keeps for up to 12 months.

MAKES 300 ml

A lovely all-purpose caramel to drizzle over all kinds of desserts.

CARAMEL ORANGE SYRUP

Combine 100 g caster sugar with 75 ml strained orange juice in a small saucepan and heat gently until it dissolves. Bring to a boil, then lower the heat and simmer until the syrup darkens to form a caramel. Remove from the heat and add a further 75 ml orange juice. Stir well and leave to cool before stirring in 2 teaspoons orange-flower water.

MAKES 150 ml

Turkish or Arabic coffee is best made in small quantities in the traditional long-handled pot called a 'rakweh', but a very small saucepan will just about do. Throughout the Middle East various aromatics may be used to flavour the coffee: a few cracked cardamom pods, a pinch of ground cardamom, a splash of rosewater, or occasionally even saffron. In North Africa they enjoy cinnamon and sometimes coriander seeds, while in Yemen they favour ginger and cloves. Sugar is always added to the coffee as it brews, not afterwards.

TURKISH COFFEE

Bring 6 small cups of water to the boil and add 3 heaped teaspoons finely ground, dark-roasted, plain Turkish coffee, 2 teaspoons sugar (or to taste) and 3 lightly crushed cardamom pods. Bring the mixture back to the boil and, as soon as the froth begins to rise, remove the pot from the heat.

Once the froth has settled, return the pot to the heat and repeat the process twice. Serve the coffee straight away, taking care to give everyone a share of the froth. Let it settle in the cup for a minute or two before sipping.

SERVES **6**

For this extremely simple lemonade, use unwaxed fruit if possible, or at least scrub them well before you start. Serve with plenty of crushed ice in tall glasses, with a drop of orange-flower water to taste. Mixed with vodka and a few shredded mint leaves, this lemonade also makes a delicious cocktail for a hot summer's day.

MIDDLE EASTERN LEMONADE

Wash 5 whole lemons very well, then cut them into eighths and place them in a large mixing bowl. Pour 1 cup caster sugar over the top and massage the lemons. The idea is to rub the sugar into the skins, as the abrasive action releases the lemon oils, and at the same time squeeze out as much juice as possible from the flesh. After about 5 minutes the sugar should have dissolved into a thick, sticky syrup. Cover the bowl with plastic wrap and chill in the refrigerator for 4 hours or so, or longer if you can.

Then add 800 ml water and return the bowl to the refrigerator to chill overnight. Strain and add a splash of orange-flower water to taste. Top with ice, garnish with edible flowers, if you like, and serve straight away.

MAKES **1 litre**

Known variously as dugh, ayran, lassi or tan, this is one of the most popular drinks throughout the hot Middle East and Indian subcontinent. Yoghurt drinks are usually sold in bottles or cartons, but in some villages they are sold churned from large wooden barrels to make the drink light and fluffy.

Yoghurt drinks in Iran and Turkey are always lightly salted, unlike some sweetened Indian lassi drinks, but it's a taste that is worth acquiring. They're certainly viewed as the only drink to go with kebabs (especially in Iran, where they place great store in the concept of a 'hot/cold' balance) and in the summer they are strangely better at slaking one's thirst than water alone. An added virtue is that the salt content is just the thing for replacing that lost through perspiration.

Homemade yoghurt drinks are easy to make. Unsurprisingly, the thicker and creamier the yoghurt you use, the richer and more delicious the result. If you make the ayran with still water, it will keep, refrigerated, for up to two weeks.

AYRAN

In a blender, whiz 500 ml chilled thick natural yoghurt, 250 ml chilled still or sparkling water, 1/2 cup crushed ice and 1 teaspoon sea salt until light and frothy. Alternatively, use a hand-held electric blender. Serve immediately in tall chilled glasses, sprinkled with dried mint to taste.

SERVES **4**

Fruit sherbets — cordials — are thought to have originated with the Persians, who for many centuries have made use of compressed snow and ice from the mountains, which was stored in ice houses, then crushed and mixed with fruit syrups or distillations made from myriad fruit, blossoms, herbs and spices. This idea spread westward in the seventeenth and eighteenth centuries, and gave rise to the refreshing fruit sorbets associated with European kitchens.

SHERBETS

MINT AND VINEGAR SHERBET Combine 350 g sugar and 400 ml water in a heavy-based saucepan over a low heat, stirring until the sugar has dissolved. Increase the heat and simmer for 10 minutes. Add 160 ml apple vinegar, the juice of 1 lemon and 12 sprigs mint and simmer for a further 5 minutes. Remove from the heat and leave to cool. When cold, fish out and discard the mint leaves, transfer the sherbet to a sterilised bottle, then seal and store in a cool place. It keeps well. To serve as a refreshing summer drink, mix 1 part syrup with 3 parts chilled water or soda water. Top with ice, garnish with fresh mint leaves and Granny Smith apple slivers, if you like, and serve straight away. Makes 400 ml.

RHUBARB-ROSEWATER SHERBET Combine 500 g roughly chopped rhubarb and 400 g sugar in a large, heavy-based saucepan and leave to macerate for 1½ hours. Add 250 ml water and bring to a boil over a low heat, stirring until the sugar has dissolved. Increase the heat and simmer gently for 20 minutes. Strain through a piece of muslin or clean Chux, return the strained juice to the pan and add the juice of 1 lime. Boil for 10–15 minutes until the syrup is thick. Remove from the heat and leave to cool. When cold, stir in 2 tablespoons rosewater and a few rose petals (optional) and transfer to a sterilised bottle. Seal and store in a cool place. It keeps well. To serve as a refreshing drink, mix 1 part syrup with 3 parts chilled water or soda water. Top with ice, garnish with edible flowers, if you like, and serve straight away. Makes 400 ml.

QUINCE-LIME SHERBET Core, peel and dice 1 large quince. Combine with 400 g sugar in a large saucepan and leave to macerate for 1½ hours. Add 250 ml water and bring to a boil over a low heat, stirring until the sugar has dissolved. Increase the heat and simmer gently for 20 minutes. Strain through a piece of muslin or clean Chux, then return the strained juice to the pan and add 1 split vanilla bean and 100 ml lime juice. Boil for 10–15 minutes until the syrup is thick. Remove from the heat and leave to cool. Transfer the cold syrup and vanilla bean to a sterilised bottle, then seal and store in a cool place. It keeps well. To serve as a refreshing drink, mix 1 part syrup with 3 parts chilled water or soda water. Top with ice, garnish with edible flowers, if you like, and serve straight away with a twist of lime. Makes 400 ml.

BITTER ORANGE SHERBET Put 500 ml freshly squeezed orange juice and 600 g sugar into a non-reactive pan and heat gently, stirring from time to time, until the sugar completely dissolves. Bring to the boil, then lower the heat, add the juice of 1 lemon and simmer for 10 minutes without stirring. Skim off any froth. Remove from the heat and cool slightly. Pour into sterilised bottles and seal. When completely cold, store in the fridge. It keeps well. To serve as a refreshing drink, mix 1 part syrup with 3 parts chilled water or soda water. Top with ice, garnish with edible flowers, if you like, and serve straight away. If you like, use Seville oranges for a slightly less sweet cordial. Makes about 800 ml.

Cocktails are really all about fun, and the many exotic flavourings from the Middle East and North Africa lend themselves perfectly to this kind of beverage. These are some of our favourites, and were dreamt up by our friend (and former MoMo barman) Tom Lovelock.

COCKTAILS

TURKISH DELIGHT MARTINI This exquisitely pretty martini combines the classic Turkish delight flavours of chocolate and rosewater. You can buy rose-flavoured syrup, which tints this cocktail the palest of pink hues. Rub the rim of an elegant chilled martini glass with ½ a lemon or lime, then dip into a saucer of drinking chocolate. Combine 45 ml vodka, 3 teaspoons white crème de cacao and 3 teaspoons good-quality rose syrup in a cocktail shaker with a handful of ice. Stir well, then strain into the martini glass.
Add 2–3 drops rosewater and garnish with rose petals, if you like.

HAZELNUT MARTINI This is a wonderful cocktail for winter evenings. Adding a stick of cinnamon to one part sugar and two parts water makes a heady sugar syrup to use here. Reserve a few tablespoons of the cinnamon syrup and candy a few chillies to use as a garnish. Rub the rim of a chilled martini glass with water, then dip into crushed hazelnuts. Combine 30 ml pepper vodka or chilli-infused vodka, 30 ml Frangelico, 3 teaspoons lime juice and 1 teaspoon cinnamon sugar syrup in a cocktail shaker with a handful of ice. Stir and strain into a chilled martini glass. Garnish with candied chillies or sprinkle with chilli flakes.

TANGERINE DREAM For this summery cocktail, try to use a gin with crisp citrus undertones, such as Tanqueray Number Ten. Put 45–60 ml gin, 5–8 mint leaves and 2–3 drops orange-flower water into a highball glass filled with ice cubes and stir well. Pour on tangerine juice to taste and garnish with a sprig of mint and a candied cumquat (optional).

POMEGRANATE CAPRIOSKA Cut ½ lime into four wedges. Place two wedges of lime in a cocktail shaker with 50 ml vodka, 30 ml pomegranate juice and 1 teaspoon caster sugar or sugar syrup. Muddle the ingredients together, then add plenty of ice and shake well. Strain into a lowball glass filled with crushed ice. Garnish with the remaining two lime wedges.

SERVES 1

GLOSSARY

BARBERRIES Popular in Persian cooking, these small red berries are dried and used in rice dishes, stuffings and omelettes. Barberries should be picked over for rogue twigs or stones, then stemmed and washed before use. Look for them in Middle Eastern food stores.

BASTOURMA/PASTIRMA Turkish air-dried beef coated in a bright red, pungent paste. Similar to pastrami, it is cut into very thin slices and eaten on its own or in savoury pastries. It is often fried with eggs as a popular breakfast dish. It is available from Turkish butchers and some delicatessens.

BRIK PASTRY A thin pastry from Tunisia, also called warka. It is used to make savoury deep-fried pastries (called brik — a derivative of börek). Available from Moroccan food stores and some good providores.

BULGUR (cracked wheat) Bulgur comes in numerous grades, from coarse to medium or fine, and is also available as the whole grain. Bulgur is a staple widely used in Middle Eastern cooking, often as an alternative to rice.

CARDAMOM There are two main varieties of cardamom — green and a larger, less common black one. The green cardamom is the one you are most likely to encounter. Cardamom is readily available from most supermarkets, and from Middle Eastern or Indian grocers. To ensure freshness it is best to buy cardamom pods in small quantities and use them fairly quickly.

CHERRIES, SOUR Sour cherries are loved all around the Middle East. They are eaten fresh in the summer months, and are also turned into sherbets, preserves and fruit pastes. Dried sour cherries are available from Middle Eastern stores and have a wonderful, almost vanilla-like quality. They can be added to rice dishes or stews, or poached until soft in a lime-spiked sugar syrup and served with rice desserts or as a topping for ice cream. Dried or fresh morello cherries may be subsituted, at a pinch.

CHICKPEA FLOUR (besan) Used as a binding agent and to make biscuits and other treats. Chickpea flour is increasingly available; it can be found in good supermarkets and in Middle Eastern or Indian food stores and good providores.

CLARIFIED BUTTER/GHEE This is butter that has been melted and strained to remove the solids. It has a lovely nutty flavour, and is often used for making sweets, desserts and pastries, or in dishes where the milk solids in hard butter might burn. Clarified butter may also be used when making rice dishes. Ghee is readily available, but it is easy to make clarified butter at home: melt butter (preferably unsalted) in a small saucepan until it froths. Strain through a fine, clean cloth (such as muslin or Chux) and discard the solids. Keep the clarified butter, covered, in the refrigerator for up to three months.

DRIED SHREDDED CHILLI This is a Korean ingredient and readily available from Asia food stores.

FENUGREEK With a mildly bitter, curry-like flavour, fenugreek is a distinctive herb in Persian cooking. Both the seeds and leaves (fresh and dried) of the plant are used. The fresh herb is used, most notably, in Fresh Herb Stew with Lamb and Dried Lime (page 211), although the dried herb can be used when the fresh is unavailable. Fenugreek seeds are notoriously hard to grind, so are often sold ready ground. Fresh and dried fenugreek leaves can be found in Middle Eastern food stores, while whole and ready-ground seeds (sold as a powder) are readily available.

FLOWERS Scented edible flower petals have always been used abundantly in the Middle East, especially in Persian cooking. Fresh or dried, they make a pretty garnish, but if using fresh, make sure they are free from insecticides. Dried petals — especially rose petals — are widely available from Middle Eastern stores. Roses and orange flowers are also used to make jams and sherbets, and are distilled to make essences and flower waters (see below).

FLOWER WATERS These distillations of flowers are an indispensable addition to the the Middle Eastern kitchen. The best known in the West are rosewater and sour orange-flower water, or neroli. Both are used to perfume sugar syrups in which sweet pastries are steeped, and they add fragrance and flavour to cordials, desserts and ice creams. Add flower waters judiciously, as some are stronger than others — taste as you go to achieve the balance that suits you.

FREEKEH Whole wheat grains harvested while 'green', or immature. They are fire-roasted, which burns the chaff but leaves the young kernels intact. Freekeh is most often used to make into pilav.

KATAIFI A type of finely shredded filo pastry. It is most often used to make crunchy, nut-stuffed, syrup-laden sweets, but works equally well for many savoury pastries. Fresh kataifi is available from Middle Eastern stores and bakeries and some good supermarkets.

LIMES, DRIED A Persian variety of lime that are left in the sun to dry, these are used plentifully for the distinctive sour flavour they add. There are two types of dried lime (limu omani), one dark, the other pale. Both types are available in Iranian and Middle Eastern stores, but either can be used for any of the recipes in this book. Dried limes should be cracked with a rolling pin before adding, whole, to stews or soups. The limes soften as they cook, and can then be squashed against the side of the pan to release their juice. Dried-lime powder is also available commercially from Middle Eastern food stores. You can make it yourself from dried

Persian limes: break them open with a rolling pin and prise out the bitter seeds, then grind the lime to a powder in a food processor and store in an airtight jar.

MAHLAB A coarse powder made from ground cherry kernels. It is often used to flavour sweet breads, cakes and biscuits.

MASTIC The resinous gum from the acacia tree. It is sold as small crystals and has a subtle pine flavour. Mastic is used in Turkish ice cream to give it a chewy consistency and is also used to flavour milk puddings and ice creams.

NIGELLA SEEDS Known in India as kolonji (and often mistakenly referred to as black cumin seeds), nigella seeds will also be familiar with anyone who knows Turkish bread — they are are sprinkled over the dough before baking, as they are in Iran also. Nigella seeds are increasingly available through providores, and can be found in Middle Eastern food stores.

PASHMAK A spun-sugar confectionery — similar to fairy floss — pashmak is eaten as a sweet treat in Iran and Turkey, but is also useful as a garnish for desserts. It is inreasingly available in high-end supermarkets, as well as in Middle Eastern stores, often in a range of flavours.

PEKMEZ (grape molasses)
A thick syrup made from boiled and concentrated grape juice. It is widely used as a sweetener, and sometimes mixed with tahini and spread on bread. It is available from Turkish food stores.

POMEGRANATE MOLASSES
A thick syrup made from boiled and concentrated pomegranate juice. It has a sweet-sour flavour, and is often added to dressings, salads or meat dishes.

SAFFRON One of the distinguishing spices of the Persian kitchen, saffron adds a golden hue and indefinable flavour to all manner of dishes. It is always preferable to buy saffron threads rather than powder, which is sometimes adulterated with safflower. Saffron threads should be lightly warmed before use to release their aroma and flavour. They may be added whole to dishes, or ground to a fine powder after lightly toasting. Iranians always prefer to use saffron liquid in cooking, which can be made easily by dissolving ground saffron threads in a little warm water (page 218).

SHANKLISH This is a strongly flavoured firm white cheese available from Middle Eastern food stores. If you can't find it, substitute a good barrel-aged feta or a hard, aged goat's cheese.

SUJUK This spicy Turkish sausage can be found in Turkish or Middle Eastern butchers and some specialist delis.

SUMAC A dried dark-red berry with a sour, citrus flavour. It may be ground and added to meats or salads. Sometimes the roughly crushed berries are steeped in water and the aromatic liquid is used in cooking or to make sherbets.

TAHINI A thick paste made from ground sesame seeds. It is used to make spreads or dressings and sometimes mixed with pekmez and spread on bread.

TAMARIND Shaped like a long brown bean, tamarind pods are popularly used as a souring agent — especially in the south of Iran. Tamarind paste is sometimes sold in jars and may be added directly to a dish. Alternatively, you may find tamarind in the form of a compressed block of solid pulp that needs to be soaked and strained to make a sour liquid paste. All forms can be found in Middle Eastern and Asian food stores, while the paste is available in some supermarkets.

TURKISH RED PEPPER PASTE
A concentrated paste of red capsicums (peppers), this is available from Turkish and Middle Eastern food stores. It comes in mild and hot versions and is used to flavour meat or vegetable stews.

TURMERIC Turmeric is a dried, ground rhizome (from the ginger family), and has a slightly acrid flavour. Ready-ground turmeric is widely available. Indigenous to Iran, it is now one of the most widely used spices there, adding a vivid yellow hue to savoury dishes. Although often considered a 'poor man's saffron', it is in fact never used as a substitute, but in its own right.

VERJUICE Made from unripe grapes, verjuice has been used widely in Persia for many centuries. It came into its own once the Islamic prohibition of alcohol started to take hold, and was used to replace wine and vinegar in cooking. Verjuice has a mildly 'grapey' flavour, as well as a much-prized sourness, although it is less harsh than vinegar and less sharp than lemon juice. Verjuice is becoming increasingly available and can be found in some supermarkets and many good providores.

YUFKA Thin pastry sheets used to make sweet and savoury pastries in Turkey. Filo pastry can be used as an acceptable substitute in some recipes, but fresh yufka pastry is increasingly available from Turkish or Middle Eastern stores.

INDEX

METRIC CONVERSIONS

WEIGHT

Metric	Imperial
10–15 g	1/2 oz
20 g	3/4 oz
30 g	1 oz
40 g	1 1/2 oz
50–60 g	2 oz
75 g	2 1/2 oz
80 g	3 oz
100 g	3 1/2 oz
125 g	4 oz
150 g	5 oz
175 g	6 oz
200 g	7 oz
225 g	8 oz
250 g	9 oz
275 g	10 oz
300 g	10 1/2 oz
350 g	12 oz
400 g	14 oz
450 g	1 lb
500 g	1 lb 2 oz
600 g	1 lb 5 oz
650 g	1 lb 7 oz
750 g	1 lb 10 oz
900 g	2 lb
1 kg	2 lb 3 oz

TEMPERATURE

C°	F°
140	275
150	300
160	320
170	340
180	350
190	375
200	400
210	410
220	430

VOLUME

Metric	Imperial
50–60 ml	2 fl oz
75 ml	2 1/2 fl oz
100 ml	3 1/2 fl oz
120 ml	4 fl oz
150 ml	5 fl oz
170 ml	6 fl oz
200 m	7 fl oz
225 ml	8 fl oz
250 ml	8 1/2 fl oz
300 m	10 fl oz
400 ml	13 fl oz
500 ml	17 fl oz
600 ml	20 fl oz
750 m	25 fl oz
1 litre	34 fl oz

LENGTH

Metric	Imperial
5 mm	1/4 in
1 cm	1/2 in
2 cm	3/4 in
2.5 cm	1 in
5 cm	2 in
7.5 cm	3 in
10 cm	4 in
15 cm	6 in
20 cm	8 in
30 cm	12 in

TEASPOONS, TABLESPOONS AND CUPS

1 teaspoon = 5 ml
1 tablespoon = 20 ml
1 cup = 250 ml

ACKNOWLEDGMENTS

I would like to start by thanking everyone who has contributed to my culinary experiences, education and efforts over the last thirty-odd years. This includes the wonderful cooks in my own family, the inspirational chefs who've taught me during my professional career and the people I've met on my travels who have shared their knowledge so generously. This book is the beautiful result.

I am also grateful for the freedom I've been given over the years to develop my own style of new Middle Eastern cooking, starting in the 1990s at O'Connell's Restaurant, through to the present day at MoMo restaurant, where I thank the Lucas and Zagame brothers for their ongoing support.

More specifically, Lucy and I thank everyone who has been directly involved in bringing this book together. We have once again been fortunate to work with a group of superbly talented and creative people. We thank Mark Roper and assistant, Peter Tarasiuk, for the absolutely gorgeous photography, and stylist Leesa O'Reilly for supplying exquisite props and clever ideas. And we also say a special thank you to designer Sarah Odgers for creating a work of such luminous beauty. All in all, we couldn't be more delighted.

We are indebted, as always, to our supportive publisher, Hardie Grant, for their continued faith in our efforts. Thanks to Julie Pinkham and Sandy Grant for suggesting that the time was right for this compilation. To Paul McNally and Gordana Trifunovic, thanks for your commitment and enthusiasm throughout the whole process. And to our eagle-eyed editor, Janine Flew, sincere thanks for helping to iron out any inconsistencies with such endless patience and close attention to detail.

We are very grateful to the following suppliers for providing us with outstanding ingredients: Elias and Rima at A1 Middle Eastern Bakery, George at Clamms Seafood, Maria and Sid at The Essential Ingredient, Peter at Flavours Fruit and Veg, Jan at Herb and Spice, Roger, Simon and Sylvio at Largo Butchers, John and George at Ocean Made and Paul from Senselle Foods. The publisher and the authors would like to thank the following prop suppliers: Kris Coad, Market Import, Hub Furniture, Izzi & Popo, The Essential Ingredient, Safari living and Country Road.

Our deepest thanks go to the following chefs who helped in preparing the food for the photoshoot: Cat Ashton, Ruamana Cobbe, Sophie Jacquelin, Brooke Payne, Simone Watts and Jess Weeks. Greg also says a huge, huge personal thanks to Brooke Payne, head chef at MoMo Restaurant, for keeping things running so smoothly during his many absences. You know he couldn't do any of it without you!

Lastly, we thank our families, for their unwavering support and love and for making everything possible.